Windows NT Server 4.0 in the Enterprise

Accelerated MCSE Study Guide

Dave Kinnaman
Theresa Hadden
Patrick Terrance Neal

McGraw-Hill
New York • San Francisco • Washington, D.C. • Auckland
Bogotá • Caracas • Lisbon • London • Madrid • Mexico City
Milan • Montreal • New Delhi • San Juan • Singapore
Sydney • Tokyo • Toronto

McGraw-Hill

A Division of The **McGraw·Hill** Companies

1 2 3 4 5 6 7 8 9 0   AGM/AGM   9 0 3 2 1 0 9 8

ISBN 0-07-067684-4

The sponsoring editor for this book was Michael Sprague and the production
supervisor was Clare Stanley. It was set by D & G Limited, LLC.

Printed and bound by Quebecor/Martinsburg.

McGraw-Hill books are available at special quantity discounts to use as
premiums and sales promotions, or for use in corporate training programs.
For more information, please write to Director of Special Sales, McGraw-Hill,
11 West 19th Street, New York, NY 10011. Or contact your local bookstore.

This book is printed on recycled, acid-free paper containing a minimum of 50% recycled de-inked fiber.

Contents

CHAPTER 1

Introduction to This Study Guide

Plan Your MCSE Process

So you want to become a *Microsoft Certified Systems Engineers* (MCSE), do you? Then you've made a good choice in purchasing this book, because it's specifically designed to prepare you for a vital MCSE examination. This introduction is designed to prepare you for planning the whole process of becoming an MCSE and to assist you in outlining the unique process for you to prepare to pass all of your MCSE examinations.

According to Microsoft, "Microsoft Certified Systems Engineers design, install, support, and troubleshoot information systems. MCSEs are network gurus, support technicians, and operating system experts." That is a central information technology role with major responsibilities in today's computer networking world.

To prepare for such a major role, it takes a solid plan. You must know all your options. So, let's begin the planning with a discussion of the components of the objective: The core and elective exams that lead toward the MCSE certificate. After identifying the core and elective exams, the remainder of this section is devoted to dispelling several myths about MCSE exams, which could derail your plan if you believed them.

Core and Elective Exams

Two tracks toward the MCSE actually exist at this writing. However, the vast majority of candidates concentrate on the more recent track. The older track is based on Windows NT 3.51, and the newer track is based on Windows NT 4.0. Because the exams for Windows NT 3.51 have been scheduled for retirement, little more will be said about Windows NT 3.51.

Microsoft Windows NT 4.0 Track

This track consists of mastering four core exams and two elective exams. All of the many current elective exams are presented after the core exams.

You must choose four core exams from these eight:

- 70-030: Microsoft Windows 3.1 (retires September, 1998)
- 70-048: Microsoft Windows for Workgroups 3.11 (retires September, 1998)
- 70-058: Networking Essentials
- 70-064: Implementing and Supporting Microsoft Windows 95
- 70-067: Implementing and Supporting Microsoft Windows NT Server 4.0
- 70-068: Implementing and Supporting Microsoft Windows NT Server 4.0 in the Enterprise
- 70-073: Microsoft Windows NT Workstation 4.0
- 70-098: Implementing and Supporting Microsoft Windows 98

You must choose two elective exams. A great number of elective exams are available. You can choose to become an expert on any 2 of these 10 software products:

- SNA Server
- Systems Management Server
- SQL Server
- TCP/IP on Microsoft Windows NT
- Exchange Server
- Internet Information Server
- Proxy Server

- Microsoft Mail for PC Networks—Enterprise
- Site Server
- Explorer 4.0 by Using the Internet Explorer Administration Kit

CAUTION
Microsoft enables you to use, as electives, exams for one, two, or three versions of several software products. Only one exam per product, regardless of version, can be counted toward the two-elective requirement. For example, if you pass both 70-013: Implementing and Supporting Microsoft SNA Server version 3.0 and 70-085: Implementing and Supporting Microsoft SNA Server *version 4.0*, these two exams will only count for one elective. *The point is that passing exams on two versions of one product won't count as two electives—just one will count as an elective.*

One of these:

- 70-013: Implementing and Supporting Microsoft SNA Server 3.0
- 70-085: Implementing and Supporting Microsoft SNA Server 4.0

or one of these:

- 70-014: Implementing and Supporting Microsoft Systems Management Server 1.0 (retired)
- 70-018: Implementing and Supporting Microsoft Systems Management Server 1.2
- 70-086: Implementing and Supporting Microsoft Systems Management Server 2.0

or *one of these:*

- 70-021: Microsoft SQL Server 4.2 Database Implementation
- 70-027: Implementing a Database Design on Microsoft SQL Server 6.5
- 70-029: Implementing a Database Design on Microsoft SQL Server 7.0

or one of these:

- 70-022: Microsoft SQL Server 4.2 Database Administration for Microsoft Windows NT
- 70-026: System Administration for Microsoft SQL Server 6.5

- 70-028: System Administration for Microsoft SQL Server 7.0

or one of these:

- 70-053: Internetworking Microsoft TCP/IP on Microsoft Windows NT (3.5-3.51)
- 70-059: Internetworking with Microsoft TCP/IP on Microsoft Windows NT 4.0

or one of these:

- 70-075: Implementing and Supporting Microsoft Exchange Server 4.0 (retired June 1, 1998)*
- 70-076: Implementing and Supporting Microsoft Exchange Server 5
- 70-081: Implementing and Supporting Microsoft Exchange Server 5.5

or one of these:

- 70-077: Implementing and Supporting Microsoft Internet Information Server 3.0 and Microsoft Index Server 1.1
- 70-087: Implementing and Supporting Microsoft Internet Information Server 4.0

or one of these:

- 70-078: Implementing and Supporting Microsoft Proxy Server 1.0
- 70-088: Implementing and Supporting Microsoft Proxy Server 2.0

or

- 70-037: Microsoft Mail for PC Networks 3.2-Enterprise

or

- 70-056: Implementing and Supporting Web Sites Using Microsoft Site Server 3.0

*Exam 70-075: for Exchange Server 4.0 retired on June 1, 1998. If you have already passed this elective exam, you will be required to take a replacement elective exam on or before September 1, 1999. Replacement exams include all current MCSE electives listed here.

or

■ 70-079: Implementing and Supporting Microsoft Internet Explorer 4.0 by Using the Internet Explorer Administration Kit

With all of these options available, MCSE candidates can surely find elective exams which fit their own career and workplace goals.

Required Software and Hardware

Many current MCSE holders earned their certificates at little or no out-of-pocket expense to themselves, because their employers paid the costs for both training and exams. Many of them also did all or almost all of their exam preparation on the clock, so that their employers actually paid them to get an MCSE certificate. These fortunate MCSEs didn't even have to pay for software or equipment, because their employers also supplied appropriate software and hardware needed to practice all the skills necessary for their MCSE exams. If your employer offers this kind of comprehensive support, wonderful. On the other hand, if your employer expects you to pay your way to the MCSE entirely by yourself, here are some thoughts on what you'll need.

Required Software

In most cases you'll need at least one copy of both the server and the client software, because most MCSE exams are about *administering networks* which contain the software in question. You'll need to know how the product works from both the client and administrator points of view, even if the exam is specifically about a client software, such as Windows NT 4.0 Workstation. As just mentioned, the MCSE exams are usually from the system support and administrator's point of view, rather than the client user's point of view.

Installing a Microsoft client software may, of course, require a pre-existing operating system or a previous version of the client software, depending on the product involved.

Similarly, several Microsoft server operating systems will require you to have *other* server operating systems already available on the network, or installed and underlying on the server computer. This means that more than one server software program may be required in order for you to use and become familiar with all the tested features of the server software required for the exam.

Minimum Required Hardware

One or more Windows NT Workstation computers:

- 12 MB. RAM
- VGA video
- Keyboard
- IDE, EIDE, SCSI, or ESDI hard disk
- 486/25 processor or faster
- 124 MB. free hard drive space (Recommended minimum: over 300 MB., including a copy of the entire I386 installation directory [223 MB.] plus Windows 95 or DOS 6.22). For hard disk controllers using translation mode to address the drive, increase these minimum sizes by 80 MB.
- CD-ROM drive, or a floppy disk drive and an active network connection

One or more Windows NT Server computers:

- 16 MB. RAM (32 MB. or more recommended)
- VGA video
- Keyboard
- IDE, EIDE, SCSI, or ESDI hard disk
- 486/25 processor (486DX2/50 or better preferred)
- 124 MB. free hard drive space (Recommended minimum: over 300 MB., including a copy of the entire I386 installation directory [223 MB.] plus Windows 95 or DOS 6.22). For hard disk controllers using translation mode to address the drive, increase these minimum sizes by 80 MB.
- CD-ROM drive (Windows NT compatible recommended), or a floppy disk drive and an active network connection
- Recommended: 28.8 v.34 (or faster) external modem, for remote debugging and troubleshooting

COSTS TO OBTAIN AN MCSE

As mentioned above, the costs of an MCSE certificate are invisible to many current certificate holders, because the costs are entirely supported by their employers. Because these advanced skills are of great value to the workplace, it's appropriate that employers provide this support, in exchange for more efficient and more productive work skills.

Some supportive employers do require a contract, to assure themselves that the newly trained MCSE will not change jobs to another employer shortly after obtaining the MCSE certificate—presumably before the current employer has had time to recoup the costs of the MCSE for their former employee. These contracts typically require the employee to repay MCSE costs on a pro-rated basis, depending on how long the MCSE candidate remained with the former employer. Often the new employer picks up the costs of buying-out the former employer's training contract, as a part of the new and more advantageous employment agreement.

Note that MCSE holders are considered more employable, and therefore more mobile in their employment. The cost efficiency of information technology workplaces has been hard hit by a mercenary, contract-worker mentality that drains the spirit from workers. In contrast, employers who provide an environment of mutual trust and employment security, by fostering loyalty and good will in all employees, will obtain the best return on their investment in employee MCSE training.

MCSE Expense Budget	**Costs**
Examinations	$600 (retests at $100 each)
Training, seminars, workshops	_____
Study time	_____
Books and materials	_____
Practice examination software	_____
Network hardware, network analysis equipment	_____
Server and client hardware	_____
Server and client software	_____

MCSE Myth #1—Everyone Must Take Six Exams To Earn The MCSE

Reality—Some People Are Exempt From One Exam
Some networking professionals are exempt from taking the Networking Essentials exam, because they already passed a similarly rigorous exam through Novell, Banyan, Sun, or Microsoft. These professionals are already skilled, and possess certificates to prove it. Microsoft grants them MCSE certificates after they pass only 5 additional Microsoft exams.

Specifically, Microsoft automatically grants credit for the Networking Essentials exam once you've passed a Microsoft Certified Professional (MCP) exam and provide evidence that you hold one of these exact certificates:

Novell

CNE—Certified Novell Engineer

CNI—Certified Novell Instructor

ECNE—Enterprise Certified Novell Engineer

MCNE—Master Certified Novell Engineer

Banyan

CBE—Certified Banyan CBE

CBS—Certified Banyan Specialist

Sun

CNA—Sun Certified Network Administrators for Solaris 2.5

CNA—Sun Certified Network Administrators for Solaris 2.6

So, if you already hold one of the above certificates, just pass one MCP exam, and provide proof of your previous networking certificate, and you'll receive credit for two exams for the price of one.

What's An MCP Exam?

An MCP exam is a Microsoft exam, first of all. Passing an MCP exam makes you a Microsoft Certified Professional, and automatically enrolls you in the Microsoft MCP program. But not all Microsoft exams are MCP exams. Networking Essentials, for instance, is not an MCP exam. The sidebar has more information about the MCP designation.

| Microsoft Certified **Professional** | **Microsoft Certified Professionals (MCPs)** |

Microsoft Certified Professionals get their certificates by passing a Microsoft exam based on a Windows server or desktop operating system. Please note: Not all MCP exams contribute to an MCSE certificate! In fact, not very many do! Be sure to check the official Microsoft requirements when you make your MCSE plans, to assure yourself that requirements have not changed since this study guide was written. Here are all the MCP exams which, as of this writing, can contribute toward an MCSE certification:

MCP Exams in the Windows NT 4.0 MCSE Track

■ 70-030: Microsoft Windows 3.1 (retires September 1998)

■ 70-048: Microsoft Windows for Workgroups 3.11-Desktop (retires September 1998)

■ 70-064: Implementing and Supporting Microsoft Windows 95

■ 70-067 Implementing and Supporting Microsoft Windows NT Server 4.0

■ 70-073 Implementing and Supporting Microsoft Windows NT Workstation 4.0

MCP Exams in the Windows NT 3.51 MCSE Track

■ 70-030: Microsoft Windows 3.1 (retires September 1998)

■ 70-042: Implementing and Supporting Windows NT Workstation 3.51 (retires as Windows NT Workstation 5.0 exam is released)

■ 70-043: Implementing and Supporting Windows NT Server 3.51 (retires as Windows NT Server 5.0 exam is released)

■ 70-048: Microsoft Windows for Workgroups 3.11-Desktop (retires September 1998)

■ 70-064: Implementing and Supporting Microsoft Windows 95

Every MCSE certificate holder has multiple MCP designations because of the nature of the MCSE requirements.

There is also a "premium" MCP certificate called MCP+Internet available. MCP certificates are considered the basic Microsoft certificate leading to a premium MCP certificate or, in many cases, to MCSE status. MCPs have a private Microsoft Web site, a free magazine, other benefits, and a special logo of their own. Here is the URL for the Microsoft MCP Web site:

Microsoft Certified Professional Web site—Certification Home Page

http://www.microsoft.com/mcp

By taking an MCP exam early in the MCSE process, you can gain access to the MCP benefits just mentioned, which are valuable to obtaining an MCSE as well.

TWO RETIRED MICROSOFT EXAMS MAY SUBSTITUTE FOR NETWORKING ESSENTIALS

In addition to the networking certificates listed above from Banyan, Novell, and Sun that can substitute for passing the Networking Essentials exam, there are two more ways to achieve an MCSE with only five (additional) exams. If you happen to have taken and passed one of the following two retired Microsoft exams, you can use that previous exam to have the Networking Essentials exam MCSE requirement waived.

■ Exam 70-046: Networking with Microsoft Windows for Workgroups 3.11 (retired)

or

■ Exam 70-047: Networking with Microsoft Windows 3.1 (retired).

Retired Microsoft exams are explained in detail later in this chapter.

MCSE Myth #2—Only One Year to Finish

Reality—Take As Long As You Like To Finish Your MCSE

Take as much time as you need to be prepared for each test. There is no stated time limit for completion of the MCSE certificate. Begin, and take examinations when you are ready. Although there is a popular misconception that you have only one year (or two years or *whatever*) to complete your MCSE certificate, there is in fact no time limit. The only limits are your own motivation and the time available in your life. As an adult, you can decide for yourself how much more of your life you want to spend working as something other than an MCSE.

So, you should plan to progress at your own deliberate or expeditious speed, depending on your needs, your personal learning style, and the amount of time, money and concentration you can devote to this project. Everyone starts their MCSE studies with different personal backgrounds, different circumstances and different knowledge. Each reader brings different expectations for this book. Some readers will want a guide:

■ To confirm they already know enough to be certified

■ To accompany a class or even a crash course

- To study on their own, reading and applying the concepts as they go

Not having an MCSE time limit is also consistent with good educational design, because adults learn best at their own rates, and in their own ways. It also keeps Microsoft away from the "bad guy" enforcer role. This way Microsoft never has to say, *"Sorry, all your work was for nothing, you're too late—you must start over."*

WHAT IF IT TAKES TOO LONG?

There is a possible down side to extending your MCSE studies. The longer you take, the more likely it is that one of the exams you've already passed will be retired *before* you finish your MCSE studies. If an exam you've passed is retired while you are still pursuing your MCSE, you'll need to replace the retired exam with a current exam, causing you more work to accomplish the same original goal.

Another reason to progress toward your MCSE with all due dispatch is in recognition of your own personal learning style. Many adults learn best if they concentrate heavily on learning, passing exams as a kind of punctuation in their study cycle. Also, each exam has areas of overlap with other exams. What you learn for one exam will help with other exams, as well. Taking Exam B soon after taking Exam A, while the learning for Exam A is still fresh in your memory, can be ideal for some adult learners. Adjust your exam strategy to accommodate your own learning style.

Establish a timeline for yourself. The longer you take to complete the MCSE track, the less likely you are to finish. Establish a study and examination schedule for yourself and make a serious effort to stick to the schedule and complete the exams in a timely manner. People generally work better if "the end is in sight," so help yourself by creating a game plan for your certification.

MCSE Myth #3—Two-Week Wait For A Retest

Reality—First Retest Anytime, Second Retest After Two Weeks
Although there have been several changes instituted to improve security around the MCSE exams, until now it is still okay to re-take a failed exam as soon as you want. So, if it happens that:

- you fell asleep during the exam,
- you just had a bad day and only missed passing by one question,
- you were coming down with the flu the day of the exam, or
- you otherwise failed an exam in a fluke event that did not represent your true level of mastery of the material,

then you can reschedule the same exam and retest as soon as you please—at full price, of course. If you fail twice, however, you will be required to wait at least two weeks before trying a third time.

TIP
Many MCSE candidates, and MCSE certificate holders, are convinced that certain questions appear on more than one exam. It seems to others that one or two questions are pulled from their "mother" exam and placed at random on other exams, without a discernable pattern. They claim that questions they expected on the TCP/IP exam turned up on the Windows NT Server or the Enterprise exam, for instance. Building a strong personal foundation of knowledge and experience is the only defense against this sort of random substitution, if it occurs.

It is clear that the exams are at least quasi-hierarchical, in that almost all Windows NT Workstation questions are legitimate fodder for the Windows NT Server exam, and all Windows NT Server exam questions are fair game for the Windows NT Server in the Enterprise exam, for instance. Likewise, all Networking Essentials questions are also fair game on the TCP/IP exam. This is another reason to take the exams in a deliberate, thoughtful order that makes sense with your own experience and knowledge.

MCSE Myth #4—You Must Pass Exam A *Before* Exam B

REALITY—THERE IS NO REQUIRED EXAM SEQUENCE
Which Exam Should You Take First?

Please understand that there is no required sequence at all. You can literally take the MCSE exams in any order you please, and achieve your certificate with no prejudice based on the order of your exams. However, there are good reasons why you might want to consider a purposeful sequence, rather than a random sequence of tests.

Here is a sample way to plan your studies. It's based on three assumptions, which may or may not be true for you. First, the assumptions are:

1. If you aren't already certifiable in one or more exam areas, and

2. If you don't have more extensive experience and knowledge in some exam areas than the others, and

3. You've decided to take these six exams, for example, to satisfy the requirements for the MCSE:

Example Core Requirements

- 70-058 Networking Essentials
- 70-067 Implementing and Supporting Microsoft Windows NT Server 4.0
- 70-068 Implementing and Supporting Microsoft Windows NT Server 4.0 in the Enterprise
- 70-073 Implementing and Supporting Microsoft Windows NT Workstation 4.0

Example Elective Requirements

- 70-059 Internetworking with Microsoft TCP/IP on Windows NT 4.0
- 70-077 Implementing and Supporting Microsoft Internet Information Server 3.0 and Microsoft Index Server 1.1

If these exams and givens fit your case, you might want to proceed in one of the exam sequences suggested below. First, check out the sidebar for basic suggestions for sequencing all MCSE exams:

SUGGESTIONS FOR MCSE EXAM SEQUENCING

- Take the exam(s) you are *already* better prepared for first, if possible, to get things rolling and to begin your benefits as a MCP. Current Microsoft MCP benefits are summarized in another sidebar.

- Take the more fundamental exam first, if one exam is a building block for another exam. This allows you to begin laying the conceptual and learning foundation for more complex ideas.

- Take exams which have Fair to High overlaps in Table 1.1 one after the other, if possible.

- Take exams that will be easiest for you either at the beginning or at the end of the sequence, or as a deliberate break between tougher exams which are more challenging to you.

Enterprise, Server, Workstation
Table 1.1 estimates the overlap of content and knowledge areas between several popular exams. Of these, the three most closely related exams are the

- Windows NT Workstation,
- Windows NT Server, and
- Windows NT Server in the Enterprise exams.

It makes sense to take these three exams in that order (Workstation, Server, and Enterprise), unless you already have an extensive or special expertise in Windows NT Server or Windows NT Server in the Enterprise.

Table 1.1. Some exams overlap more than others. The Windows NT Server and the Windows NT Server in the Enterprise Exams have a high degree of overlap.

Perceived Exam Overlaps	Networking Essentials	Windows NT Workstation	Windows NT Server	NT Server in the Enterprise	TCP/IP
Networking Essentials					
NT Workstation	Low				
NT Server	Low	High			
NT Server/ Enterprise	Fair	Low	High		
TCP/IP	High	Low	Low	Low	
IIS and Index Server	Low	Low	Fair	Fair	High
Windows 95	Low	Low	Low	Low	Fair
Exchange Server 5.0	Low	Low	Fair	Fair	Fair

Of the exams listed in Table 1.1, these four are generally considered to be the toughest exams:

- Windows NT Server in the Enterprise
- TCP/IP on Microsoft Windows NT (any version)

- Windows 95 (retired)
- Exchange Server 5.0

As usual, the exam that will be the toughest for you is the exam for which you are unprepared.

TCP/IP, Networking Essentials, IIS and Index Server

The next strongest relationship among the exams is the high degree of overlap between TCP/IP and both the Networking Essentials exam and the IIS and Index Server exam. Because Networking Essentials is considered the foundation of standards and definitions needed for networking concepts used in other exams, Networking Essentials is often taken early in the exam sequence.

As said, TCP/IP is judged to be one of the more difficult exams, even after the exam was re-designed to moderate the impact of subnetting.

And IIS and Index Server is commonly considered one of the most straightforward MCSE exams, largely because MCSE candidates are familiar with how to prepare for Microsoft exams by the time they attempt IIS and Index Server. IIS and Index Server also covers a more limited amount of material than the other exams, making it a quicker study.

So, combining all these information sources, here are some acceptable proposed exam sequences:

Exam Sequence A

1. Networking Essentials
2. Workstation
3. Server
4. Enterprise
5. TCP/IP
6. IIS and Index Server

Exam Sequence B

1. Networking Essentials
2. TCP/IP
3. Workstation
4. Server
5. IIS and Index Server
6. Enterprise

Exam Sequence C

1. Workstation
2. Networking Essentials
3. Server
4. Enterprise
5. TCP/IP
6. IIS and Index Server

If you selected other exams for your MCSE, rather than the six used in these examples, use these same principles to find your own ideal exam sequence.

SOME NETWORKING EXPERTS FIND MICROSOFT EXAMS DIFFICULT

It is not uncommon for networking professionals, with years of actual experience, to fail the *Networking Essentials* exam. Likewise, it is often heard that the *TCP/IP* exam is considered tough by seasoned Internet experts. Why is this so?

The most satisfying explanation is that these professionals already *know too much* about real-world networking, and they "read into" the exams real-world facts that are not stated in the question. Many Microsoft exam questions are stated ambiguously, and the resultant vagueness seems to force these professionals to make assumptions. They assume that if the question says X, and they know that X is almost always because of Y, that Z must be true—only to find that Z is not even an available answer!

Network professionals advise that, for their colleagues taking the Networking Essentials or TCP/IP exams from Microsoft, nothing from the real-world should be assumed. Read the questions at face value only, to avoid reading anything real into the question. Often the questions that are the most troubling to these experts are simply testing their factual knowledge, rather than testing their troubleshooting expertise and network design experience.

Therefore, networking professionals with extensive prior experience often hold these two exams (Networking Essentials and TCP/IP) to the end of their exam sequence, hoping to get into the flow of the Microsoft testing manner of thinking before encountering these too familiar topics.

BETA EXAMS ARE HALF PRICE!

When a new Exam is under construction, Microsoft *tests* the exam questions on folks like you and me. For $50.00, rather than the regular, full price of $100.00, we can take, and possibly pass an exam while it is still in its "beta" stage.

You should expect beta exams to have between 150 and 200 questions, because they contain all the questions being considered for all versions of that exam. On a beta exam, you'll have *only* 3 hours to answer all the questions. This means that on a beta exam you must work at least at the same rapid pace you would use on a regular exam, if not faster.

Although beta exams can save you some money, they can also be frustrating, because it takes 6 to 8 weeks to get your scores back from Microsoft. Waiting that long can be quite a trauma when you're used to having immediate results as you leave the testing room!

Important—Please Note: Beta Exams are designated with a *71* at the beginning of the exam code number, rather than the regular exam codes which begin with a 70.

To find out if any beta exams are available, check this URL:

MCP Exam Information

```
http://www.microsoft.com/mcp/examinfo/exams.htm
```

Another point should be made about the Web page just cited. The dynamic links on the page jump to the official Microsoft Preparation Guides for each upcoming examination. Notice that the Preparation Guides become available *even before* the beta exams. This means you can actually be studying for an exam at the same time that they're preparing the exam to test your skills.

However, to study before the beta exam exists will sometimes require you to have access to the beta software product that the exam is based on. One of the many benefits of obtaining an MCSE certificate is a one-year subscription to the Microsoft Beta Evaluation program—free monthly CDs containing Microsoft beta software.

As of April 1998, these exams were *expected soon* in beta form:

■ Beta Exam Expected *July 1998*

Beta Exam 71-098 Implementing and Supporting Microsoft *Windows 98* for Exam 70-098 Implementing and Supporting Microsoft *Windows 98*

Preparation Guide at:

Exam Preparation Guide for exam 70-098

http://www.microsoft.com/mcp/exam/stat/SP70-098.htm

■ Beta Exam Expected *Summer 1998*

Beta Exam 71-028 System Administration for Microsoft *SQL Server*
7.0 for Exam 70-028 System Administration for Microsoft *SQL Server*
7.0

Preparation Guide at:

Exam 70-028: System Administration for Microsoft SQL Server 7.0
Status Page

http://www.microsoft.com/mcp/exam/stat/SP70-028.htm

■ Beta Exam Expected *Summer 1998*

Beta Exam 71-055 Developing Solutions with Microsoft *FrontPage 98*
for Exam 70-055 Developing Solutions with Microsoft *FrontPage 98*

Preparation Guide at:

Exam 70-055: Developing Solutions with Microsoft FrontPage 98
Status Page

http://www.microsoft.com/mcp/exam/stat/SP70-055.htm

■ Beta Exam Expected *Fall 1998*

Beta Exam 71-086 Implementing and Supporting Microsoft
Systems Management Server 2.0 for Exam 70-086 Implementing
and Supporting Microsoft *Systems Management Server* 2.0

Preparation Guide at:

Exam Preparation Guide for exam 70-086

http://www.microsoft.com/mcp/exam/stat/SP70-086.htm

■ Beta Exam Expected *Fall 1998*

Beta Exam 71-029 Implementing a Database Design on
Microsoft *SQL Server* 7.0 for Exam 70-029 Implementing a
Database Design on Microsoft *SQL Server* 7.0

Preparation Guide at:

Exam 70-029: Implementing a Database Design on Microsoft SQL
Server 7.0 Status Page

http://www.microsoft.com/mcp/exam/stat/SP70-029.htm

Old Exams Are Eventually Retired

Yes, Microsoft retires old exams. However, they take several specific measures to mollify the effect of obsolete exams on certified professionals—including giving 6 months advance warning in writing, and substantially cutting the cost of replacement exams for at least 6 months *after* the former exam is retired. Read on for the details.

When an operating system (OS) is no longer commonly in use, supporting the old operating system becomes increasingly expensive. If new and better operating systems are available at reasonable prices, and the migration path for the majority of users is not too burdensome, it stands to reason that the manufacturer would want to withdraw the old OS from support. Similarly, Microsoft examinations are withdrawn and retired when their use has waned, especially when the OS they are based upon is becoming obsolete.

In explaining Microsoft's policy on retirement of exams, it's useful to know that they highly value the relevance of the *skills measured by the exams*. If your skills are still good in the marketplace, there will be less reason to retire the exam that certified those skills. Microsoft explains that their exam retirement decisions are based on several factors, including:

- Total number of copies of the product ever sold (the customer base)
- Total number of exams ever taken (the MCP base)
- Ongoing sales of corresponding Microsoft products
- Ongoing sales of corresponding Microsoft courseware

By considering this broad framework, Microsoft can retire only exams which have fallen from use and have truly become obsolete.

Microsoft announces which exams are being withdrawn and retired, at this URL:

Microsoft Certified Professional Web site—Retired MCP Exams Information

http://www.microsoft.com/mcp/examinfo/retired.htm

If your MCSE certificate is based on an exam that is being, or has been retired, you'll probably need to find a replacement exam to prepare for and pass, to position your certificate for renewal.

WHAT HAPPENS WHEN ONE OF MY EXAMS IS RETIRED?

Although there are no guarantees that these policies will always be the same, here are the current Microsoft policies on exam retirements:

- First, you'll be mailed a notification in writing at least 6 months *before* your certification is affected.

- You'll be given a date deadline to pass specific replacement exam(s).

- You may take all replacement exams at a 50 percent discount until at least 6 months after the exam retirement date.

For any questions or comments about Microsoft exam retirements, or if you ever want to check your certification status or ask about the MCSE program in general, just send e-mail to mcp@msprograms.com or call one of the regional education centers below:

Microsoft Regional Education Centers

North America	800-636-7544
Asia and Pacific	61-2-9870-2250
Europe	353-1-7038774
Latin America	801-579-2829

In addition, there are many more toll-free numbers for Microsoft International Training & Certification Customer Service Centers in several dozen countries worldwide at this URL:

Microsoft Training & Certification Programs—International Training and Certification Customer Service Centers

http://www.microsoft.com/train_cert/resc.htm

One more thought on retiring exams: Because an MCSE certificate is good for life, or until exams are retired, the *only way* to be sure that MCSE professionals are keeping up with the real world information technology market is for Microsoft to retire exams. For the MCSE to continue to signify the highest level of professional skills, old exams must be retired and replaced with more current exams based on skills currently in demand.

EARLY WARNING OF EXAM RETIREMENT

One of the earliest warnings that an exam you've taken may become obsolete is that the development of a new exam is announced for the next version of the software, or a beta exam is announced for a new version of the exam. Once beta software or a beta exam has appeared, watch for further signs more closely.

Usually there is advance warning that an exam is being withdrawn many months before the event. If you subscribe to the following monthly mailing lists and read the Web pages mentioned, you'll have the longest forewarning to choose how you'll prepare for any changes.

- *MCP News Flash* (monthly)—Includes exam announcements and special promotions

- *Training and Certification News* (monthly)—About training and certification at Microsoft

To subscribe to either newsletter, visit this Web page, register with Microsoft and then subscribe:

Personal Information Center

```
http://207.46.130.169/regwiz/forms/PICWhyRegister.htm
```

Don't be caught off guard. Stay in touch with the status of the MCSE exams you've invested in mastering!

FREE SAMPLE EXAM SOFTWARE CD-ROM

Microsoft will ship (by UPS—United Parcel Service—so that an ordinary United States Postal Service post office box address won't work) a CD containing a dated snapshot of the Microsoft Certified Professional (MCP) Web site and sample examination software called Personal Exam Prep (PEP) exams.

By calling Microsoft in the United States or Canada at (800) 636-7544, you can request the most recent CD of the MCP Web site. *Ask for the "Roadmap CD."* They may protest greatly—don't worry. They'll say the *"Roadmap to Certification CD"* is no longer available, and that you would be much better off to check the Microsoft Web site for more up-to-date information. However, they'll also still (as of this writing) ship a CD if you insist, and if you provide an address *other than a post office box.*

Of course, if you're in a hurry, you can always download the free sample exam software directly from the Microsoft Web site at:

Personal Exam Prep (PEP) Tests

`http://www.microsoft.com/mcp/examinfo/practice.htm` (mspep.exe) (561K)

The free PEP exam download currently covers these Microsoft tests:

- 70-018 Implementing and Supporting Microsoft Systems Management Server 1.2
- 70-026 System Administration of Microsoft SQL Server 6
- 70-058 Networking Essentials
- 70-059 Internetworking with Microsoft TCP/IP on Windows NT 4.0
- 70-063 Implementing and Supporting Microsoft Windows 95 (retired)
- 70-067 Implementing and Supporting Microsoft Windows NT Server 4.0
- 70-068 Implementing and Supporting Microsoft Windows NT Server 4.0 in the Enterprise
- 70-073 Implementing and Supporting Microsoft Windows NT Workstation 4.0
- 70-075 Implementing and Supporting Microsoft Exchange Server 4.0
- 70-077 Implementing and Supporting Microsoft Internet Information Server 3.0 and Microsoft Index Server 1.1
- 70-160 Microsoft Windows Architecture I
- 70-165 Developing Application with Microsoft Visual Basic 5.0

FREE PERSONAL EXAM PREP (PEP) TEST SOFTWARE

The PEP sample exam software has many values. First, you should take the appropriate PEP exam as the *beginning* of your studies for each new exam. This mere act commits you to the course of study for that exam, and offers you a valid taste of the depth and breadth of the real exam. Seeing what kind of material is on the exams also allows you recognize the actual level of detail expected on the exams, so that you can avoid studying too much or studying too little to pass the exam.

Later, by taking the PEP examination again from time to time, you can generally gauge your progress through the material. The PEP exam also gives you practice at taking an exam on a computer. Perhaps best of all, it allows you to print the questions and answers for items you may have missed, so that you can concentrate on areas where your understanding is weakest.

Although the PEP tests are written by Self Test Software, they are distributed free by Microsoft to assist MCP candidates in preparing for the real exams. Take advantage of this generous offer!

Several other sources of practice exam software, including several more free samples, are provided in a sidebar later in this chapter.

Prepare For Each Exam

FREE TECHNET CD

The value of this offer cannot be over estimated. The free TechNet Trial CD includes the entire Microsoft knowledge base, plus many evaluation and deployment guides, white papers, and all the text from the Microsoft resource kits. This information is straight from the horse's mouth, and is therefore indispensable to your successful studies for the MCSE certificate. And the price can't be beat. Do not delay, get this free TechNet CD today!

Of course, Microsoft is hoping you'll actually subscribe to Tech-Net. Once you have earned the MCSE certificate, you probably will be sure to convince your employer to subscribe, if you don't subscribe yourself. TechNet can help you solve obscure problems more quickly, it can help you keep up to date with fast paced technology developments inside and outside of Microsoft, and it can help you keep your bosses and your users happy.

Microsoft TechNet ITHome—Get a Free TechNet Trial Subscription

```
http://204.118.129.122/giftsub/CltlForm.asp
```

On the same Web page you can also register for ITHome and for other free newsletters.

Remember, Microsoft exams generally don't require you to recall obscure information. Common networking situations and ordinary administrative tasks are the real focus. Exam topics include common circumstances, ordinary issues, and popular network problems that networking and operating system experts are confronted with every day.

USE PRACTICE EXAMS

Taking a practice exam early helps you focus your study on the topics and level of detail appropriate for the exam. As mentioned, taking another practice exam later can help you gauge how well your studies are progressing. Many professionals wait until their practice exams scores are well above the required passing score for that exam, then they take the real exam.

There are many sources of practice exams, and most of the vendors offer free samples of some kind. Microsoft supplies free sample exams from Self Test Software, and the MCSE mailing lists on the Internet often recommend products from Transcender. Both of these and several other practice exam sources are listed in the sidebar.

PRACTICE EXAMS AVAILABLE—FREE SAMPLES!

BeachFrontQuizzer
E-Mail: info@bfq.com
http://www.bfq.com/
Phone: 888/992-3131

A free practice exam (for Windows NT 4.0 Workstation) is available for download.

LearnKey
http://www.learnkey.com/
Phone: 800/865-0165
Fax: 435/674-9734
1845 W. Sunset Blvd
St. George, UT 84770-6508

MasterExam simulation software—$800 for six exam simulations, or $150 each.

NetG
info@netg.com
support@netg.com
http://www.netg.com/
800/265-1900 (in United States only)
630/369-3000
Fax: 630/983-4518

NETg International
info@uk.netg.com
1 Hogarth Business Park
Burlington Lane
Chiswick, London
England W4 2TJ
Phone: 0181-994-4404
Fax: 0181-994-5611

Supporting Microsoft Windows NT 4.0 Core Technologies—
Part 1(course 71410—Unit 1—7.7 MB.) and Microsoft FrontPage
Fundamentals (course 71101—Unit 2—8.1 MB.) are available as free
sample downloads.

Prep Technologies, Inc.
Sales@mcpprep.com
Support@mcpprep.com
http://www.mcpprep.com/
1-888/627-7737 (1-888/MCP-PREP)
1-708/478-8684 (outside US)

CICPreP (Computer Industry Certification Preparation from ITS, Inc)

A free 135 question practice exam is available for download (5+ MB.).

Self Test Software
feedback@stsware.com
http://www.stsware.com/
Americas
Toll-Free: 1-800/244-7330 (Canada and USA)
Elsewhere: 1-770/641-1489
Fax 1-770/641-9719
Self Test Software Inc.
4651 Woodstock Road
Suite 203, M/S 384
Roswell, GA 30075-1686

Australia / Asia
Email address stsau@vue.com
Phone: 61-2-9320-5497
Fax: 61-2-9323-5590
Sydney, Australia

Europe/Africa
The Netherlands
Phone: 31-348-484646
Fax: 31-348-484699

$79 for the first practice exam, $69 for additional practice exams ordered at the same time.

Twelve free practice exams are available for download. These are the same free practice exams which Microsoft distributes by download or CD.

Transcender
Product Questions: sales@transcender.com
Technical Support Questions: support@transcender.com
Demo download problems: troubleshooting@transcender.com
http://www.transcender.com/
Phone 615/726-8779
Fax 615/726-8884
621 Mainstream Drive Suite 270
Nashville, TN 37228-1229

Fifteen free practice exams are available for download.

VFX Technologies, Inc
sales@vfxtech.com
support@vfxtech.com
http://www.vfxtech.com/
Phone 610/265.9222
Fax 610/265.6007
POB 80222
Valley Forge, PA 19484-0222 USA

Twenty-two free practice MCP Endeavor exam preparation modules are available for download.

ORGANIZE BEFORE THE DAY OF EXAM

Make sure you have plenty of time to study before each exam. You know yourself. Give yourself enough time to both study *and* get plenty of sleep for at least two days before the exam. Make sure co-workers, family and friends are aware of the importance of this effort, so that they will give you the time and space to devote to your studies.

Once you have the materials and equipment you need, and study times and locations properly selected—force yourself to study and practice. Reward yourself when you finish a segment or unit of studying. Pace yourself so that you complete your study plan on time.

SURVEY TESTING CENTERS

Call each testing center in your area to find out what times they offer Microsoft exams. Jot down the center's name, address, and phone number, along with the testing hours and days of the week. Once you've checked the testing hours at all the centers in your local area you're in a better position to schedule an exam at Center "B" if Center "A" is already booked for the time you wanted to take your next exam.

The Sylvan technician taking your registration may not easily find all other testing centers near you, so be prepared to suggest alternative testing center names for the technician to locate, in the event that your first choice is not available.

Plan to take your MCSE exams at times of your own choice, after you know when exams are available in your area. This puts you in control, and allows you to take into account your own life situation and your own style. If you are sharpest in the early morning, take the exams in the morning. If you can't get calm enough for an exam until late afternoon, schedule your exams for whatever time of day, or phase of the moon that best suits you. If you really need to have a 'special' time slot, schedule your exam well in advance.

SAME DAY AND WEEKEND TESTING

You may be able to schedule an exam on the same day that you call to register, if you're lucky. This special service requires the test vendor, Sylvan or VUE, to download the exam to or store the exam at the testing site especially for you, and it requires the testing site to have an open slot at a time acceptable to your needs. Sometimes this works out, and sometimes it doesn't. Most testing centers are interested in filling all available exam time slots, so if you get a wild hair to take an exam *today,* why not give it a try? VUE testing centers can schedule exams for you, and they store popular exams onsite, so they are especially well positioned for same day testing.

SHOP AROUND FOR THE BEST TESTING CENTER AVAILABLE

Shop around your area for the best testing center. Some testing centers are distractingly busy and noisy at all times. Some official testing centers have slow 25 MHz. computers, small 12" monitors, cramped seating conditions, or distracting activity outside the windows of the testing rooms. Some centers occasionally even have crabby, uninformed staff. Some centers actually limit testing to certain hours or certain days of the week, rather than allowing testing during all open hours.

Because these MCSE exams are important to your career—you deserve to use the best testing environment available. The best center costs the same $100 that a less pleasant center does. Shop around and find out exactly what is available in your area.

If you are treated improperly, or if appropriate services or accommodations were not available when they should have been, let Sylvan or VUE, and Microsoft, know by e-mail and telephone.

CHECK FOR AVIATION TESTING CENTERS

Some of the best testing centers are actually at airports! Aviation training centers, located at all major airports to accommodate pilots, are frequently well equipped and pleasant environments. Aviation training centers participate in Microsoft testing in order to better use their investment in computer testing rooms, and to broaden their customer base.

The best thing about aviation training centers is that they are regularly open all day on weekends, both Saturday and Sunday. The staff at some aviation training centers actually like to work on weekends! One verified example, for instance, of an aviation training center and excellent Microsoft testing center available all day every weekend is Wright Flyers in San Antonio, Texas, telephone: 210/820-3800 or e-mail: Wflyers@Flash.Net.

OFFICIAL EXAM REGISTRATION AND SCHEDULING

VUE exam scheduling and rescheduling services are available on weekends and evenings; in fact they're open on the World Wide Web 24 hours 365 days a year. Sylvan's telephone hours are Monday through Friday 7:00 A.M. through 7:00 P.M. Central time, and the new Saturday telephone hours are 7:00 A.M. through 3:00 P.M.

As mentioned, many testing centers are open weekends on both Saturday and Sunday. If something goes horribly wrong at a Sylvan testing center after 3:00 P.M. on Saturday, or anytime on Sunday— you'll have to wait to talk to Sylvan when they open on Monday morning. As has happened, if a testing center simply fails to open its doors for your scheduled exam while Sylvan is closed for the weekend, you can do nothing until Monday morning.

INSTALL THE SOFTWARE AND TRY EACH OPTION

Make sure you know the layout of the various options in the software's graphical user interface (GUI), and which popular configuration options are set on each menu. Become "GUI familiar" with each software product required in your next exam by opening and studying each and every option on each and every menu. Also, for whatever they're worth, read the Help files, especially any context-sensitive Help!

Commonly tested everyday network features, like controlling access to sensitive resources, printing over the network, client and server software installation, configuration, troubleshooting, load balancing, fault tolerance, and combinations of these topics (such as security-sensitive printing over the network) are especially important. Remember, the exams are from the network administrator's point of view. Imagine what issues network designers, technical support specialists and network administrators are faced with every day —those are the issues that will be hit hardest on the exams.

MCSE candidates are expected to be proficient at planning, renovating, and operating Microsoft networks that are well integrated with Novell networks, with IBM LANs and IBM mainframes, with network printers (with their own network interface cards), and with other common network services. Microsoft expects you to be able to keep older products, especially older Microsoft products, running as long as possible, and to know when they finally must be upgraded, and how to accomplish the upgrade or migration with the least pain and expense.

Pass One Exam At A Time

Microsoft exams are experience-based and require real know-how, not just book learning. Don't be fooled by anyone—you must have real experience with the hardware and software involved to excel on the exams, or as an MCSE holder in the workplace.

Passing a Microsoft exam is mostly a statement that you have the experience and knowledge that is required. And there is also an element in passing of knowing how to deal with the exam situation, one question at a time. This section describes the various kinds of questions you'll encounter on the MCSE exams, and gives you pointers and tips about successful strategies for dealing with each kind of question.

This section then walks you through the process of scheduling an exam, arriving at the test center, and taking the exam. There is also a brief resource list of additional sources of information related to topics in this chapter.

Choose The Best Answer

These questions are the most popular, because they are seemingly simple questions. "Choose the best answer" means *one* answer, but the fact that there is only one answer doesn't make the question easy—unless you know the material.

First, try to eliminate at least two obviously wrong answers. This narrows the field, so that you can choose among the remaining options more easily.

SOME QUESTIONS INCLUDE EXHIBITS

Briefly look at the exhibit when you *begin* to read the question. Note important features in the exhibit, then finish a careful reading of the whole question. Then return to the exhibit after you've read the entire question to check on any relevant details revealed in the question.

Some exhibits have nothing to do with answering the question correctly, so don't waste your time on the exhibit if it has no useful information for finding the solution.

Choose All That Apply

The most obviously tough questions are those with an uncertain number of multiple choices: "Choose all that apply." Here, you should use the same procedure to eliminate wrong answers first. Select only the items which you have confidence in—don't be tempted to take a wild guess. Remember, the Microsoft exams do not allow partial credit for partial answers, so any wrong answer is deadly, even if you got the rest of it right!

Really Read The Scenario Questions!

There is no better advice for these killer questions. Read the scenario questions carefully and completely. These seemingly complex questions are composed of several parts, generally in this pattern:

1. First, there are always a few short paragraphs describing the situation, hardware, software, and the organization involved, possibly including one or two exhibits that must be opened, studied and then minimized or closed again.

2. The required results

3. Two or three optional desired results

4. The proposed solution

5. Four multiple choice answers you must choose among

"Pay close attention to the number of optional results specified in answer B"

Most scenario questions have an opening screen which warns that you should "Pay close attention to the number of optional results specified in answer B." This instruction is to accommodate the fact that there are sometimes two, and sometimes three, optional results, and to accommodate occasional proposed solutions that only satisfy the required result and some (but not all) of the optional results.

Often two scenario questions in a row will differ only in their proposed solution. They'll have the same scenario, the same exhibit, the same results, but different solutions will be proposed. Sometimes some other slight difference might be introduced in the second scenario. Compare those similar questions, noting the differences to see what's missing, or what's new in the second question. If the second question satisfies all the required and desired results, that tends to imply that the *previous* scenario did not satisfy all optional results, at least.

Also, it is common to encounter another scenario question later in the same exam which clarifies the situation in the previous scenario. Some people jot down the question numbers and topics of each scenario, to enable them to return and reconsider a question after reading other, related questions and perhaps having a flash of memory that might help.

TIP
The scuttlebutt is that, if you just don't have a clue on a complex scenario question, or if you're out of time, you should select answer A (meets all results) or D (meets none), because these are the most frequently correct answers. The recommended method, of course, is to know the material better, so that you never need to resort to this kind of superstitious advantage.

For most people, your first priority should be to note the required results. If the proposed solution does not satisfy the required result, you're done with the question and you can move on. There is no need to focus on the optional desired results unless the required result is satisfied.

There can be up to three optional desired results, and each one must be evaluated independently. Usually, if an optional result is satisfied there are specific words in the question that deal with the optional result. Use the practice exams to sharpen your skills at quickly identifying which optional results are satisfied by which words in the question.

Another strategy which works for some people is to focus first on the question and results (both required and optional), writing down all related facts based on the question's wording. This strategy then evaluates the proposed solution, based on the previous question analysis. Because some people find the scenario questions to be ambiguously written and vague, this strategy can also lead to time wasted on unimportant or unnecessary analysis, especially if the proposed solution does not meet the required results.

Some people work at exams differently. Aside from intelligence, there are also very different learning and understanding styles among adults. Some people, for instance, find that they deal better with the scenario questions by working backwards from the required results, and later, if necessary, from the optional results. They break the question into its elements, find their own solutions, and then finally compare notes with the solution proposed by the exam.

For example, they might start from the required results, building the case that would be required to create that final required result. Once they have built their own solution which does meet the required result, they then check their solution against the exam's proposed solution. By checking their conclusions against the exam's proposed solution and the givens offered in the question, they then easily decide which required and optional results are achieved. If they know the material, they can answer the scenario questions, they just do it in a way others would call backwards!

It's important for candidates to see the forest *and* the trees, and to know when to see each. In a question about a congested network, the candidate must decide whether the question is trying to ferret out the factual knowledge that FDDI is faster than 802.3 10 Mbps. Ethernet, or knowledge about the technical standards for installation and configuration details of FDDI. Candidates with extensive networking experience may be tempted to show off and choose the latter, when only the simple knowledge that FDDI is faster than Ethernet was required. Don't read information into the question that is not there!

EXAM INTERFACE QUIRKS—SYLVAN INTERFACE

The Sylvan exam interface has a peculiar quirk on long questions, that can hurt you if you're not careful. This is particularly true if the testing center uses small monitors, so that many questions are longer than one screen. On these long questions there is an elevator or scroll bar on the right side of the screen, so that you can use the mouse to move down to read the remainder of the question. When you reach the bottom of the question, but not until you reach the bottom, the left hand selection box on the outside bottom of the screen changes from "More" to "Next." There is a built-in assumption that if you are not looking at the bottom of the screen when you select your answer, you've made a premature answer.

If you have moved back up the screen, to re-read the question, for example, and the very bottom of the screen is *not visible,* and you then check very near but not exactly on your answer, sometimes the box above your selection actually gets selected, rather than the box you intended to check. To correct for this quirk you should either be sure you are always looking at the very bottom of the screen before you select the answer, or you should back up from the next question, by clicking on the "Previous" question box, to double-check your previous selection.

SELECT THE WRONG ANSWERS!

Okay, it sounds nuts. But the best advice around is to begin analysis of each question by selecting the answers that are clearly wrong. Every wrong answer eliminated gets you closer to the correct answer(s)! Often there are two answers that can be quickly eliminated, leaving you to focus your attention and time on fewer remaining options.

By carefully structuring your time, you can answer more questions correctly during the allotted exam period. Eliminate wrong and distracter answers first, to narrow your attention to the more likely correct answers.

INDIRECT QUESTIONS

Microsoft exams are not straightforward. They often use questions that *indirectly* test your skill and knowledge, without coming straight out and asking you about the facts they are testing. For example, there is no exam question that actually asks "Is the Windows NT 4.0 Emergency Repair Disk bootable?" and there is no question that says "The Windows NT 4.0 Emergency Repair Disk is not bootable, True or False?" But you had better know that the Emergency Repair Disk (ERD) is *never* bootable. By knowing that the ERD cannot be booted, you can eliminate at least one wrong answer, and therefore come closer to the right answer, on one or more exams. *By the way, after you've once had an unfortunate experience that calls for actually using the Windows NT ERD, you'll never again have a doubt about whether you can boot to it—the ERD repair occurs considerably later, well after booting the computer.*

After you've taken a Microsoft exam or two, if you think you would be good at composing their kind of indirect question that tests many facets and levels at the same time, check out this URL, where you can get information about being a contract test writer for Microsoft:

Microsoft Certified Professional Web site—Become a Contract Writer

`http://www.microsoft.com/Train_Cert/Mcp/examinfo/iwrite.htm`

Scheduling An Exam

Register by exam number. Say "I want to register to take Microsoft exam number 70-073." Also know the exact title of the exam, so that it's familiar when the test registrar reads it back to you.

The Microsoft MCSE exams are administered by or through VUE (Virtual University Enterprises, a division of National Computer Systems, Inc.) or Sylvan Prometric. Either Sylvan or VUE can provide MCSE testing. Both VUE and Sylvan have access to your records of previous MCSE tests, and both vendors report your test results directly to Microsoft. Taking an examination through either vendor organization does not obligate you to use the same organization or the same testing center for any other examination.

VUE began testing for Microsoft in May, 1998 after requests for another vendor from throughout the Microsoft professional community. They began by offering exams only in English, and largely in North America. VUE projects significant growth during 1998 and 1999, with worldwide coverage available by June 1999.

Call back the day before the exam to confirm your appointment. Anything could have gone wrong, and you want to know *before* you get to the testing center.

SYLVAN PROMETRIC

To schedule yourself for an exam through Sylvan, or for information about the Sylvan testing center nearest you, call 800-755-3926 (800-755-exam) or write to Sylvan at:

Sylvan Prometric
Certification Registration

2601 88th Street West
Bloomington, MN 55431
Phone: 800-755-3926

To register online:

Sylvan Prometric (Nav1)
http://www.slspro.com

Sylvan also offers 16 short sample online exams, called Assessment Tests, on various Microsoft products. (Although Sylvan has offered online registration for several months, reports have continued that would-be exam candidates are unable to use the online registration, despite valiant attempts—good luck!)

VIRTUAL UNIVERSITY ENTERPRISES (VUE)

To schedule yourself for an exam through VUE, or for information about the VUE testing center nearest you, call 888-837-8616 or visit VUE's Web site to register online 24 hours a day, 365 days a year:

Virtual University Enterprises (VUE)
To register online: http://www.vue.com/ms
North America: 888-837-8616 toll-free
5001 W 80th Street Suite 401
Bloomington, MN 55437-1108

VUE is a new kid on the block, but never fear, they are seasoned test people, and their promise to the industry has been new thinking in technology and service, and higher levels of candidate and testing center service. They have a "we try harder" attitude, and back it up with higher standards for testing centers (800x600 video resolution on Windows 95 machines) and an agile new, 32-bit testing engine. While VUE is in expansion mode, you should expect some growing pains, but also watch for some new thinking and professional amiability.

For instance, VUE immediately found a way to offer live online 24 hour, seven days a week exam scheduling and re-scheduling of Microsoft exams for busy professionals. And VUE offers on-site exam scheduling and re-scheduling *at testing centers*. These conveniences will be tremendously valuable to individual candidates. Because VUE's operation is based on heavy Internet bandwidth, they are able to use secure Java-based system management and site administration software to handle all testing and services. Also, VUE stores popular exams onsite and delivers new exams quickly to testing centers over the Internet, rather than by modem and telephone lines, as Sylvan does.

When You Arrive At The Testing Center

Arrive early. It can put you at ease to check in 30 to 60 minutes early. Relax a bit before you actually sit for the exam. Some exam centers won't complete your check in until the last minute before your scheduled time, and others will get you all signed up and then tell you to "let them know" when you're ready to begin. Sometimes they'll offer to let you begin "early." Starting a little bit late is also sometimes tolerated, if you want to review your notes one more time—be sure to ask first.

To check in, you'll be asked to provide proof of your identity. Two pieces of ID with your name and signature are required, one must have a photograph of you—a driver's license or passport and a credit card are adequate. There are testing center rules you'll be asked to read, sign, and date. Microsoft has also begun to require, on all new exams, that the candidate agree to a non-disclosure statement, discussed in the next section.

Testing center staff will explain their procedures and show you to the testing computers. This is the time to ask any questions about the testing rules. Find out, for instance, if you'll be allowed to leave the exam room to visit the restroom (with the *clock still running* on your exam) if your physical comfort demands a break.

CARRY WATER ONLY

Some folks bring bottled water, vitamins, or medications into the exam room, for their own comfort. You should consider what will make you most productive during the 90 minutes of your exam, and prepare accordingly.

Of course, the down-side to drinking soda, coffee or water during or even before the exam occurs later, when you are nearing the end of the 90 minute exam, and really need to visit the restroom instead.

WRITING MATERIAL IN THE EXAM ROOM

This is a touchy area. Testing centers are required to be very picky about *cheat notes* carried *into or out of* the exam. There is a story of a candidate who had an ordinary napkin wrapped around a can of soda in the exam room, and carried it out for disposal at the end of the exam. S/he was challenged about the napkin, and would probably have been disqualified or worse had the napkin contained any writing.

Always ask for writing implements. Paper and pen are easier to use, but some testing centers will not allow them. Those centers that do not allow pen and paper will issue you marking pens and plasticized writing cards that are hard to use.

The marking pens commonly have a wide tip that makes writing difficult, and they dry out very quickly between uses if they will write at all—you must remember to replace the cap or the pen will refuse to write the next time you try. Get the finest tipped pens available. The tips seem to widen with use, so newer pens are better. Ask the testing center to open a *new* package of pens, and ask for two or three pens in case they go completely dry.

Also ask for another sheet or two of the 8" by 10" plasticized writing material. If you have a large network drawing in mind, for instance, use the back of the card—two inches of the card's front are already in use by Sylvan Prometric. Don't force yourself to try to use those awkward marking pens in a small space—start another side or another sheet!

TIP

Don't waste your precious exam time writing down any memorized notes on the exam room writing material. Write down any memorized notes during the time *before the exam* you could use for taking the how-to-use-this-exam-software tutorial (discussed next). Some exams call for more memorization than others, and some exams have a tremendous amount of minute detail. Use your time wisely by recording any easily forgotten formulae, rules of thumb, and mnemonics *before* you begin the exam, *after* you enter the exam room.

The day before the exam, practice writing down all those notes you've decided will help you on your exam. Force yourself to write from memory only, to prove you can remember it long enough to write it down in the exam room.

ONLINE TUTORIAL

There is an optional exam tutorial available before each MCSE exam. The tutorial is designed to show you how the computer-administered exam software works and to help you become familiar with how the exam will proceed *before the clock starts on your real exam.* Don't become confused by the presence of the tutorial—if the clock in the upper right corner is ticking, you are taking the real exam, not the tutorial!

NERVOUS?

If you happen to be nervous before an exam, it might help reduce your anxiety to take some off-the-clock time with the optional tutorial to breathe deeply and calm yourself down and get into the right mood for passing the exam. Even if you've already seen the tutorial, and know exactly how to run the exam software, the tutorial can be a safety valve to give you a little time to adjust your attitude. Controlling your own use of time around the exam can give you just the boost you need!

REQUIRED NON-DISCLOSURE AGREEMENT

Microsoft requires certification candidates to accept a Non-Disclosure Agreement before taking some exams. If you take an exam that was first released after February 1998, you'll be required to provide an affirmation that you accept the terms of a brief, formal non-disclosure agreement. This policy will eventually cover all MCSE exams. Microsoft says this policy will help maintain the integrity of the MCP program. The text of the agreement is provided in the sidebar and is also available at this URL:

Microsoft Certified Professional Web site—Certification Non-Disclosure Agreement for MCP Exams

> http://www.microsoft.com/mcp/articles/nda.htm

NON-DISCLOSURE AGREEMENT AND GENERAL TERMS OF USE FOR EXAMS DEVELOPED FOR THE MICROSOFT CERTIFIED PROFESSIONAL PROGRAM

This exam is Microsoft confidential and is protected by trade secret law. It is made available to you, the examinee, solely for the purpose of becoming certified in the technical area referenced in the title of this exam. You are expressly prohibited from disclosing, publishing, reproducing, or transmitting this exam, in whole or in part, in any form or by any means, verbal or written, electronic or mechanical, for any purpose, without the prior express written permission of Microsoft Corporation.

Click the Yes button to symbolize your signature and to accept these terms. Click the No button if you do not accept these terms. You must click Yes to continue with the exam.

Mandatory Demographic Survey

Microsoft says they appreciate your participation in the mandatory demographic survey before each exam. For years the survey was optional—now it is mandatory. Microsoft estimates the survey will take most candidates less than 5 minutes. Of course, the survey time does not count against your clocked exam period.

To motivate you to furnish sincere and valid answers on the mandatory survey, Microsoft stresses that the survey results are vital to the program and useful for setting the passing score of each exam, validating new exam questions, and in developing training materials for MCSE candidates. Microsoft says "By providing accurate and complete information on this survey, you will help Microsoft improve both the quality of MCP exams and the value of your certification."

The mandatory demographic survey collects information, keyed to your Social Security Number, about your work experience, your work environment, the software tested by the exam, and information about your exam preparation methods. The survey has three components. One portion is common to all exams, another is keyed to the exam track, and the third portion is specific to that one exam. Carefully note the wording of any promises of confidentiality, data cross-matching or disclosure of your personal information.

CHECK THE EXAM NUMBER AND EXAM TITLE

Although it is unlikely, there have been stories about the wrong test being loaded for an exam candidate. The first task of taking a Microsoft exam is to be sure you are beginning the exam *you intended to take.* By double-checking the exam number and exam title, you might save yourself and the testing center hours of difficulty, if somehow the wrong exam showed up for you. So, be sure you check the exam title before you begin the clock on the exam— checking the exam title doesn't need to be part of your timed exam.

ITEM REVIEW STRATEGIES

In the upper right-hand corner, there is a small square box with the word "Mark" next to it. This little box is your key to another method to better manage your time during MCSE exams. When you encounter a question that stumps you, or leaves you feeling like you didn't study the right material *at all,* check an answer with the best guess you can quickly make, check the "Mark" box, and move on to the next question. At the end of the exam there is an item review option that will allow you to revisit only the questions you marked!

When you reach the end of the questions, a page that summarizes your answers to all the questions is shown. It has red marks where you have not yet completed the question or skipped it entirely. Try to fill in at least a best guess as you go through the exam the first time—you can't get a question right which was left blank or incomplete!

The end-of-exam summary page also shows which items you marked for later review. If you click on the box for Item Review, you will be taken back through your marked questions from the beginning of the exam, without needing to see the other, non-marked questions intervening. Or, if you double-click on any answer on the summary page, you'll be taken to that question, marked or not.

After you're quite comfortable with the testing process, you might want to consider this advanced strategy for dealing with marked questions. As you go through the exam, remember to jot down topics that are in the "stumper" questions you've marked. Then, if a later question includes that same topic, make a note of what the question number is, right next to your 'tough topics' list. This way, when it comes time for you to review the questions you marked, you'll have the numbers of informative or "clue-filled" questions to review on that same topic. Although the final summary screen allows you to access any question, unless you've recorded the question number as you go along it may be too time consuming to find that informative question during item review.

SOURCES OF ADDITIONAL INFORMATION

Microsoft maintains a large staff to handle your questions about the MCSE certificate. Give them a call at:

Microsoft MCP Program: 800/636-7544

If you have a CompuServe account, you can access the Microsoft area with this command:

```
GO MSEDCERT
```

Microsoft Newsgroups

By pointing your Internet news-reading software to the NNTP news server at Microsoft, you can read ongoing news, questions, answers and comments on dozens of topics close to Microsoft products.

Microsoft Public NNTP server: msnews.microsoft.com

Two typical hierarchies for your attention are these:

```
microsoft.public.windowsnt
microsoft.public.inetexplorer
```

The Saluki E-mail Mailing List

Saluki is a very active majordomo Internet e-mail mailing list. Some days have 50 to 100 messages about MCSE studies and related topics. To subscribe send an e-mail message to:

```
majordomo@saluki.com
```

In the body of the message write:

```
subscribe mcse Yourfirstname Lastname
```

For example:

```
subscribe mcse Scott Armstrong
```

You may use an alias if you wish.

For further information about Saluki, write to Scott Armstrong at `<saluki@gate.net>` or Dean Klug at `<deano@gate.net>`.

The Windows NT 4.0 Enterprise Exam

The Enterprise exam is primarily composed of scenario questions. For this reason, some people think it is one of the hardest exams. If you learn how to approach these questions, you should do well. Remember, if you take each question one at a time you will be done before you know it.

When reading the questions, diagram the situation. This will help you not be misled. Frequently, having a graphical representation of the situation before you will make the correct answer obvious.

One additional strategy is to ignore the offered answers. Instead plan out what you think would be the best solution. Next compare your proposed solution to those offered. By focusing on the differences, if any, you have a better chance of answering the question correctly.

Exam Room Notes

For the Windows NT Server in the Enterprise exam, here are typical items to memorize and write down as soon as you enter the exam room, before the clock starts:

- Networked HP printer or Jet Direct—DLC protocol
- Minimum hardware requirements—120MB Disk, 12MB RAM (I386),16MB RAM (RISC), and 486-DX33

- Internet Information Services—FTP, Gopher, WWW
- Hosting a virtual domain requires an additional IP address
- MRS.

  M—Move

  R—Retain

  S—Same (partition)

  This is the only time permissions or attributes are retained. All other files inherit the target folder's (not target partition's) permissions and attributes.

- Winnt32—3.51 upgrade, winnt new install
- Regedt32—security, Regedit—search values
- Novell 3.x user—password change setpass
- Novell 4.x NDS—password change ALT+CTRL+DEL
- A single domain has only one PDC
- Add an additional BDC for every 2,000 users
- A single domain can handle up to 26,000 users
- A master domain can handle up to 40,000 users
- A trust is one way and not transitive
- Installing a BDC on the far side of a WAN link will improve the speed of a user's logon
- When installing a WINS server on the far side of a WAN link, configure it for pull replication
- Using Last Known Good and ERD for troubleshooting

CHAPTER 2

Microsoft NT 4.0
Directory Services

When planning a large, enterprise network, the relationships among domains, computers, users, and groups will determine the type of directory services that best meet your needs. This chapter presents an overview of the various components of a Microsoft Windows NT Server-based network and some central concepts to be applied when administering Windows NT Server domains.

Directory Services

User accounts are tracked using a secure database called a *directory*. The network operating system component that manages the user account database is called *directory services*. When using Windows NT server 4.0, the domain is the administrative unit of the directory services. The domain structure provides several features that simplify network administration. These features include the following:

- A single user logon enables users to connect to multiple servers with a single username/password.

- The single user logon enables access to all available resources whether located in the same domain or a different domain.

- Network administration is centralized and simplified. Multiple servers can be administered from any workstation on the network.

Various administrative tools enable the administrator to manage users, groups of users, and resources. Each of these tools function through the directory services.

Each single user account includes user information and group memberships. In addition, the directory services include security information.

Domains

A domain is defined by a single directory database that stores user, group, and computer accounts. This database, the *Security Accounts Manager* (SAM), contains security information, the role of each computer and user, and account properties.

A domain, therefore, is a logical grouping of computers with a common security policy and a single database of user information. A domain may cover a single geographic location or cover several locations separated by great distances. The computers in a domain may be connected via a *local area network* (LAN) or include other types of connections such as dial-up lines, ISDN, leased lines, or wireless connections such as satellites.

> **NOTE**
> Account properties are set using the User Manager for Domains and applied globally to all user accounts in your domain. These properties include password policies—discussed further in Chapter 9, "Policies and Profiles."

Domain Controllers

The domain controllers are computers running Windows NT Server, which share one directory database or SAM. Domain controllers use the information in this database to validate users logging onto the domain. Only two types of domain controllers exist:

- Primary
- Backup

The *Primary Domain Controller* (PDC) has control of the SAM. The PDC is responsible for tracking any and all changes made to the SAM. In fact, because a domain can have only one PDC, by installing Windows NT Server in the role of the PDC, you create a domain and that domain's SAM.

The PDC has the only editable copy of the SAM and has the responsibility of ensuring that the *Backup Domain Controllers* (BDCs) have an up-to-date copy. A BDC contains a read-only copy of the SAM that is synchronized regularly with the original on the PDC. When necessary, a BDC may be promoted to act as the PDC.

> **TIP**
> When promoting a BDC to the PDC, the copy of the SAM on the BDC is automatically updated (*synchronized*) to include the latest changes *before* the promotion takes place. When a BDC has been promoted to PDC, the old PDC is automatically demoted to a BDC.

The PDC's functions are the maintenance of trusts between domains, synchronization of domain controllers, and user authentication if the BDCs are overloaded. Both trusts and synchronization are covered later in this chapter.

Although only one PDC can exist, no limit is placed on the number of BDCs in a domain. Microsoft recommends that one BDC be installed for every 2,000 users to optimize user logons. If an adequate number of domain controllers are not available, domain users will probably experience unacceptable delays at logon. When logon delays are occurring, one of the solutions you can consider is the addition of one or more BDCs to the domain.

Remember, the primary role of a BDC is user authentication. The PDC can provide auxiliary user authentication support, if the BDCs are too busy or unavailable. User authentication is a BDC's main role.

If the PDC is not available, a BDC will continue to validate user logons. However, changes cannot be made to a BDC's read-only SAM. If the PDC is unavailable, even administrators will be unable to make any changes to the SAM including being unable to do the following:

- Create user accounts
- Change passwords
- Create groups
- Add or remove computer accounts
- Add or change account policies
- Create trusts

TIP
If the PDC is offline, users cannot change their passwords, and administrators cannot add or delete user accounts. Nobody can add computers to the domain, create or change user or group accounts, trusts, policies, etc., while the PDC is off the network.
Central control, security, and administration are the biggest advantages of Windows NT domains. When the central, most important security and administrative computer for the domain is out of service, the domain continues to function; the users continue to work and use resources; but in terms of security and administration, the domain servers sort of hold their breath until the PDC is again available.

Domain controllers can have additional roles, such as functioning as a print server or as a location for users' home directories. An administrator's decision to assign additional roles to a domain controller is dependent on the size of the network, the anticipated workload, and the capability of the computer hardware itself.

Member Servers

Not all Windows NT Servers are domain controllers. Windows NT 4.0 also allows two additional kinds of servers—the stand-alone server and the member server.

As the name *stand-alone server* implies, each of these servers is an entity to itself. Stand-alone servers may be configured to participate in a workgroup. If a stand-alone server that has been participating in a workgroup is later connected to a domain, it then becomes a member server.

A member server is a Windows NT Server that is part of a domain and does not receive a copy of the SAM or validate domain user logons. Rather, these servers are used as the following:

- File servers, such as a location for users' home directories
- Print servers
- Application servers, such as providing mail services using Microsoft Exchange or database access using Microsoft SQL

Unlike domain controllers, member servers may move from one domain to another. Stand-alone servers can be moved from a workgroup to a domain as well; thereby becoming member servers. This process is accomplished via the Control Panel | Network applet. For a computer to join a domain, it must first have an account in that domain. This account can be created in one of two ways:

- Using Server Manager, an administrator can create an account for the computer. Then from the Member Server computer, the administrator uses the Network applet to join the domain.

- From the Member Server computer, a computer account can be created at the same time that the server joins the domain. This action requires a user with an account username and password that has the right to create computer accounts in the domain.

Figure 2.1 shows the Identification Changes dialog box that is used to move a Member Server from one domain to another. A Member Server can belong to only one domain or workgroup at a time. However, resources from other domains may be accessed through the use of trusts, which are discussed later in this chapter.

TIP
A member server cannot be promoted to be either a PDC or BDC. If a situation develops that you want to use the Member Server computer to validate user logons, it *must* become a domain controller, and Windows NT Server *must* be reinstalled.

CAUTION
Although Windows NT Member Servers may be moved from one domain to another as described earlier, Primary Domain Controllers and Backup Domain Controllers *cannot be moved* outside of their original domain. If a computer configured as a domain controller is needed in another domain, you must reinstall the operating system.

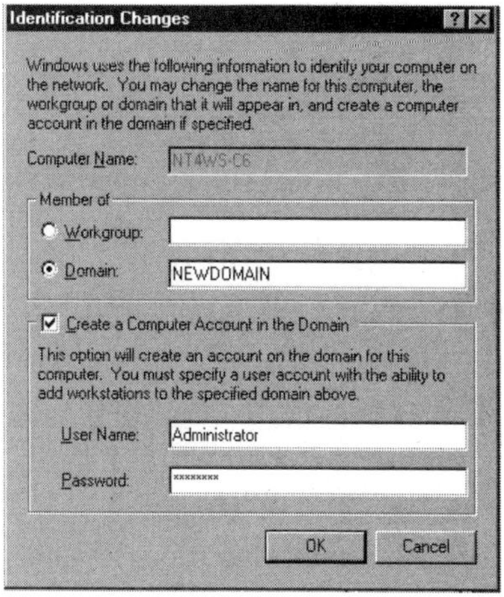

Figure 2.1   A computer account may be created at the same time that a Member Server joins a new domain.

On the exam, you may encounter scenarios that describe instances when you might want to move a domain controller from one domain to another or to otherwise change its role to something other than a domain controller. These things cannot be done. When a domain becomes defunct, all the domain controllers must go down with the ship. The only way to reuse a computer that was once installed as a domain controller is to reinstall Windows NT Server.

Netlogon Service

The Netlogon service runs on every Windows NT workstation and server. Its main function is user authentication. In addition, the Netlogon service on the PDC is responsible for the maintenance of trusts. The Netlogon services on all domain controllers synchronize the BDCs to the PDC.

Synchronization refers to the process that takes place when the copy of the SAM that is on the BDC is updated to include the latest changes from the PDC.

User Authentication

Because user authentication is accomplished through the Netlogon service using the domain's SAM, this centralized user authentication enables Windows NT users to have a single login (one user account and one password) to gain access to all the network's resources.

On a computer running Windows NT Workstation or Windows NT Server, which also is a Member Server (not a domain controller), you have the option of either logging on locally to the computer or to a domain. If the computer name is selected in the Logon Information dialog box, the Netlogon service processes requests via the Local Directory Services on the member server.

If the request is to log onto a domain, the request is passed through to the Netlogon service of a domain controller:

- A domain controller must be located by broadcasting the request or by requesting a list of domain controllers from a WINS server.

- A secure channel is established between the computer making the request and the domain controller.

- The computer sends the logon request to the domain controller to check account authentication. When the account has been identified as valid, the information is returned to the logon computer, and the user gains access.

If the preceding request is made to a WINS server, the WINS server returns the addresses of the first 25 domain controllers that registered with that WINS server. As a result, validation may not be made by the closest domain controller. To directly address this lack, you can use an LMHOSTS file to preload the name and IP address of the closest domain controller in the NetBIOS cache. This process causes the computer to send its validation logon to the preloaded domain controller rather than broadcasting or requesting a list from the WINS server. See Chapter 13, "Windows Internet Name Service (WINS)," for more information on using an LMHOSTS file.

Synchronization

The Netlogon service is responsible for synchronizing the SAM on the PDC with the read-only copies of the SAM that reside on the BDCs. The PDC sends periodic pulses to the BDCs and notifies the BDCs that changes have been made to the SAM since the last synchronization. This periodic interval is five minutes by default and can be altered by changing the Pulse value in the registry under the following:

```
\HKEY_LOCAL_MACHINE\SYSTEM\CurrentControlSet\Services
\Netlogon\Parameters
```

CHANGE LOG

As changes are made to the SAM, they are noted in the change log. This information is used to determine whether a BDC needs to be updated. When a BDC requests updates from the PDC, the change log is used to determine which changes must be sent.

The size of the change log determines how long the changes are available. By default, the change log can contain approximately 2,000 changes before the older entries are overwritten. This log is usually large enough to prevent having to do a full synchronization.

FULL SYNCHRONIZATION

A full synchronization occurs when the entire SAM is sent to a BDC. If a BDC has been offline for a period of time, then changes may have been deleted from the change log. In this case, a full synchronization will be performed. A full synchronization also is performed when a new BDC is added to the domain.

PARTIAL SYNCHRONIZATION

A partial synchronization occurs when only the changes are communicated. This default action occurs when the PDC synchronizes a BDC or when Server Manager is used to force a synchronization. Partial synchronization is quicker and more efficient than full synchronization.

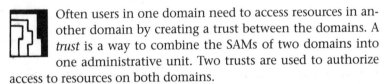

Server Manager may be used to force a partial synchronization to occur. You may select to either synchronize the entire domain or synchronize a single BDC, which is helpful after doing many changes if you need to have the changes available to your users. Figure 2.2 shows the Server Manager being used to synchronize the domain.

Trusts

Often users in one domain need to access resources in another domain by creating a trust between the domains. A *trust* is a way to combine the SAMs of two domains into one administrative unit. Two trusts are used to authorize access to resources on both domains.

Trusts are one way and nontransitive; access rights are not inherited from a trusting domain. Figure 2.3 shows the SantaFe domain as trusting the Albuquerque domain. If a third domain trusted the SantaFe domain, SantaFe users would be able to access resources in this new domain, but users from the Albuquerque domain would not have any access.

NOTE
When diagramming trusts, Microsoft's convention is to draw the arrow from the trusting domain to the trusted domain. The arrow shows the

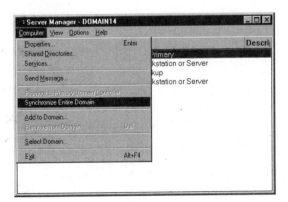

Figure 2.2 Select the Primary Domain Controller to force synchronization of the entire domain or select a Backup Domain Controller to synchronize only that copy of the SAM.

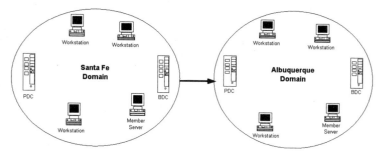

Figure 2.3   The SantaFe domain is the trusting domain, and Albuquerque is the trusted domain.

direction the resources flow. The trusting domain grants access to its resources to users from the trusted domain.

With this arrangement, users from the Albuquerque domain can access resources located in the SantaFe domain. However, users in the SantaFe domain cannot access files located on a server in the Albuquerque domain.

TIP
When answering questions that involve using trusts to access resources, draw a diagram of the domains and their trusts. Then indicate the location of the user and the location of the resource. This diagram will assist you in identifying how to grant the user access to the resource.

When a user from Albuquerque (trusted domain) logs on from a computer in SantaFe (the trusting domain) the request for authentication is forwarded to the PDC of SantaFe domain. Because that user does not exist in the SAM of the SantaFe domain, the SantaFe PDC forwards the authentication request to the Albuquerque PDC using pass-through authentication. The Albuquerque PDC authenticates the user and passes this information back to the SantaFe PDC. The SantaFe PDC then enables the user to log on.

PASS-THROUGH AUTHENTICATION

Pass-through authentication is used when a user from a trusted domain logs on from a computer located in the trusting domain. This process occurs when the user initially logs on and when a user accesses a resource located in the trusting domain. Figure 2.4 illustrates this process. The steps are as follows:

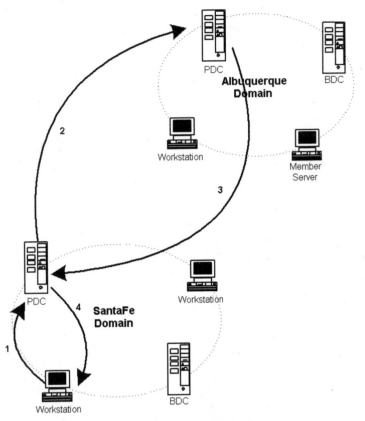

Figure 2.4 Four steps occur when a user is validated via pass-through authentication.

1. A user from the Albuquerque domain tries to log on using a computer in the SantaFe domain.
2. The request is forwarded to the PDC of the SantaFe domain. The SantaFe PDC cannot authenticate the user because the user account resides in the Albuquerque domain.
3. The SantaFe PDC passes the request to the Albuquerque PDC via the trust.
4. The Albuquerque PDC sends back the authentication information to the SantaFe PDC, which then completes the logon process. When this process is completed, the user is known as follows: *DomainName\Username*, or in this case *Albuquerque\user*.

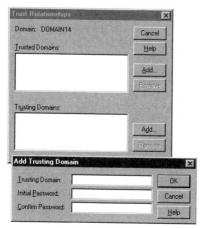

Figure 2.5 Enter the name of either the trusted or trusting domain depending on which side of the trust you are establishing.

Trusts are created using the User Manager for Domains. Select Policies | Trust Relationships from the menu. Figure 2.5 shows the dialog box used for configuring a trust. Here, you designate whether or not your domain will trust another domain (trusting) or whether your domain will allow another domain to trust you (trusted).

The trust must be configured by an administrator *from each domain* before it is established. As shown in Figure 2.5, the trusted domain's administrator may provide a password if desired. This password then must be entered by the administrator of the trusting domain to finish establishing the trust. This password is not required but may be implemented as an additional form of security.

TIP

To establish a trust immediately, first configure the trust from the trusted domain and then configure it from the trusting domain. If the trust is created on the trusting domain first, the trust won't be established for up to 15 minutes.

Domain Models

Windows NT networks are fully scalable and can be used to create large networks of thousands of computers. Depending on the size of the network, administrators may choose various domain models to accomplish various administrative goals:

- Optimizing efficient use, distribution, and availability of resources
- Security and access control
- Budgeting and cost control
- Innovation, version control, license control
- Expanding or shrinking network capacities
- Providing access from remote sites

Microsoft considers management and cost issues important. Network managers have an immense and pivotal role in software and hardware purchasing decisions. Therefore, any MCSE candidate should expect to understand how these issues are addressed by the various Windows NT and domain models.

 Four different domain models can be used to organize your network:

- Single Domain Model
- Master Domain Model
- Multiple Master Domain Model
- Complete Trust Domain Model

Single Domain Model

As in any domain, the single domain model has one PDC that contains the SAM for that domain. The SAM contains all of the accounts: users, groups, and computers. One or more BDCs are used to assist with user authentication.

TIP
As a rule of thumb, the domain should have a BDC for every 2,000 users to ensure efficient user validation.

The single domain model can contain approximately 20,000 user accounts as well as the associated group and computer accounts. The number of user accounts may be as high as 26,000, depending on the number of groups used. Figure 2.6 diagrams the Albuquerque domain, which is a single domain.

When the organization has grown larger than approximately 20,000 to 26,000 users, another domain model must be used. The limiting factor is the size of the directory database that contains the

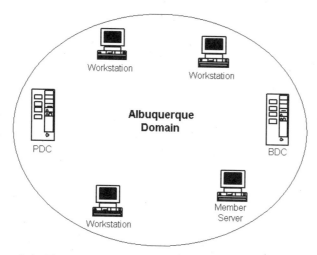

Figure 2.6   The Albuquerque domain, a single domain, has one PDC that contains the SAM. One or more BDCs provide for a faster login process.

user accounts. The maximum recommended size of the SAM is 40M. If the SAM is larger than this, then synchronization becomes inefficient. Each of the objects contained in the database takes up space. Table 2.1 shows the size of each of these objects. The sum of the objects determines the size of the SAM.

Table 2.1   Object Space Taken in the SAM.

Object	Size
User account	1.0K
Computer account	0.5K
Group account	4.0K

Single Master Domain Model

When an organization has exceeded 20,000 users, a Single Domain will not be adequate. Also, if the network needs to be split into separate domains for organizational reasons, then the Single Master Domain Model may be implemented. With this model, all user accounts are contained in the master or account domain.

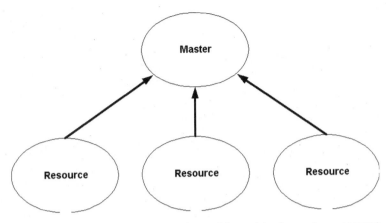

Figure 2.7 The single master domain model consists of a master or account domain and one or more resource domains.

Additional domains are created as resource domains. These resource domains contain application servers, print servers, file servers, and other network resources. They also contain the accounts for all computers including the workstations. Each resource domain trusts the master domain.

TIP
Remember that each resource domain also has a PDC and one or more BDCs and contains all the computer accounts. The only user accounts in a resource domain should be administrative accounts.

Users log on to their accounts located in the master domain using a computer in one of the resource domains. The authentication request is passed through (via the trust) to the master domain PDC that approves the user's access. Figure 2.7 illustrates a Master Domain Model.

The biggest advantage of the single master domain model is centralized user administration. Even if the organization is composed of several sites, because all user accounts are contained in the master domain, users can access resources located at any site.

The other major advantage of this model is the ability to delegate administrative tasks. An individual at one of the resource domains can be empowered to manage those resources without being granted administrative rights to resources located at other sites.

The maximum number of users in a single master domain also is limited by the size of the SAM. Because a single master domain has no resource accounts, a 40M SAM can accommodate approximately 40,000 user accounts (40,000 times 1 Kilobyte).

TIP

When presented with the need to select a domain model, first note the type of user and resource administration required. If centralized user administration is needed while still allowing for local administration of resources, select the Single Master Domain model.

Multiple Master Domain Model

If an organization spans multiple locations, it may be cumbersome to have all account administration in one location. The multiple master domain model addresses this issue by providing for more than one master or account domain. In addition, this model removes the overall limit of 40,000 users and will support networks of any size by adding a new master domain for each 40,000 users.

As in the master domain model, resource domains are used to manage network resources, such as shared files and printers. Each resource domain must trust each master domain, greatly increasing the number of trusts that must be maintained. In addition, the master domains must trust each other. Figure 2.8 illustrates a multiple master domain model.

As illustrated in Figure 2.8, each master domain trusts the other master domain, which is a two-way trust. Actually, this is two one-

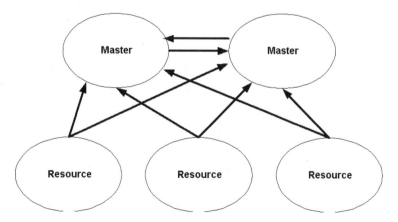

Figure 2.8 The multiple master domain can contain two or more master domains and as many resource domains as are necessary.

way trusts. By configuring these trusts, every user can access all resources, which simplifies account administration as domain administrators from one master domain may be granted administrative rights in the other master domains.

TIP
The formula for computing the number of trusts in a multiple master domain model is

$$m \times r + m(m - 1)$$

where *m* is the number of master domains, and *r* is the number of resource domains.

Complete Trust Domain Model

The maximum number of users in a multiple master domain is similarly limited by the size of the SAM. Each master domain can contain up to 40,000 user accounts.

The most complex and difficult to maintain domain model is the complete trust. This model consists of two or more single domains that trust each other. As the number of domains increases, the number of trusts that need to be maintained increases significantly.

This model often is used when divisions or departments want to have administrative control over users and resources but still need to share some resources. Figure 2.9 shows a diagram of a complete trust domain.

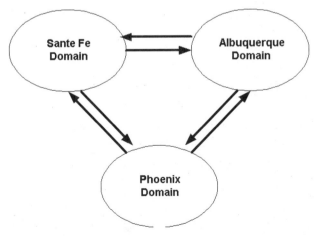

Figure 2.9 The complete trust domain model consists of multiple single domains that trust each other.

TIP
The formula for computing the number of trusts in a complete trust model is

$n(n - 1)$

where *n* is the number of domains.

Because the number of trusts needed to maintain a Complete Trust Domain grows rapidly as the network grows and because the work of maintenance is increasingly demanding, Microsoft no longer recommends this model. However, when departments want to maintain control of users and resources, the Complete Trust Domain Model is the correct choice.

Your choice for organizing your network is dependent on many factors. The most important being the type of network administration you want to implement. In addition, the number of users and computers will need to be considered. If the number of users is greater than 6–10 or if centralized administration is desired, one of the four domain models is a better choice than a workgroup.

For Review

- Workgroups are for 6–10 computers and users.

- Domain models allow centralized administration, enhanced security, and simplified access to shared resources.

- PDCs and BDCs cannot be moved to another domain—just reinstalled.

- Member Servers *cannot* be promoted to domain controllers.

- Member Servers can be moved from one domain to another.

- Plan for one BDC for every 2,000 users.

- The Netlogon Service is responsible for user authentication, domain synchronization, and the maintenance of trusts.

- Plan a maximum of 26,000 users per domain for Single Domains and 40,000 users for each Master Domain.

- Each trust is one way and involves only two domains.

- Creating a trust requires action in both domains.

- The trusting domain grants access to its resources for users from the trusted domain—the arrow shows the direction in which resources flow.

What's Next

See Chapter 7, "User Manager for Domains," for information on
configuring and using account policies and Chapter 13, "Windows
Internet Name Service (WINS) for how to use LMHOSTS files.

CHAPTER 3

Planning for Fault Tolerance

A basic part of planning the installation of Windows NT Server is planning how to partition your hard disk or disks. Not only is the size of the partition important, but the type of files to be placed in each partition is vital to the decision process.

The system partition is the partition that contains the files necessary to initialize the operating system (i.e., to boot). The boot partition also helps start the operating system and contains the operating system files. The system partition must be on a primary (also called *active*) partition; however, the boot partition may be a primary or logical partition. System and boot files may, in fact, be placed on the same or different partitions.

Providing for fault tolerance is another important consideration. Three types of *Redundant Arrays Of Inexpensive Disks* (RAID) are supported by Windows NT. RAID can be either hardware- or software-based. The Windows NT operating system provides for sofware-based RAID with the following options:

- RAID 0— Striping
- RAID 1—Mirroring or Duplexing
- RAID 5—Striping with Parity

Of these, only RAID 1 and RAID 5 provide fault tolerance.

For the exam, you should remember that RAID 0 means *not fault tolerant*. System and boot files may be placed on a mirrored partition but not on a stripe set. Stripe Sets are faster than mirrors. They also are more economical of disk space in that they have a lower cost per megabyte of data stored. The cost issue is addressed as each type of disk management is discussed in this chapter.

An additional type of partition is the *Volume Set*. Volume sets enable expansion of a partition on the fly, but they do not provide any fault tolerance.

Disk Administrator

Disk Administrator is a graphical tool for administrating disk resources. Figure 3.1 shows the Disk Administrator, which enables you to create or delete partitions and replaces the DOS fdisk utility. The properties of your hard disks may be changed using Disk Administrator, including changing drive letter assignments, changing a volume label, and formatting the partition. Disk Administrator also can create and manage various disk configurations including mirror sets, stripe sets, stripe sets with parity, and volume sets.

Volume Sets

A Volume Set gives you the option of extending a full partition on the fly. A Volume Set can be composed of from 2 to 32 sections of

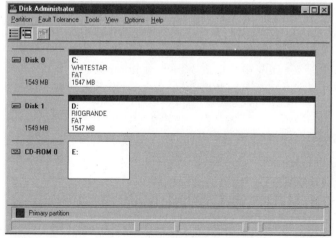

Figure 3.1   Disk Administrator is used to manage disk resources.

disk space and may span from 1 to 32 physical drives. Each of these pieces may be a different size. The resulting combination appears as one logical drive.

TIP

Although a Volume Set can provide needed space immediately, it does not provide any fault tolerance. If any disk that contains a portion of the Volume Set fails, then the *entire* Volume Set is lost. The only way to re-cover your data if this occurs is to restore from a backup.

You create a Volume Set by selecting two or more areas of free space. Select Partition from the Disk Administrator menu and select Create Volume Set. You then type the size of the Volume Set and click on the OK button. You then must format the drive before it can be used. Figure 3.2 illustrates a Volume Set.

A Volume Set may be formatted as either FAT or NTFS. If you want to later extend a Volume Set, however, it must be formatted as NTFS. Neither system nor boot files can be placed on a Volume Set.

TIP

If a scenario is presented in which you need to extend a partition to allow for additional space, first determine the file system being used for that partition. If it is FAT, you first must convert the file system to NTFS before extending the partition.

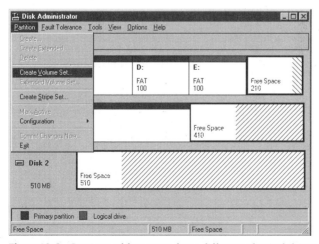

Figure 3.2 Portions of free space from different physical drives may be used to create a Volume Set.

Extending a Volume Set

A Volume Set can be extended, either by adding free space from the same hard drive or by incorporating free space from a separate hard drive. To extend a Volume Set, select the Volume Set. Then, while holding down the Control key, select additional area(s) of free space. Remember, a Volume Set has to be formatted as NTFS in order to be extended.

TIP

A Volume Set is read sequentially— making it the *least efficient* way to organize your disks, and it has no fault tolerance. Only consider using a Volume Set when you unexpectedly need additional space immediately.

Stripe Set

A Stripe Set combines 2 to 32 sections of space from separate physical disks to create one logical partition. Data is written in 64K chunks sequentially across the disks. The advantage to this arrangement is faster read and write access to your drives. This makes the Stripe Set the fastest and most economical way to store data. Figure 3.3 illustrates how data is written to a stripe set.

 Use the Disk Administrator to create a Stripe Set. Select the first area of free space and then while holding down the Control key, select 1 to 31 additional areas of free space, each of which must be on a separate physical disk.

On the Partition Menu in Disk Administrator, select Create Stripe Set. Next, Disk Administrator displays the minimum and maximum sizes for the stripe set you are creating based on the amount of free space.

Type the total size of the stripe set you want to create and click OK. These changes will not be saved until you commit the changes.

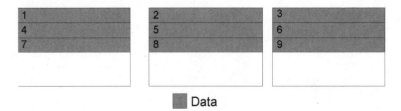

Data

Figure 3.3   Data and parity information is written sequentially across a Stripe Set.

After creating the stripe set and committing the changes, you need to format the new logical partition in either FAT or NTFS.

TIP
Each section of free space comprising a stripe set must be the same size. To calculate the maximum size of available space, multiply the size of the smallest section times the total number of sections selected. Each stripe must be on a separate physical disk drive.

CAUTION
Stripe Sets do not provide any fault tolerance. Therefore, in the case of a disk failure, you must replace the failed disk, recreate the stripe set, and restore your data from a backup.

Stripe Set with Parity

A stripe set with parity consists of 3 to 32 sections of disk space, each of which must be on a separate physical drive, and the whole set appears as one logical drive. Data is written in 64-byte segments sequentially across all the drives as in a Stripe Set, except that one segment on each stripe contains parity information.

The segment containing parity information is not written to the same disk, but rather rotates. This information is calculated from the data chunks on that row, and the parity information can be used to recover lost data in the case of a single disk failure. See Figure 3.4 for an illustration of how data is written to a stripe set with parity.

TIP
Read each question on the exam very carefully. If the question involves a stripe set, never assume that the stripe set is a *stripe set with parity*, unless it is stated in the question. Some questions might lead you to be-

Figure 3.4 Data and parity information is written sequentially across a Stripe Set with parity. Notice that the location of the parity section varies with each stripe.

lieve that the situation involves a stripe set with parity from the context, but without the words *with parity*, a stripe set is not fault tolerant.

The steps for creating a stripe set with parity are similar to creating a Stripe Set. Select a minimum of three physical disks with free space, up to a maximum of 32; each stripe must be on a separate physical disk. Create the stripe set by selecting Create Stripe Set With Parity from the Fault Tolerance menu.

TIP

When asked for the largest size stripe set, be sure to consider all the different combinations. Don't be taken in by the urge to use space from all available disks. Remember that the size of the set is limited by the smallest available stripe. Combining three large segments of available space might not create a larger stripe set than smaller portions of four or five drives due to the parity overhead.

For example, if you have FOUR disks with sections of free space of 75M, 100M, 100M, and 100M, you could create a stripe set of 300M by using the three 100M sections. The available storage space would be 200M. However, if you select four sections of 75M each, the total size of the stripe set also is 300M, but the available storage space is 225M.

When planning the configuration of a stripe set with parity, always pay attention to whether the question asks for the size of the stripe set or the amount of storage space that would be available.

Mirror Set

Mirroring a partition results in automatically creating an exact copy of a partition or disk. This is a fault-tolerant technique that helps ensure that your computer will stay up and that you will not lose your data. If the primary side of the mirror fails, your system will continue to function from the mirrored side.

Use Disk Administrator to create a mirror set by selecting the two partitions you want to use while pressing the Control key. Select Fault Tolerance | Establish Mirror as shown in Figure 3.5. Commit your changes or quit Disk Administrator. You must format each partition before it is usable, and the mirrored or second portion must be on a different physical disk, must be available (unused) space, and must be the same size.

To boot from the second side of the mirror, you must create a fault tolerance boot disk that contains ntldr, ntdetect.com, and boot.ini. You also need ntbootdd.sys if you are using a SCSI drive without BIOS

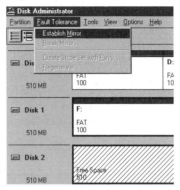

Figure 3.5   After selecting the two partitions, use Fault Tolerance / Establish Mirror to establish the mirror set.

enabled. The `boot.ini` file needs to be changed to reference the mirror partition. For example, if your operating system boots from the following line

```
multi(0)disk(0)rdisk(0)partition(1)\WINNT="Windows NT Server Version 4.00"
```

you will need to change this to the following:

```
multi(0)disk(0)rdisk(1)partition(2)\WINNT="Windows NT Server Version 4.00"
```

The first example refers to the first controller card that is IDE, EIDE, or SCSI with the BIOS enabled [`multi(0)`], the first disk attached to that controller card [`rdisk(0)`], and the first partition on that disk [`partition(1)`]. The second entry refers to the first controller, the second disk [`rdisk(1)`], and the second partition on that disk [`partition(2)`]. See the sidebar on "ARC Naming Conventions" for further information.

ARC NAMING CONVENTIONS

Advanced RISC Computing (ARC) Naming conventions refer to the method used to identify the path to the operating system you want to start in the `boot.ini` file. It consists of the following four parts:

multi or *scsi* refers to the type of controller you are using. Multi refers to an IDE, EIDE, or SCSI adapter with BIOS enabled. SCSI refers to a SCSI adapter without the BIOS enabled. The number contained in the parentheses refers to which controller, with the first one being referred to as 0.

disk is used if the first entry is SCSI and refers to which hard disk is attached to that controller. Disks ordinally are numbered so that the first disk is 0.

rdisk is used when the first entry is *multi* and also designates which disk to use. The first disk is referred to as 0.

partition refers to which partition on that disk. Partitions are numbered starting with 1, *not* 0.

TIP

Know how to create a boot disk so that you can boot from the second half of your mirror set. See the Microsoft Knowledge Base Article Q119467, "Creating a Boot Disk for an NTFS or FAT Partition," for more information on creating a Windows NT boot disk.

To recover from a failed mirror, replace the failed drive, and reboot your machine. Using Disk Administrator, you first must break the mirror by selecting Fault Tolerance | Break Mirror. After breaking the mirror, commit your changes. When these steps have been completed, you then create the mirror set.

Mirroring is a more expensive method of fault tolerance because the amount of available storage on the mirrored partitions is cut in half. Mirroring is the most expensive type of fault tolerance because each megabyte of storage costs twice as much as a single drive.

TIP

Disk duplexing is mirroring using two disk controllers rather than one. If one disk controller fails, you can still boot your system. Also, duplexing reads and writes faster than a mirror, because it uses two disk controllers working at the same time.

Backup Server

One other type of fault tolerance is to have a duplicate or backup server. This configuration is accomplished by connecting the two servers together in such a way that if the main server should go down, the backup server is made available for network clients.

Both the name and address of the two servers are identical, which is accomplished via various third-party hardware/software combinations. Windows NT can be the operating system, although it does not directly control this failover configuration.

Planning how to provide for data protection and integrity is a vital part of planning your network. One of the major components of this data integrity plan is how you organize your hard disk(s). Administering a Windows NT-based network includes the planning and implementation of such a plan. This topic is covered on the certification exams, so you should understand and remember each of the concepts presented in this chapter.

For Review

- Volume sets need 2 to 32 sections of free space, which can be from 1 to 32 separate physical drives.

- A Volume set must be formatted in NTFS to be expanded.

- A mirror set is composed of two physical drives or two partitions (each on a separate drive) of equal size.

- A stripe set is composed of 2 to 32 sections of free space of equal size, each located on separate physical drives.

- A stripe set with parity is composed of 3 to 32 sections of free space of equal size, each located on separate physical drives.

- A mirror set and a stripe set with parity are fault tolerant.

- A Volume Set and a Stripe Set are *not* fault tolerant.

- If a part of a mirror set fails, you must first break the mirror before establishing a new one.

From Here

An important part of planning a server is providing for data protection. The use of fault tolerance on each server is an important part of addressing this issue. When the planning is completed, you can begin installing.

CHAPTER 4

Windows NT 4.0 Installation

The exam content for Windows NT 4.0 Server installation requires you to know about the computer hardware and the network configuration. Microsoft goes to great pains to ensure that you understand the importance of planning the installation. Here is a summary of the topics covered in this chapter:

- Installation preparation

- Hardware compatibility list

- System requirements

- Primary Domain Controllers

- Backup Domain Controllers

- Member Servers

- Different ways to install Windows NT 4.0

- Unattended installations

- Uniqueness database files

- Sysdiff.exe

- Removing Windows NT 4.0

Preparation for Installation: Hardware Compatibility List (HCL)

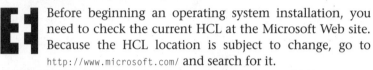 Before beginning an operating system installation, you need to check the current HCL at the Microsoft Web site. Because the HCL location is subject to change, go to http://www.microsoft.com/ and search for it.

The HCL list is updated daily on the Web site and references to the HCL may be on the MCSE test. You'll need to know that Microsoft *only* supports Windows NT 4.0 Server on hardware shown on the official list. Otherwise, hardware not listed is not guaranteed to work with Windows NT.

Preparation for Installation: NT Hardware Qualifier, or NTHQ

Included on the Windows NT installation CD is the *NT Hardware Qualifier* (NTHQ). The NTHQ is a tool that can be used only on Intel-based computers, however. NTHQ, found on the Windows NT Server Setup CD-ROM in the \Support\Hqtool directory, creates an MS-DOS boot floppy when you execute the makedisk.bat file. This floppy is used to boot the system before installation of Windows NT and will detect all hardware, helping to create a system inventory to diagnose potential problems before installing Windows NT.

Minimum Hardware Requirements

For the exam, know the minimum hardware requirements for Windows NT Server; Table 4.1 shows the minimum requirements.

> **NOTE**
> The faster the processor and the more RAM, the better Windows NT Server will perform.

 On the MCSE exam are long, involved questions that conclude by asking about installing Windows NT 4.0 on a 386 computer. You must know your minimum requirements to get the answer correct.

 Also, keep the distinctions between Windows NT Server and Windows NT Workstation clear. Specifically, Windows NT Workstation requires a minimum of 12M RAM, and

Windows NT Server requires 16M. The differences are slight but *important* to know.

Table 4.1
Windows NT Server Requires 16M of RAM

NT Server 4.0 Requirements	INTEL-based	RISC
CPU	486/33 MHz or higher	RISC processor: Alpha, MIPS, or PowerPC
Memory	16M RAM minimum	16M RAM minimum
Hard disk space	125M on a single disk	160M on a single disk
Display monitor	VGA or higher	VGA or higher
Mouse	Pointing device	Pointing device
Drive requirements	HD 3.5″ floppy and CD-ROM or 3.5″ floppy with network connection**	CD-ROM drive*

---

*RISC—must initiate installation from the CD-ROM
**Intel-based systems can install Windows NT without the CD-ROM using a network connection; however a 3.5″ floppy drive is still required.

CAUTION—BEFORE BEGINNING ANY INSTALLATION
Backing up is mentioned throughout the MCSE tests. It's also a smart habit to develop. Back up data from the disk drive before beginning any installation. Also, the following drive configurations will *not* be recognized by the Windows NT Setup procedure:

- Fault-tolerant Setups
- Stripe sets
- Volume sets

You also should do a backup before you change any partition configurations. When you have created or changed partitions so that they are as you want them to be, then restore the data. The process of creating partitions is covered later in this chapter.

Another smart habit to get into is to start a written log of installation information, including passwords, and store the log in a secure place.

Server Roles

E: Nothing is more important to Windows NT network planning than understanding the role(s) the server(s) play in the network. You choose the role of the server during installation. Windows NT Server can be installed as the following:

- Primary Domain Controller
- Backup Domain Controller
- Stand-alone or member server

If partitions need to be changed, first back up the data on the drive in case you need to restore it later.

Neither the PDC, nor a BDC can become a member server without reinstalling Windows NT. Nor, can a member server become the PDC or a BDC without reinstalling Windows NT.

Figure 4.1 illustrates the relationships between the different servers in a Windows NT domain.

I recommend you have at least one BDC so that the domain will still function if the PDC should fail. Microsoft recommends installing at least one BDC for every 2,000 users.

The PDC controls the domain's master account database. All changes are registered to that one database. Therefore, the PDC must be installed and running before any other computer.

A BDC also is installed with Windows NT Server and keeps a copy of the PDC's master account database. This process enables a BDC to log on users. Nevertheless, changes are always made to the PDC and synchronized with BDCs.

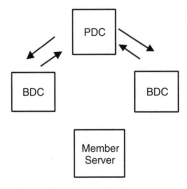

Figure 4.1 PDCs and BDCs both authenticate domain users; member servers do not.

Throughout the MCSE exam are numerous questions about logons. These questions often are in a scenario format and concern the role of a BDC in logons, as well as the relationship between a BDC and the PDC.

PDC's and BDC's are *almost* interchangeable. If the PDC *does not* crash, and you need to take it offline for maintenance, do the following:

1. *Promote* a BDC to become the PDC, which *automatically* demotes the original PDC to a BDC

2. Perform maintenance on the PDC while it is temporarily a BDC.

3. *Promote* the original PDC when it is ready to come back online, which automatically demotes the replacement PDC to a BDC

 There probably will be a scenario test question about promotion and demotion. This question may ask you about the need to perform a synchronization of the domain before promoting a BDC. This synchronization is *not necessary* because synchronization occurs automatically as part of the BDC promotion procedure.

A *member server* also can be created during the Windows NT Server Setup. However, a member server cannot become either the PDC or a BDC, without Windows NT Server being reinstalled and its role redefined at time of Setup.

A *stand-alone server* can be created if it "stands alone" and does not join a domain. However, stand-alone servers may participate in a workgroup.

Member servers do not maintain a copy of the master account database and do not process logons. Instead, they maintain applications and provide file and print services, etc.

 For the purposes of this exam, the distinctions between the types of servers is important as well as their roles within the Windows NT network environment. See Chapter 3, "Microsoft NT 4.0 Directory Services," for more information on server roles.

Windows NT Domains

The Windows NT Setup program requires you to enter a *domain name* when creating the PDC. A domain name should be unique and is created only during the Windows NT Server PDC Setup.

E Microsoft tests use traditional domain names like FINANCE and ACCOUNTING. In the real world, how you create domain and computer names should not be too creative either. Instead, a clear naming system should be created and maintained.

Most likely, domains are created according to geographic regions or department functions. So, a name like ACCOUNTING works well. In addition, if two domains are to communicate, they should not have the same domain name. Not only would this be confusing, but it will interfere with NetBIOS name resolution. The key is planning. A system is vital, or the organization will experience network chaos.

After you enter a domain name, that name is assigned *a Security Identifier* (SID). This SID corresponds to a unique number kept in the Windows NT registry and is the true, secure identifier of the domain. Think of the domain name as the alias of the SID. The domain name is what will be visible to the user, because remembering the lengthy SID number would be difficult if not impossible.

It is important to create a domain name you will want to use for a long time. (You can change the name later. However, in addition to changing it on the PDC, you must change the domain name on *every* computer in the domain—a daunting task indeed!) Regardless of whether the domain name is changed or not, the SID, stays the same.

You need to know one other important bit of information about the SID. The SID must be *unique*.

The importance of the SID cannot be stressed. After the PDC is installed, the domain name, secretly referencing a SID number in the registry, is used throughout the network as a reference point for all other computers. As you can see, its importance is critical.

The concept of domains is covered on the test in a variety of ways—generally in the scenario questions. What is important in preparing for the exam is understanding the Microsoft Windows NT domain concept and the fact that a Windows NT domain is not the same as an Internet domain. From the standpoint of this test, however, knowing that the meanings of the word *domain* are not identical is sufficient.

Creating and Joining a Domain

Understand the concept of creating and joining domains. Also, be sure to make a distinction in your mind between creating a computer account and creating a domain name.

When joining a domain, a *computer account* must be created in the domain. The easiest way to do this is during installation by checking the Create a Computer Account in the Domain option.

 Restrictions are imposed for joining a domain and creating computer accounts, and most likely, you will see a question on the test about this. Specifically, the appropriate rights must be assigned for a user to create a computer account or join a domain. By default, only *administrators, domain administrators,* and *account operators* have the right to create a computer account.

You can create a computer account after installation in two ways. The first is by going to Control Panel | Network | Identification | Change. The Identification Changes dialog box can be used both for joining a domain and creating a computer account.

The second way to create a computer account is with Server Manager. When Server Manager is used, an administrator first creates the account, and then the domain is joined *from* the client computer.

Installation Options

You can install Windows NT 4.0 Server in several ways:

- Dual boot with other operating systems, such as Windows 95 or Windows 4.x

- Fresh installation on a computer without an operating system

- Installing over Windows 3.x

- Upgrade from Windows NT 3.51

For the MCSE Server exam, you need to be aware of these four options, how to start each of them, and how to configure them.

Windows 95

 A question about how to upgrade from Windows 95 to Windows NT may be asked on the test. Do not be fooled by this. There is *no* upgrade procedure from Windows 95 because of incompatibility issues with the Windows 95 registry and the Windows NT registry. What you do in this instance is install Windows NT by following this procedure:

1. Install Windows NT into a separate folder.

2. Remove the Windows 95 folder after Windows NT is installed if a dual boot is not desired.

All applications and hardware previously installed in Windows 95 must be reinstalled in Windows NT. Naturally, they must be Windows NT compatible. You can check the HCL as discussed in the beginning of this chapter for hardware compatibility issues.

Upgrading from Windows NT 3.51 to Windows NT 4.0

Setup will detect previous versions of Windows NT and give you the option of upgrading to the newer version. Some important limitations must be considered, and you need to know these for the test. Specifically, these considerations deal with the concepts we have discussed already about how the PDC and a BDC are almost interchangeable. Member servers may not be promoted to either the PDC or a BDC without reinstallation of Windows NT.

During the upgrade process from Windows NT 3.51, the Registry, network settings, and all accounts are preserved for Windows NT 4.0.

For the exam, you will need to know that some limitations exist during a Windows NT upgrade. Generally, upgrade installations work only if the computer will fulfill the same role in the network. The only exception is that Windows NT 3.51 Workstations may be upgraded to become either a Windows NT 4.0 Workstation or a Windows NT 4.0 Member Server, as shown in Table 4.2.

Table 4.2 Upgrades from Windows NT 3.51 to Windows NT 4.0

From Windows NT 3.51	Upgrade to Windows NT 4.0
PDC or BDC	PDC or BDC
Workstation	Workstation or Member Server
Member Server	Member Server

Dual Booting Options

The Windows NT Server exam may make reference to dual booting; however, a full-fledged question about dual booting is not asked. The concepts involved in dual booting should be understood, nevertheless.

Microsoft does not recommend a dual boot configuration between Windows 95 and Windows NT. However, this configuration is possible. One significant drawback is that applications must be installed twice, once for each operating system. This is especially true if the application has dual versions for 95 and Windows NT and neither is compatible with the other. Keeping the application files in one place and accessing them from either operating system is possible. Hardware devices also must be installed twice on a computer with a dual boot between Windows NT 4.0 and Windows 95.

If you create a computer with a dual boot configuration, it is required that each operating system be installed in separate folders. If you have multiple hard disks, you may elect to keep each operating system separate by placing one on Disk 0 and the other on Disk 1, etc.

Partitioning the Disks

Windows NT Setup can create partitions during the Setup process. You are prompted during installation for this option. Partitions are logical units on the hard disk, distinguished by sequential drive letters.

You also may partition the disk before installation by using the DOS `fdisk` command at a command prompt. After installation, use Disk Administrator to create, delete, and format partitions. Keep in mind that partitioning disks removes *all* data on the disk area in question.

Boot and System Partitions

For the exam, it is important to have an understanding of the differences between these two partitions.

Windows NT requires a system partition *and* a boot partition. The Boot Partition is where the Windows NT operating system files are installed. The System Partition contains the files necessary to boot Windows NT. So, if Windows NT is on Drive C, Drive C becomes the System Partition.

On an Intel-based computer, the active partition is the System Partition, which is usually Drive C, but not always. Table 4.3 may help you understand this. The operating system files are on the boot partition. Guess where files needed to boot the computer are? Paraphrasing Jack Friday, the names have been changed to *confuse* the innocent.

Table 4.3 Boot versus System Partitions

Boot Partition	System Partition
For the Windows NT operating system files, often C:\Winnt*.*	For the hardware-specific files needed to boot Windows NT

If the Windows NT operating system files are on the same partition with the System Partition, that partition also becomes the Boot Partition.

Suppose that two partitions are on the hard disk, Drives C and D. The Winnt folder can be on Drive D, and the system partition containing the boot files can be on Drive C. This configuration is common in a dual boot situation. See Chapter 3 for more information on managing partitions.

File Systems

When beginning your installation, you may find yourself dealing with three file systems, depending upon which, if any, operating system was installed already. The three file systems are FAT, FAT32, and NTFS. Table 4.4 should help you understand which operating systems support which file systems.

Table 4.4 Supported File Systems

Windows95	Windows NT*
FAT	FAT
FAT32	NTFS

*Note: HPFS is no longer supported in Windows NT 4.0.

NOTE

These incompatibilities are for local (dual-boot) computers and do not apply for remote access. For purposes of the exam, treat these file systems as if they are interacting locally. What Microsoft stresses on the tests are the incompatibilities.

Two caveats before proceeding with your decision about which file systems to use:

- Locally, Windows 95 does not support NTFS.
- Locally, Windows NT 4.0 does not support FAT32.

And here's what this means: Let's say that you configured your local computer with a dual boot of Windows 95 and Windows NT. Also assume that you have four partitions. If each partition is configured with a different file system as shown in Table 4.5, here is how each operating system will or will not recognize the file systems. In this example, Windows NT can read drives C, E, and F. Windows 95 can read only Drives C and D.

Table 4.5 Recognized File Systems

Partition	File System	Windows 95	Windows NT
DriveC	FAT	Yes	Yes
DriveD	FAT32	Yes	No
DriveE	NTFS	No	Yes
DriveF	NTFS	No	Yes

In this instance, Drive D cannot serve as the Boot Partition for the Windows NT file system because FAT32 is an unrecognized file system to Windows NT 4.0. To work as a dual boot, install Windows NT to Drives C, E, or F. This arrangement can become complex, so it is understandable why Microsoft might not recommend a dual-boot configuration.

When selecting a file system for a dual-boot system, the prime question is which operating system needs to access data files. That is, if in the preceding situation, only Windows 95 needs to access information on Drive D, then FAT32 is acceptable. On the other hand, if Windows 95 needs to access data from Drives E and F, their file systems would need to be changed.

To avoid this situation on a dual-boot system, each partition or drive should be configured with the FAT file system. However, this configuration may not be ideal because many of the advanced features that are available in FAT32 and NTFS are lost.

Fat File System

As a good all-around file system, *FAT* can be accessed by all Windows operating systems, plus MS-DOS and OS/2. Microsoft does not recommend using the FAT file system for Windows NT installations except when required by a dual-boot situation.

In addition to the variety of access the FAT file system allows, FAT also provides less security, which can be a plus or a minus depending upon your needs. More about this subject is presented in Chapter 8, "Managing Files and Directories."

NTFS File System

New Technology File System (NTFS) is a new file system created by Microsoft for Windows NT. Consequently, Windows NT is the only operating system that can work with NTFS. Windows NT also can recognize FAT (but not FAT32). In a configuration booting with Windows NT only, this will be fine. A dual boot, however, requires more planning.

NTFS was designed by Microsoft to create a more secure file system environment than was possible in the FAT system. Unfortunately, the redesign created incompatibilities with the other file systems. Nevertheless, NTFS provides more features and should be used whenever possible. Among the enhancements are the following:

- File-level security
- File compression
- Extended volumes
- Preserves permissions during a NetWare Migration
- Macintosh file sharing support

Table 4.6 is a quick comparison of the features available in the two file systems you should be aware of for the exam.

If you're not sure which file system to use during installation, choose FAT. You can convert FAT to NTFS at any time; however, you cannot convert NTFS to FAT. Converting FAT to NTFS is performed at a command prompt, and the utility to run is Convert.exe. If you need help with the utility, type help convert or convert /? at a command prompt.

Windows NT 4.0 Setup defaults to the FAT file system.

Table 4.6 NTFS Can Do Everything FAT Can Do, and More

	FAT	NTFS
Allows shared folders	Yes	Yes
File/folder level security	No	Yes
Share level security	Yes	Yes
Auditing	No	Yes
MAC support on the server	No	Yes
MAC support on workstation	No	No
POSIX support	Yes	Yes
Long filenames	Yes	Yes
File compression	No	Yes

Planning the Installation

You should plan your installation of Windows NT before beginning. Not only is it wise, but planning is one of the six test scoring categories.

If you are doing a single Windows NT installation (in other words, a non-dual boot), create the Windows NT system and boot files with the following configuration:

- Drive C
- On the primary partition
- Fat file system

If this computer is RISC-based, there *must* be at least 2M of free space on the disk formatted as FAT for the boot partition.

Otherwise, for Intel-based computers, the size of the partition depends on how large you want to make your initial page file, if you have alternate disk drives, and how you want to organize your applications and files.

 For the test, remember the importance of keeping a FAT partition for booting between MS-DOS, Windows 95, or any 16-bit Windows operating systems, such as Windows 3.x.

Again, if you are installing Windows NT on a computer that has applications and data on it already, back up everything important in case of a problem with the installation. A total failure is unlikely, but better safe than sorry.

Windows NT server also installs as a *Custom Setup* that enables you to pick only the components you want to install.

Here are the options you can choose from in the Custom Setup:

- Accessibility options—for individuals with disabilities
- Accessories—Wordpad, Paint, Hyperterminal, Write, Clock, etc.
- Communications programs—anything that uses the modem
- Games—Solitaire, FreeCell, Pinball (new in Windows NT, not in 95, except PLUS!)
- Windows messaging—e-mail services
- Multimedia—programs for multimedia presentations

Installation Phases

Without a doubt, you must know the *four* phases to the Windows NT installation. They are as follows:

1 Initializing Installation

During this phase, Setup determines whether a previous version of Windows NT is installed and will ask you whether you want to upgrade or install the new version of Windows NT without upgrading. Hardware detection also takes place during this phase. Finally, Setup asks you where to install the Windows NT files as well as what type of file system to use and the partition information.

2 Gathering Information

Setup initializes this portion of the installation using the Windows NT Setup wizard. During this phase, you will be asked the following:

- Are you using Per Server or Per Seat licensing?
- Is installation for the PDC, a BDC, or member server?
- Would you like to create an Emergency Repair disk?
- Which optional components would you like to install using the Custom Setup?

- What password would you like to use for the Administrator Account?

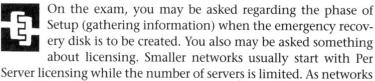 On the exam, you may be asked regarding the phase of Setup (gathering information) when the emergency recovery disk is to be created. You also may be asked something about licensing. Smaller networks usually start with Per Server licensing while the number of servers is limited. As networks grow, a one-time, one-way conversion to Per Seat licensing eventually may become appropriate.

3 Installing Windows NT Networking

This portion of Setup asks you several more, nonetheless, important questions. The first question is about your Network configuration; specifically, whether you are wired to the network or accessing the network via a dial up connection?

NOTE

If you answer NONE when asked about your network configuration, Setup will end and go to *finishing setup*. Otherwise, you will finish setting up this section.

Among the other responses you will be prompted for are the following:

- Which Domain to Join (see earlier section about creating and joining domains).

- Information about your network adapter card. You will be given the option to allow Setup to automatically detect and install the hardware. However, because Windows NT is not yet fully Plug-n-Play, you must verify the information obtained through automatic detection.

- Protocols to install and any necessary protocol or network configuration parameters.

- Additional services to install.

4 Finishing Setup

At this point, you have installed Windows NT Server. In the final brief stage, you set the time zone for your system and configure your video monitor.

Specific Setup Issues

A remote installation and local installation are distinguished only by the location of the Setup files. Throughout the following explanations, to begin a server-based installation, you will locate the system files you'll need for installation by connecting over-the-network to a network share.

When installing Windows NT Server locally, the installation files may be located on the CD-ROM or already copied to the hard drive. You may access the installation files and run the installation from either the CD-ROM or the hard drive.

Two different forms of the command are used to install Windows NT. They are as follows:

- winnt.exe
- winnt32.exe

Use winnt32 when upgrading from a prior version of Windows NT; use winnt in all other cases. An installation is faster using winnt32 than when you use winnt because Windows NT already is configured and running and fewer files must be copied.

For the test, it is important to be familiar with several installation *switches*, or command extensions and how to use them. To study all the options, at the command prompt, change to the directory containing winnt and winnt32 and type the executable filename followed by the /? switch for a fuller listing.

- /x—Prevents Setup from creating the startup disks

- /ox—Creates a set of startup disks—useful for CD-ROM installations

- /b—Prevents the necessity of using startup disks. Rather, these files are written to the hard disk and require about 5M additional hard drive space. Requires /s.

- /s—Specifies the location of the installation files. Multiple /s switches may be used to speed up a network-based installation.

- /t—Specifies the partition to use for temporary files

- /f—Speeds installation by preventing file verification

- /u:answer_file—Designates the answer file to use with an unattended installation

■ /udf:id—Identifies the udf file to be used during an unattended installation

 Be sure to understand the use of the /ox and /b switches. It is not always necessary to boot with the three startup floppies. If the system BIOS supports booting from the CD-ROM drive, and if the CD-ROM drive is Windows NT compatible, you often can start installation directly from the Windows NT CD-ROM.

Doing a Fresh Install of Windows NT

If no previous operating system exists, Windows NT uses three floppy disks to begin the Setup process. The disks first install a condensed version of Windows NT on the hard drive that then allows the CD-ROM to be accessed for continuing the installation.

Begin your installation of Windows NT, whether locally or server-based, by using the winnt.exe /x command. You will use the /x switch to prevent the boot disks from being created again. If you are doing a network install, you can use winnt.exe /b to bypass the need for Setup disks.

If the Windows 95 or DOS CD-ROM Drive Is Not Supported by Windows NT

If the CD-ROM does not appear on the HCL, this situation is not as hopeless as it may first appear. Begin the Windows NT installation by using Windows 95 or DOS and this procedure:

1. Start the operating system that supports the CD-ROM.

2. Connect to a network share, or copy the installation files from the CD-ROM to the hard drive.

3. Start the installation from either the hard drive copy of the installation files or the network share.

RISC-Based Computer Setup

In most cases, after inserting the Windows NT CD, the Setup program will initiate itself, and installation begins automatically. A RISC computer uses a program on the CD called Setupldr. If this doesn't happen, use the RUN A PROGRAM option to enter a path to the SETUPLDR program.

Don't forget RISC computers require a minimum 2M boot partition formatted as FAT.

Doing a Server-Based Installation from the Installation Files

It is simple to set up Windows NT to install over a network. Over-the-network installation is an excellent way for sites with multiple client computers to install Windows NT. This installation also is faster because installation is from files on the server and doesn't necessarily require reading from a CD or floppies.

Server-based installations work only with Intel processors. RISC-based computers cannot do an initial installation of Windows NT from a server, they must be individually installed. Server-based installations can be used for RISC computers, however, for upgrading or reinstallations.

You can use two methods to distribute the installation files over the network.

Using the XCOPY command

- Create a folder on the Server for the files. Share the folder.

- Use the "XCOPY /s" command to copy the appropriate folder and subfolders based on the type of processor. Note that using /s is crucial to ensure that the installation subfolders are copied.

Sharing the CD-ROM

- Share the server's CD-ROM and insert the Windows NT Server CD.

- Change the share permissions on the server CD-ROM from Everyone to Read.

Using XCOPY requires more room on the server; however, using the CD-ROM may slow the installation.

Performing an Unattended Installation

The test covers unattended installation in some depth. If you want to do additional research, the Microsoft materials you may consult are the Windows NT Workstation Resource Kit and TechNet.

The command for an unattended installation is as follows:

```
winnt.exe /u:unattend.txt
```

or

```
winnt32.exe /u:unattend.txt (for Windows NT upgrades)
```

unattend.txt is an *answer file* you create to answer the Setup questions posed during installation. In a single installation of Windows NT Server, you normally would answer these questions while sitting in front of the computer. By doing an Unattended Installation, the questions are answered automatically, eliminating user input.

Creating an answer file is easy. The Windows NT Server installation CD-ROM includes the setupmgr.exe program. This program will help you create the custom replies you need for your answer file.

The /u switch specified in the preceding command actually indicates that this is an unattended installation. Other switches are covered earlier in this chapter.

NOTE
Using /u *requires* use of the /s switch to specify the location of the installation files.

For the exam, remember that winnt32.exe *does not support* the following switches:

- /f–Do not verify files as they are copied to the Setup boot floppies
- /c—Skips free-space check on Setup boot disks
- /l—Creates the log file $winnt.log

Uniqueness Database File (UDF)

For the exam, you need to understand that you can use *both* an Answer File and a UDF. Although the Answer File, or unattend.txt, creates a global installation with default settings for all computers, the UDF enables you to create specific information for a certain computer.

Let's say that you need to specify the user name and computer name for some computers during installation. The UDF does that by overriding the %username% and %computername% section of the answer file. The command would be written as follows:

```
WINNT(32).exe /u:unattend.txt /udf:ID[filename]
```

A UDF is created using a text editor such as Notepad. You can have more than one UDF, although this level of information is not needed for the test.

Sysdiff.Exe

An unattended installation also is called a *scripted installation*. The sysdiff.exe utility is used to install applications that don't support scripted installations. sysdiff.exe has three modes:

- **SNAP**—Records a snapshot of a computer's registry, files, and folders.

- **DIFF**—Records difference between the SNAP configuration and after the desired applications have been installed.

- **APPLY**—The method of applying the DIFF configurations recorded.

The procedure for using the sysdiff utility is as follows:

1. After installing Windows NT, run the sysdiff /snap snapshot_file utility, in which 'snapshot_file' is a filename you invent. This will create a model of your source computer.

2. Next, configure the source computer *exactly* as you will eventually configure the destination computers, remembering:

   - Microprocessors of the source and destination computers must be identical.

   - The system root folder, or winnt folder, must be located identically on source and destination computers.

3. Run the sysdiff /snap snapshot_file difference_file utility, in which snapshot_file is the file created in the first step and difference_file is a filename you create. This difference file designates the distinctions between the beginning model and ending model of the source computer.

4. The last step is to run sysdiff | apply difference_file on the target computer.

 What's important to know for purposes of the test: The differences recorded during this procedure include the creation of binary versions of the application files that enable the unattended installation to occur.

Removing Windows NT 4.0

Just as important as installing Windows NT is knowing how to remove it. The test does contain questions about this special process. Here are the steps you'll need to take to remove Windows NT from a computer:

1. Create a boot disk for the alternative operating system and copy the `sys.com` utility to the boot disk. Be sure and test the boot disk before going any further.

2. Get rid of any NTFS partitions. This can be done in one of three ways:

   - Disk Administrator
   - Run the Windows NT Setup disks
   - *fdisk* from MS-DOS 6.x

3. Delete the `WINNT` folder and its contents and subfolders.

4. Delete the following files:

   - `Ntldr`
   - `Ntdetect.com`
   - `Boot.ini`
   - `Ntbootdd.sys`
   - `Bootsect.dos`
   - `Pagefile.sys`

5. Reboot the computer using the boot disk created in Step 1.

6. Type `sys c:` (This places the necessary boot files back on the Drive C boot track.)

7. When you reboot your computer, Windows NT will be gone, and you will have reverted to the alternative operating system.

For Review

Although the installation is straightforward, there is still quite a bit of material to remember. As you prepare for the exam, keep the following in mind—these items are sure to pop up on a test:

- Planning the installation is crucial.
- HCL defines what is compatible with Windows NT.

- NTHQ can be created from the Windows NT Setup disk.
- NT Server requires a 486/33 microprocessor or higher.
- Only one PDC can exist per domain.
- More than one BDC can exist per domain.
- Every device, user, and resource in the domain has a unique SID to identify it.
- Computers must have Accounts to join a domain.
- Windows NT can be installed as an upgrade or a fresh install over previous versions of Windows NT.
- Windows NT replaces Windows 95 but is *never* upgraded from it.
- Windows NT can dual boot with other operating systems.
- The boot and system partitions can be the same or different partitions.
- Know these three file systems and compatibility issues: FAT, FAT32, NTFS.
- You can convert from FAT to NTFS, but never from NTFS back to FAT without reinstalling Windows NT.
- Installs are begun with either `winnt.exe` or `winnt32.exe` (for upgrades).
- `winnt.exe /ox` creates the three Setup disks, including the Setup boot disk (#1).
- You must create a share on the server or share the CD-ROM before doing a server-based installation.
- Unattended installations use answer files and UDFs.
- `sysdiff.exe` creates a snapshot of a reference computer to install applications.
- When removing Windows NT and returning to Windows 95, always remove the NTFS partition after you create the Windows 95 boot disk.

From Here

For more information on server roles and domains, see Chapter 2, "Microsoft NT 4.0 Directory Services." Chapter 3, "Planning for Fault Tolerance," provides additional information on managing partitions. Managing file systems is covered in Chapter 8, "Managing Files and Directories."

CHAPTER 5

Network Configuration

T his chapter covers important details of the Windows NT 4.0 Server network configuration process:

- Configuring network protocols
- Configuring network adapters
- Configuring the network Browser Service
- Securing your computer on the network

The Network dialog box enables you to install, remove, or configure various network components. This dialog box can be accessed via the Network Applet in the Control Panel or by right-clicking on the Network Neighborhood icon and selecting properties. Figure 5.1 shows the Network dialog box and its tabs.

Identification

This tab displays the computer's name and its domain. Identification also is used to change the computer's name or to join another domain. When joining a domain, an account must be created for the computer.

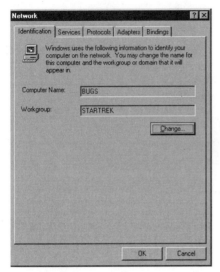

Figure 5.1 The Network dialog box has five tabs: Identification, Services, Protocols, Adapters, and Bindings.

A computer account can be created in one of two ways. Either use Server Manager to create the account or create the account at the same time the computer joins the new domain. This process will require entering an account and password with the right to create an account.

Protocols

A protocol is a piece of software that embodies a set of rules which allows communication over the network. A protocol may be thought of as the language a computer speaks. If two computers speak different languages (protocols), then communication cannot occur. Three protocols are supported with Windows NT: NetBEUI, NWLink, and TCP/IP.

Each of these protocols has advantages and disadvantages. The network environment needs to be considered when selecting a protocol or protocols for your network. The protocol considerations you can expect to find on the exam are reviewed in this chapter.

NetBIOS Extended User Interface (NetBEUI) was introduced in 1985 by IBM. NetBEUI is a small, fast protocol that is an excellent choice for a small network. Although it is broadcast based, for the network with less than 200 nodes, it is often the best choice.

NetBEUI's major drawback is the fact that it is not routable. Therefore, it will not work on the routed network. Also, if your network includes computers running other operating systems, such as NetWare or Unix, another protocol must be selected, because NetBEUI is not supported by these operating systems.

NWLink

NWLink is Microsoft's own IPX/SPX compatible transport protocol. NWLink requires minimal configuration. Because it is routable, NWLink is an excellent choice for the routed network. If NetWare servers are part of the network, then NWLink is required to provide for communication between the Windows NT computers and these NetWare servers.

TIP

By installing the NWLink protocol on a Windows NT computer, that Windows NT client computer can run applications on the NetWare server.

When NWLink is installed on a Windows NT server, it is configured to automatically determine the IPX frame type to use. If you need to connect to different NetWare servers that are using different frame types, you will need to manually configure the frame type. The frame type is configured using the NWLink IPX/SPX Properties dialog box.

TIP

The standard frame type for NetWare servers running NetWare 3.11 or older is 802.3. If the NetWare server is running Version 3.12 or newer, then the default frame type is 802.2.

The disadvantage of the NWLink protocol is that it is not supported by Unix computers. In addition, NWLink by itself will not provide your network with communication to the Internet or your company's intranet. See Chapter 16, "NetWare Connectivity," for a more detailed discussion of integrating NetWare servers in your network.

TCP/IP

TCP/IP is the protocol of choice for access to the Internet or an intranet. TCP/IP is routable and provides instant communication with computers running Unix. Although rapidly becoming the most popular protocol, especially for

Wide Area Networks (WANs), TCP/IP is somewhat more difficult to configure and to maintain on a network.

 When installing TCP/IP on a Windows-based network, the two minimum parameters needed are as follows:

- IP address
- Subnet mask

The subnet mask determines the part of the IP address that is the Network ID and the part that is the Host ID. For two computers to communicate, they must be on the same network or have a router between them.

In a routed environment, a default gateway address is a third item also needed to configure TCP/IP on a Windows-based computer. The gateway address is the IP address of the local router that provides for nonlocal delivery.

To open the TCP/IP Properties dialog box, highlight TCP/IP on the Protocols tab of the Network Properties dialog box and click on the Properties button. Figure 5.2 shows the TCP/IP Properties dialog box.

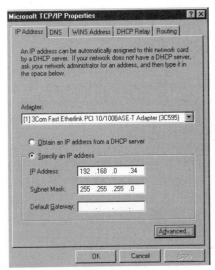

Figure 5.2   The Properties dialog box for TCP/IP is used to assign an IP address, subnet mask, and other parameters.

Other TCP/IP parameters that may be configured include:

- *Domain Name System* (DNS)—Enter the IP address for one or more DNS servers to be used for host name resolution.

- Windows Internet Name Service (WINS Address)—Enter the IP address of the primary and secondary WINS servers. This tab also is used to enable DNS for Windows resolution. See Chapter 13 for further discussion of WINS.

- DHCP Relay—This tab is used to configure the server as a DHCP Relay Agent. See Chapter 12, "Dynamic Host Configuration Protocol," for further discussion of DHCP.

- Routing—This tab is used to enable IP forwarding on the multihomed computer. (Multihoming is described later in this chapter.)

DLC

 Data Link Control (DLC) is not a transport protocol. DLC is used to communicate with IBM mainframes and HP printers using Jet Direct network cards. DLC is small and is not routable. Install DLC only on the computer that needs to communicate with a resource using DLC. An example is a print server that needs to communicate directly with one of these special network printers.

 TIP
If you are installing an HP Printer attached directly to the network on a Windows NT Server and do not see the HP Printer port, you need to install the DLC protocol.

Point-to-Point Tunneling Protocol (PPTP)

PPTP can be used to establish virtual private networks using multiple protocols. PPTP provides secure access via the Internet by encapsulating the data before transmission. Remote users can securely access the company's network by connecting through the Internet. These users can send any type of packet over the network allowing the use of IPX, for example, to communicate over the Internet.

Adapters

Adapters refer to the software/hardware devices that provide physical access to your network. The two most common adapters are a *network adapter card* (NIC) and a modem. See Chapter 15, "Remote Access Server," for information on installing and configuring modems.

Although Windows NT will attempt to detect and configure your NIC, it is not a true plug-and-play operating system. As such, you must verify the settings for your NIC when installing your card and its device driver.

 TIP
If you cannot access network resources, be sure and verify the IRQ and I/O address. Also if you are using a combo card, be sure and verify the transceiver settings.

Multihoming

A multihomed computer is configured with more than one IP address. You can configure your computer with more than one IP address in two ways. One way is by binding multiple IP addresses to one network card by clicking the Advance button on the IP address tab of the TCP/IP Properties dialog box. Figure 5.3 shows the addition of multiple IP addresses.

The second way to configure a multihomed computer is to install multiple network cards—with each network card attached to a different network segment. By enabling IP forwarding, this configuration allows the Windows NT server to route information between different segments.

Bindings

Network bindings connect NICs, protocols, and services. In Windows NT, the bindings can be disabled and/or reordered. Changing the binding order will alter the way information is obtained across the network.

 TIP
To optimize network performance, change the order that protocols are bound to the workstation service so that the most frequently used protocol is first on top of the list.

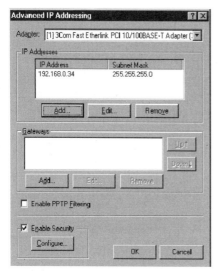

Figure 5.3 Multiple IP addresses can be configured to be bound to one NIC.

Due to the modularity of the Windows NT operating system and the use of *Network Driver Interface Specification* (NDIS), multiple protocols may be bound to one NIC. This is especially useful in the multiplatform environment that includes Windows NT, Unix, and NetWare-based computers. The order that the protocols are bound has an impact on efficiency of communication, so binding order is important to fine-tuning performance.

Default Services

During Windows NT Server installation, several services were installed, but what is a service? Think of a service as a piece of software that provides specialized functionality for the operating system. The default services, which are always installed, include the following:

- Workstation service
- Server service
- NetBIOS service
- Remote Procedure Call service

The two services with the most confusing names are the server service and the workstation service. These names are not the same as Windows NT Server or Windows NT Workstation, which are operating systems. These two services provide for the sharing and use of network resources. Both the server and workstation services are installed with both Windows NT Server and Windows NT Workstation.

The server service provides network access to your computer's resources, such as files or printers. The server installs the *Server Message Block* (SMB) protocol. This language is used by Windows NT based computers to communicate with each other.

The workstation service is actually the SMB client. All user requests are handled by the workstation service. This service enables you to use your computer to access resources located on other computers via the network.

Two other services necessary for network operations are the *Network Basic Input/Output System* (NetBIOS) Interface and *Remote Procedure Call* (RPC) Configuration, which consists of two major parts as discussed later in this chapter.

NetBIOS defines the naming convention that is used on the network and can communicate over NetBEUI, NWLink, and TCP/IP. NetBIOS enables communication *sessions* between networked computers and the transfer of information between them.

The RPC Configuration actually consists of several different services including the RPC Locator and RPC Endpoint Mapper. This configuration provides access to the RPC Name Service database. RPC is the interface for applications to establish a secure connection to perform procedures on one or more remote computer such as user authentication.

RIP (Routing Information Protocol)

The *Routing Information Protocol* (RIP) is actually a service that runs on *Internet Protocol* (IP) or *Internetwork Packet Exchange* (IPX) or both. Use the Services tab of the Network Properties dialog box to install RIP.

RIP forwards network packets between two or more connected networks and exchanges routing information with other RIP enabled routers. RIP also periodically broadcasts all the routing information that it knows. Due to the high amount of traffic, RIP routers are best used on a relatively small network.

Computer Browser Service

The browser service simplifies locating network resources by maintaining a list of resources and converting the NetBIOS names for these available resources to network addresses. Windows NT assigns browser tasks to specific computers on the network. The computers work together to provide a centralized list of shared network resources, eliminating the need for all computers to maintain their own resource lists.

The Windows NT Browser system consists of a master browser, backup browsers, and browser clients. The computer that is the master browser maintains the browse list and periodically sends copies of the list to the backup browsers. The browser client obtains the current browse list by sending a request to either the master browser or a backup browser.

 The browser status of a Windows NT Server can be configured via the registry. You can decide whether or not your computer will become a browser. The key is

```
\HKEY_LOCAL_MACHINE\System\CurrentControlSet\Services\Browser\
Parameters\MaintainServerList
```

and may be set to Yes, No, or Auto. If set to Auto, the Master Browser will determine whether this particular computer will function as a browser. On any computer with an entry of Yes or Auto for the MaintainServerList parameter, Windows NT Setup configures the Browser service to start automatically when the computer starts.

TIP

Changing the value for the MaintainServerList registry entry only changes the role of the computer—whether it can be a browser or not. The capability for the server to query a browser is not affected by turning off its participation in browsing.

Browser Roles

All Windows NT domain controllers are automatically configured to be a browser. The PDC is always the *domain master browser*. Any BDCs are configured to be backup browsers. As a rule, member servers will become a backup browser only when needed.

DOMAIN MASTER BROWSER

The domain master browser is responsible for collecting announcements for the entire domain, including any network segments, and for providing a list of domain resources to master browsers.

MASTER BROWSER

The master browser is responsible for collecting the information necessary to create and maintain the browse list. The browse list includes all servers in the master browser's domain or workgroup and the list of all domains on the network. Individual servers announce their presence to the master browser. When the master browser receives the announcement, it adds that computer to the browse list. The PDC will always be the master browser. If the PDC becomes unavailable, then a backup browser, normally a BDC, becomes the master browser.

BACKUP BROWSER

The backup browser receives a copy of the browse list from the master browser. Backup browsers call the master browser every 15 minutes to get the latest copy of the browse list and a list of domains. If the backup browser cannot find the master browser, it forces an election of the master browser. BDCs always are backup browsers unless located on a network segment separate from the PDC. In this case, the BDC becomes a master browser for that segment.

Because browsing is broadcast based and does not cross a router; browsing across the *wide area network* (WAN) to other subnetworks requires at least one browser on the domain for each subnetwork. The PDC typically functions as the master browser on its subnetwork.

Browser Elections

Browser elections occur to select a new master browser under the following circumstances:

- When a computer cannot locate a master browser
- When a preferred master browser comes online
- When a Windows NT domain controller system boots

The Browser service must be notified by a resource when the resource is available. Each networked computer periodically announces itself to the master browser. The computer announces its availability in intervals of 1 minute, 2 minutes, 4 minutes, 8 minutes, 12 minutes, and then announces to the master browser only every 12 minutes.

If the master browser has not heard from the computer for three consecutive announcement periods, the master browser removes the computer from the browse list. This system of automatic browser database refreshment is designed so that users have immediate access to all available resources.

Backup browsers, by default, call the master browser every 15 minutes to obtain updated network resource browse lists and lists of workgroups and domains. Because it can take up to 15 minutes for a backup browser to receive an updated browse list, a missing computer may appear in the browse list for as long as 51 minutes after it is no longer an available resource on the network. The time period consists of 36 minutes, which is three 12-minute announcement cycles for the master browser to automatically remove the resource from the database for lack of announcement, plus 15 minutes for the backup browser to receive an updated resource list.

Securing Your Computer on the Network

 The first and foremost action you must take to secure your network is to control *physical* access to your servers, especially the domain controllers. Another action to take on all your Windows NT-based computers in order to prevent unauthorized access via the network is to stop any unnecessary services.

The most common unneeded service is the server service. If a workstation or server computer is not hosting resources that others need access to over the network, then stopping the server service will stop all outside access without reducing network usefulness. However, turning off the server service also prevents remote administration of that computer.

Other basic actions that you may take to improve the security of your Windows NT computers include *renaming* the administrator account and disabling the guest account. Implementation of password policies also can improve your network's security. These are discussed in Chapter 7, "User Manager for Domains."

Frequently, the little things leave your network open to intruders. Always be sure to implement and enforce password policies. Limit membership to the administrator group to those who need it. And, most important, keep your user accounts up to date. Remember, the most frequent source of data corruption occurs from within —either on purpose by disgruntled employees or by accident.

For Review

- Use the Identification tab of the Network dialog box to change the computer's name or to join a domain.

- NetBEUI is a nonroutable protocol that works well for the smaller network.

- NWLink is routable and is used to communicate with NetWare servers.

- If you are having trouble communicating with a NetWare server using NWLink, check the frame type.

- TCP/IP is the protocol of choice for communicating with the Internet.

- The minimum parameters required to configure TCP/IP is an IP address and a subnet mask.

- If configuring a routed network, TCP/IP requires an IP address, a subnet mask, and a default gateway.

- Use DLC to communicate with an HP printer connected directly to the network with a JetDirect card.

- A multihomed computer has two or more IP addresses.

- Change the order protocols are bound to the workstation service to optimize network communication.

- Change the value of `\HKEY_LOCAL_MACHINE\System\CurrentControlSet \Services\Browser\Parameters\MaintainServerList` to control a computer's browser role.

- Stop unnecessary services to better secure your computer against outside intrusions.

From Here

For more information on network services, see Chapter 12, "Dynamic Host Configuration Protocol," and Chapter 13, "Windows Internet Name Service (WINS)." Chapter 16, "NetWare Connectivity," details integrating NetWare servers in your network, and account policies are discussed in Chapter 7, "User Manager for Domains."

CHAPTER 6

Network Services

Directory Replication

When planning a domain with more than one domain controller, a method of ensuring that logon scripts and system policies are consistently applied is needed. This method should address issues, such as administrative overhead, network traffic, and ease of user access.

In addition, replication may be used to provide user access to various templates or other documents while providing for load balancing. An additional advantage of placing these files on separate servers is that the load placed on a server by multiple users accessing these files is reduced, and response time is improved.

Microsoft Directory Replication was designed for this purpose. The Directory Replicator service is used to maintain copies of folders and the files contained in them on multiple computers. The organizational scheme of the folders and files is retained.

Both Windows NT Server and Windows NT Workstation may participate in directory replication. The master directory, however, must reside on Windows NT Server. As updates are made to the master directory, these changes are duplicated to all the copies. Figure 6.1 shows how directory replication occurs.

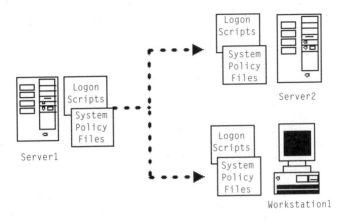

Figure 6.1 Folders and files, such as logon scripts and system policies, are copied from the master directory on Server1 to their destinations on Server2 and Workstation1.

Files to Replicate

Basically, an administrator may replicate three types of files to multiple locations: logon scripts, system policies, and shared files.

E Both logon scripts and system policies generally are replicated from the Primary Domain Controller to each Backup Domain Controller. In this way, no matter which domain controller authenticates a user, the appropriate parameters are applied.

For example, suppose that a user is a member of a group with a system policy. In order for this policy to be applied, the policy file must be present on the domain controller that authenticates that user. If the system policy is not present, the appropriate policy will not be applied.

The same is true of logon scripts. The domain controller that authenticates a user looks in its netlogon share for the appropriate logon script. If the script does not exist, then the user may not have access to necessary network folders or printers.

The third type of file that may be replicated are those files accessed by a larger number of users. These files include online information such as in-house telephone lists and templates used to maintain consistency in document production.

These files should be designated as read-only in order to prevent changes. If any change is made, those changes are copied over the next time replication occurs.

The two sides to directory replication are the export server and the import computer.

The Process

The Directory Replicator Service is responsible for controlling how and when replication occurs. The first step in enabling directory replication is to designate the directories to be replicated on the export server (i.e., the computer that contains the master copies). The import computer also must be configured as to the destination location for the replicated files.

When changes occur to the files contained in the directories, the new versions are copied to the destination computer (import computer). This update occurs as the result of a three-step process and is illustrated in Figure 6.2.

- The export server periodically checks for updated files. If newer versions are found, it notifies the import computer that changes have been made.

- After receiving the update notice, the import computer contacts the export server and checks for newer versions by reading the directory structure on the export server.

- The import computer copies any files that have newer versions on the export server. In addition, the import computer deletes any files it contains that no longer exist on the export server.

If no changes have been made to the export server, no update notification is sent. The frequency that an export server checks for changes is configurable by editing the registry.

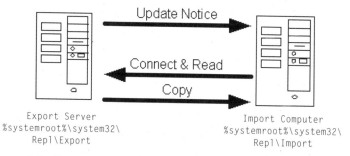

```
    Export Server                Import Computer
%systemroot%\system32\        %systemroot%\system32\
   Repl\Export                    Repl\Import
```

Figure 6.2   The export server notifies the import computer that changes have been made. The import computer then copies those new files.

Export Server

The Export Server maintains the master directory structure. This directory structure is copied to the designated import computer(s). Only Windows NT Server may be configured as an export server. The default path for the directories to be exported is %SYSTEMROOT%\ System32\Repl\Export. This directory automatically is shared as Repl$ when the directory replicator service is started. The administrator must create the subdirectories under this location.

TIP

Only *subdirectories* located under the %SYSTEMROOT%\System32\Repl\ Export directory are replicated. If any individual files are located in this directory, they will *not* be replicated.

When Windows NT Server and Workstation are installed, the replication path is created. In addition, a subdirectory called Scripts is created under both the Export and Import subdirectories. This subdirectory is used for logon scripts and system policies.

Additional directories may be configured to be exported, such as when replicating a phone book or a collection of document templates. The directory replication service creates the directory structure automatically on the destination or import computer.

To serve as an export server, the computer must be running Windows NT Server. Configuring the export server consists of four steps:

1. A user account must be created that the Directory Replicator Service uses to access the designated folders. Add this account to the Backup Operators and Replicators built-in groups.

   When creating this account, be sure to uncheck the User Must Change Password at Next Logon option. Failure to do this will result in directory replication failing.

   Also, be sure to check the Password Never Expires option. Otherwise, directory replication will fail later when a notification of impending password expiration is created.

2. Configure the Directory Replicator Service to use the account you just created. In addition, make sure that the Service is configured to start automatically.

3. Place the directories to be replicated under the %SYSTEMROOT%\ System32\Repl\Export directory.

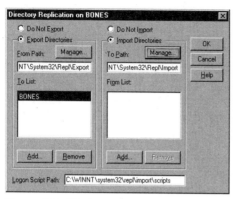

Figure 6.3 The Directory Replication dialog box is used to configure the directories to export as well as the destination import computer.

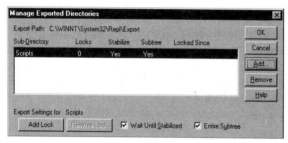

Figure 6.4 The Manage Exported Directories dialog box is used to designate which subdirectories are to be exported and whether a lock should be applied.

4. Use Server Manager to designate which directories the export server should export. Figure 6.3 shows the Directory Replication dialog box used to configure the export server.

In addition to selecting the directories to export and their destinations, additional parameters may be designated such as Locks, Export Subtrees, and whether the directory should be stabilized as shown in Figure 6.4.

- *Locks*—Prevents a directory from being exported

- *Subtrees*—Whether all subdirectories also should be exported

- *Stabilize*—Indicates how long after changes are made before a file is exported

TIP

If the Wait Until Stabilized **option is checked on the export computer, it causes the export server to wait a period of time before notifying the import computer that changes have been made.**

The disadvantage to using this option is that the import computer copies the entire subtree when *any* file changes. If this option is not checked, the import computer examines each of the files and copies only the files that have been changed.

Two additional parameters are configurable on the Export Server but not by using Server Manager. Rather, these parameters are configured via the Registry. These parameters are located at

```
HKEY_LOCAL_MACHINE\System\CurrentControlSet\Services\Replicator
\Parameters
```

and are *Interval* and *GuardTime*.

- *Interval* indicates how frequently the export server checks for file changes. The default is 5 minutes with a range of 1 to 60 minutes.

- *GuardTime* is how long after changes are made before a directory may be exported. This condition is referred to as being stabilized. The default is 2 minutes and may range from 0 to one-half of the interval value.

Import Computer

The Import Computer receive updates from the export server. An Import Computer may be Windows NT Server, Windows NT Workstation, or a LAN Manager OS/2 server.

The default path for the directories to be imported to is %SYSTEMROOT%\System32\Repl\Import. The Directory Replicator Service creates the appropriate subdirectories to correspond to the directory structure on the export server.

 Configuring the import computer consists of three steps.

1. A user account must be created if the import computer is not part of the export server's domain. This account must have the same username and password as the account created for replication on the export server. In addition, make this account a member of the local Backup Operators and Replicator groups.

When creating this account, be sure to uncheck the User Must Change Password at Next Logon option. Failure to do this will result in directory replication failing.

Also, be sure to check the Password Never Expires option. Otherwise, directory replication will fail later when a notification of impending password expiration is created.

2. Configure the Directory Replicator Service to use the account you just created. In addition, make sure that the Service is configured to start automatically.

3. Use Server Manager to configure to receive the files from the export server. You also must configure which computers will be accepted as export servers. Figure 6.5 shows the Directory Replication dialog box used to configure the import computer.

In addition to selecting where to import the directories, you also select which directories to import. A directory may be locked, which prevents automatic replication, but it may be manually replicated. Figure 6.6 shows the Manage Imported Directories dialog box, which also shows the status of replication.

Managing Enterprise Directory Replication

When administering an enterprise network, directory replication may be necessary across WAN links, especially if domain controllers are located on the far side of the link. If the link is slow,

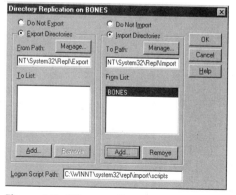

Figure 6.5 When configuring the import computer, the Directory Replication dialog box is used to designate what export server will be accepted and where to save the replicated files and directories.

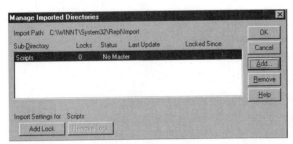

Figure 6.6   The Manage Imported Directories dialog box shows the status of replication as well as allowing a lock to be placed on a specific directory.

this replication may have a detrimental effect on the apparent speed of the network.

If the only thing being replicated is logon scripts and/or system policies, this effect is usually not significant. These files are generally rather small and do not frequently change; thereby not requiring replication very frequently.

If, however, other types of files are replicated, this may result in considerable network traffic. Sometimes this traffic is large enough to adversely effect users' ability to access needed resources across this link.

The replication traffic across a WAN link consists of the following:

- Update notification from the export server to each import computer. By default, this notification occurs every 5 minutes.

- If changes have occurred, the import computer establishes a connection to the export server.

- The import computer then copies the updated files.

- If the import computer fails to hear from the export server after a period of time, the import computer contacts the export server to determine whether updates have occurred. This interval defaults to 10 minutes.

Some parameters may be changed to decrease the amount of traffic. Two of them, Interval and GuardTime, are discussed earlier in this chapter. In addition, the Pulse parameter controls how frequently the import computer contacts the export server.

If an import computer fails to hear from an export server after a specified period of time, the import computer contacts the export server. The amount of time that must elapse before this happens is determined by multiplying the Interval parameter times the Pulse parameter.

If default values are used (Interval = 5 min. and Pulse = 2), then the interval is 10 minutes. Lengthening the Pulse parameter causes the import computer to wait longer before contacting the export server. This wait is very helpful in the case of slow, unreliable WAN links.

The other option to consider is whether to configure the Wait Until Stabilized option. This option causes the entire subtree to be copied if any file changes. Leaving this option unchecked reduces the replication traffic as only the changed files are copied.

DIRECTORY STRUCTURE

An additional way to reduce how much traffic the Directory Replicator Service generates is how you organize the directories to be replicated. The Directory Replicator Service checks the top-level directories for changed files. If one is found, the entire structure is replicated.

If the directory structure is deep, this replication results is a large number of files and directories being replicated that have not been changed. These replications, in turn, results in large amount of network traffic being generated.

Using a shallow top-level directory structure results in replication generating less network traffic. In this way, less chance exists for files and directories that have not changed to be replicated.

Troubleshooting Directory Replication

 When errors occur as a result of directory replication, these errors are recorded as events in the Application Log, which is viewable using the Event Viewer. These events contain information about the Status column displayed in the Manage Import Directories dialog box. The most common errors that may occur are as follows:

- Access Denied

- Exporting to Specific Computers

- Replicating Over a WAN Link

- Logon Scripts and/or System Policies are Not Working

Each of these types of errors should be approached in a logical manner.

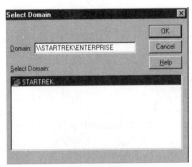

Figure 6.7 Enter both the domain name and the computer name to ensure replication to a specific computer.

If `Access Denied` messages are received, verify that the user account being used for replication has the correct rights. In addition, verify that the Directory Replicator Service on both export server and import computers are correctly configured with this user account.

If replication is to be to a nondomain controller, then use Server Manager to identify the correct computer by entering both the domain name and the computer name. This information should be configured on both the Export and Import sides and is accomplished using the Select Domain dialog box as shown in Figure 6.7.

Sometimes when replicating across a WAN link, a secure connection is not established. One way to improve connections is to designate both the domain name and server name when configuring both the export server and the import computer.

Because directory replication is most frequently used to replicate logon scripts and system policies, the failure of these to function properly is one of the most common problems that an administrator must solve. Be sure that the export server is configured to export to `%SYSTEMROOT%\System32\Repl\Export\Scripts` and that the import computer is configured to import to `%SYSTEMROOT%\System32\Repl\Import\Scripts`.

For Review

- Directory replication occurs between an export server and an import computer.

- To act as an export server, the computer must be running Windows NT Server.

- An import computer may be Windows NT Server, Windows NT Workstation, or a LAN Manager OS/2 server.

- The export server sends a notice when changes have occurred.

- The import computer connects to the export server to copy files and directories that need to be replicated.

- Save logon scripts and system policy files to %SYSTEMROOT%\System32\ Repl\Export\Scripts in order to replicate them.

- The user account used for replication should be a member of both the Backup Operators and Replicators built-in groups.

- Parameters for the replicator service are found in the registry under the key HKEY_LOCAL_MACHINE\System\CurrentControlSet\Services\ Replicator\Parameters.

- The Interval parameter controls how often the export server checks for changes in the replication subtree.

- The GuardTime parameter controls how long a directory must be stable before it is replicated.

- The Pulse parameter is a factor used by the import computer to determine when it should contact the export server if no message has been received.

- To optimize replication across a WAN link, configure a shallow top-level directory structure.

- Using the Wait Until Stabilized option causes the entire subtree to be replicated. Do not configure this option across a WAN link.

From Here

For more information on configuring services see Chapter 5, "Network Configuration." Creating user accounts using User Manager for Domains is covered in Chapter 7. Logon scripts and system policies are covered in Chapter 9, "Policies and Profiles."

CHAPTER 7

User Manager for Domains

The exam for Windows NT 4.0 Server in the Enterprise will test you at length on administering users and groups. In Windows NT Server, these functions are administered through the User Manager for Domains. The following is a summary of the topics covered in this chapter:

- Default user accounts
- Creating user accounts
- Local versus domain accounts
- Home folders
- Local and global groups
- Built-in groups
- Creating groups

Any introductory explanation of User Manager for Domains must include explanations of what a user account is and why you need them. Without a user account, users cannot log on to a computer to access the network's resources.

A user account defines the user's rights on the network and establishes the operating guidelines while the person is logged on.

When a user logs onto a computer, whether it is part of a domain or not, a profile is created locally for that user. By saving the user's profile to a network server, that profile is available for the user no matter what computer is used to log onto the domain. When stored on the server, the profile is a *roaming profile*. These functions are covered more in Chapter 9, "Policies and Profiles."

User Manager for Domains

The test questions may try to trick you about the actual location of the utility called User Manager for Domains. Remember, this utility is on the Server, not the workstation (that utility is called User Manager). You start User Manager for Domains by going to the following:

```
Start | Programs | Administrative Tools | User Manager for
Domains
```

The Windows NT Workstation's User Manager is different than User Manager for Domains installed with Windows NT Server. *The Workstation version can't do as much.* User Manager cannot be used to remotely manage either a domain's SAM or the SAM of a remote NT Workstation or Windows NT Server.

Windows NT Directory Services

The purpose of directory services is to manage network resources and provide a single user logon. This process, called *authentication*, enables access to the network's resources. More about this topic is in Chapter 2, "Microsoft NT 4.0 Directory Services."

Local versus Domain

One of the most important concepts that you will need to know for the MCSE exam is how a *local* account differs from a *domain* account. The test questions are indirect. Mostly, they refer to the terms *local* and *domain* rather consistently throughout the exams. As you study, develop a working knowledge of these concepts.

You also need to know about remote and local logons. See Chapter 2, "Microsoft NT 4.0 Directory Services," for more information about logons.

Default User Accounts

When you install Windows NT 4.0 Server, two accounts are created:

- Administrator
- Guest

The Administrator account is vital to further management of all the functions needed to keep Windows NT working. The Guest account is for visitors to the domain, and use of this account enables you to control their actions on their network, which you do by assigning appropriate permissions. Table 7.1 shows you how these two accounts are configured when Windows NT is installed:

Table 7.1 Default Settings at Creation

	Administrator	Guest
Rights Assigned?	All	None
Acct. Disabled?	No	Yes

You will notice that the Guest account is disabled when created. Remember that you create the other accounts for the domain.

Planning Your Accounts

Although the user accounts you create are pre-equipped with *user rights,* you must plan a strategy for the entire domain. This strategy not only involves the new user accounts that you create, but also involves any modifications you need to make to the default *Administrator* and *Guest* accounts:

- *Rename* the Administrator account and give it a complex password. Moreover, don't forget to write the name down and store it in a secure location.

- If the default rights of the Guest account don't suit the needs of your organization, you should review and modify that account's rights.

When creating or modifying user accounts, devise a set of standards, which you can apply consistently throughout the organization. Consider these three essential elements: *names, passwords,* and *restrictions.*

When preparing for the MCSE test, remember that a focus is placed on a *best policy* strategy. These policies are comprised not only of how you create each of the preceding elements, but why. All of this, and what is required for the tests, is reviewed in Chapter 8, "Managing Files and Directories," and Chapter 9, "Policies and Profiles."

Creating or Renaming User Account Names

1. *Be consistent.* If you start out with JOHNSONT (or last name, first initial of first name) as the method you use for user names, d*o not deviate!* Nothing creates more confusion than trying to understand usernames that do not follow a standard.

   If your organization uses a lot of temporary employees, create a standard for these account names to make them easily identifiable. As further examples, you may want to distinguish administrative assistants with AA*username* or lawyers with an L*username*.

2. *Be unique.* What will you do if you have a *Johnson*S in the Accounting Domain and a *Johnson*S in the Finance Domain?

   How will you merge them into the same domain?

   Identical usernames cannot be in the same domain. In the preceding scenario, you need to rename one or both of the user accounts if you combine the Accounting Domain and the Finance Domain into a single domain. Although unfortunate, this is a good example of why it is best to plan. You can avoid these situations by creating unique user account names.

   As with all things, basic rules must be followed when creating user account names:

   ▪ Maximum of 20 characters, upper- or lowercase
   ▪ The following are illegal characters: / \ [ ] : ; | = , + * ? < >

Renaming a User Account

You might have a test question about this function. More than likely, you will be asked about an employee leaving the company and being replaced by another. For purposes of the test, remember that renaming an account is a useful way of keeping all of the permissions and group memberships of an account.

Suppose that Frank left the company last month. Rather than delete his account, you disabled the account, knowing that a replacement would be found for Frank. When Susan was hired as Frank's replacement, you *renamed* Frank's User Account to Susan.

RENAMING SAVES TIME

Remember SID, the Security Identifier, from Chapter 4? In the preceding example, a SID was assigned to Frank's account when it was originally created. Putting Susan's name on the account doesn't change the SID. You accomplish a lot and save time by renaming the account. You also avoid the hassle of having to create an account with the necessary rights, permissions, groups, and so on.

Deleting User Accounts

Be very cautious when deleting user accounts. All of the account information is deleted, and the SID is deleted as well. Luckily, Windows NT does not allow the Administrator or Guest account to be deleted.

TIP
Use User Manager for Domains for *creating, renaming,* and *deleting* user accounts.

Creating a User Account Template

 Here are some quick tips on how to create and use a User Account template:

- Create templates by functions (i.e. secretary, VP, temporary, etc.)
- Check the `Account Disabled` box
- Check the `Password Never Expires` box
- Copy the template when creating new users
- Create the new user from the copied template

PLAN YOUR TEMPLATES
Have a template ready for the different types of employees you have in your organization. You also may want to consider a naming

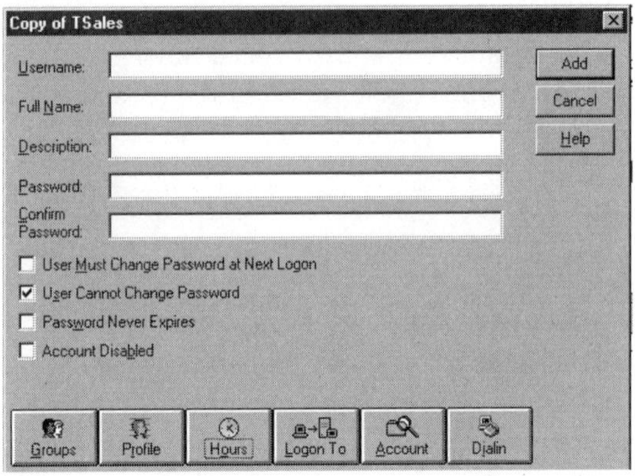

Figure 7.1   Create a user account by using a template

practice for templates, by beginning each template with the same letter, number, or phrase.

After you have your User Account template, create a user account by selecting the Template account. Next select User | Copy from the menu in User Manager for Domains. The great thing about using the copy function is that it copies some things and not others. Here's a brief description of what is and isn't copied:

Copies	Doesn't Copy
Description	User Name
Group memberships	Password information
Password Never Expires field	*Account Disabled field*
Home directory path	Modified rights and permissions
Profiles, Hours, Logon To, Account, Dialin	
Default rights and permissions	

USING A TEMPLATE IS THE BEST OPTION

You could copy another user's account, but if that user has had their default rights modified, you can run into problems. Copied rights and permissions revert to their defaults. The copying process ignores any changes that have been made.

On the other hand, a template, when configured correctly, is an exceptional tool, especially if you're confronted with setting up lots of new employees. It's also a great way to maintain consistency.

Creating and Modifying User Accounts without a Template

Use this path to get to User Manger for Domains:

```
Start | Programs | Administrative Tools | User Manager for
Domains
```

NOTE

When modifying user accounts, you use the same path and the same screen, however the words "User Properties" are on the title bar and not NEW USER. Also, the username is displayed.

The fields for this screen are self-explanatory. What is important about this screen is how it is a launching pad to other user account functions.

Familiarize yourself with the functions of the five boxes on the side of this screen:

```
USER MUST CHANGE PASSWORD AT NEXT LOGON
```

If you choose to use this option, the user has to change his password on his first logon.

```
USER CANNOT CHANGE PASSWORD
```

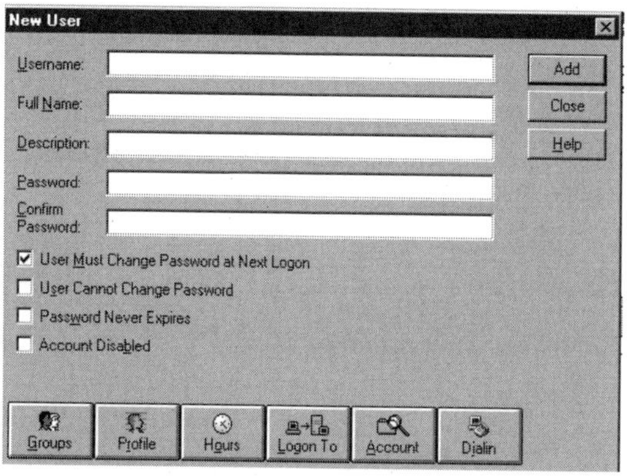

Figure 7.2   When creating a user, all the text boxes are blank.

If you check this option, make sure that you make a record of the password you assign.

PASSWORD NEVER EXPIRES

This option is best for low or no security organizations.

ACCOUNT DISABLED

This option is the default setting for Guest accounts and also recommended for templates.

ACCOUNT LOCKED OUT

When the account is locked out, only the Administrator, or a user with the proper rights, can uncheck this box. This option is grayed out when the account is not locked out.

Managing Your User Account Passwords

Windows NT, unlike Windows 95, requires a password, or the pressing of the Enter key indicating a blank password.

You can use many methods, depending on your organization's needs, for creating and controlling passwords. For instance, you can allow the users to determine their own passwords but require them to change them periodically. You also can determine how often the password is changed.

From the screen shown in Figure 7.3, you can see the numerous options available. This dialog box is reached by selecting Policies | Account from the menu in User Manager for Domains.

For the administrator, planning a password policy is important. Factors to consider are as follows:

- Password expirations
- Account lockouts for improper passwords
- Password structure
- Maximum 14 characters
- Case-sensitive, basically, "what you type is what it is"

Review passwords thoroughly in preparation for your MCSE exam. Read Chapter 8, "Managing Files and Directories," for more information.

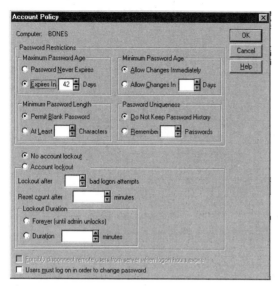

Figure 7.3 The Account Policy dialog box allows configuration of a password policy for your domain.

Managing User Accounts

Before moving on to the description of the items on the User screen, you need to understand the *Universal Naming Convention* (UNC), which is a way to access network resources by specifying both the name of the computer containing the resource and the share name. The UNC is designated as \\servername\sharename.

User Accounts

You can configure user accounts in numerous ways. The buttons at the bottom of the User screen, as shown in Figure 7.2, enable you to create these user features.

- Groups
- Profile
- Hours
- Logon To
- Account
- Dialin

GROUPS

Through this option, you add users to groups in the domain. Groups are explained later in this chapter.

PROFILE

A default user profile is created when a new user logs onto Windows NT for the first time. This profile is associated with that user and is kept in a special directory. By default, that directory is %SYSTEMROOT%\ Profiles\%USERNAME%. Basic configurations, such as the desktop setup and network configurations, are included in the profile.

Three types of profiles are possible: Roaming, Mandatory, and Local. These profiles are discussed in detail in Chapter 9, "Policies and Profiles." By specifying a path for a user profile on the PDC, you are telling the network that this is a roaming profile.

Although user profiles are stored locally in a default directory, the directory path may be configured in User Manager for Domains. Use the Profile button, which brings up the screen shown in Figure 7.4.

In this dialog box, you also enter the path for a logon script. See Chapter 9, "Policies and Profiles," for more discussion on logon scripts.

Home Folders are storage places for users' personal files, and they are configured in the User Environment Profile. Remember two things about Home Folders:

- Creating Home Folders is optional.
- Store a Home Folder anywhere, local or remote.

The screen you see in Figure 7.4 enables you to specify that location. The two major issues that justify using Home Folders are *security* and *backup*.

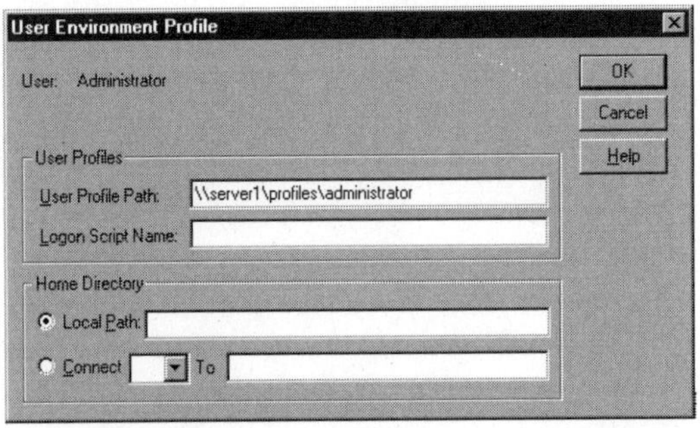

Figure 7.4 The User Environment Profile dialog box is used to specify the location of roaming profiles.

By placing Home Folders on a network server, the network can maintain copies of all user files, personal and business. This strategy also allows for central administration of backups. Otherwise, when files are stored locally, the user must do the backups. For the MCSE exams, you need to understand the concept of Home Folders thoroughly. For purposes of backing up Home Folders, keeping all of them in a central location makes the most sense. Keep in mind that if you place a Home Folder directory on a network server, you must share the directory and grant the appropriate permissions.

Additional considerations regarding Home Folders are the available disk space, both local and remote, and the performance of both server and network.

Obviously, the space available on a disk, whether locally or remotely, will determine whether a bounty of home folders can be placed there. Conversely, both server and network performance could be compromised if numerous users access their Home Folders on a server. Keep all of this in mind when planning your Home Folders.

A Home Folder also can be created on the local computer by specifying the *local path*, which is the partition drive letter and directory path.

NOTE
Because putting Home Folders on the server can increase network traffic, place the folders on a partition other than the partition containing the user's operating system.

Using the variable %USERNAME% causes Windows NT to automatically create the user's home directory providing the Profiles directory has been previously shared.

HOURS

When you create a user in User Manager for Domains, by default, you give them the right to access the network at any time, as shown in Figure 7.5. As the administrator, you can restrict the access by changing the logon hours for a user.

This is a powerful tool. One option you have for Hours, configured in the Policies menu, is to allow users already logged on to remain on the network after hours or to be forcibly disconnected from the network. Otherwise, a user with restrictions of hours cannot make a new connection to the network but can continue to use any previously established connections.

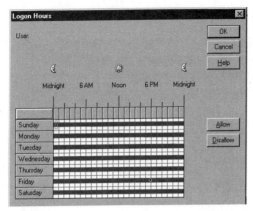

Figure 7.5 Restrict the logon hours for those users who do not need access to the network 24 hours a day.

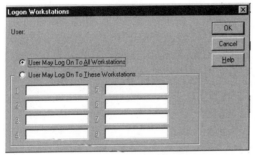

Figure 7.6 With Logon To, you can allow a user to log on to all workstations or as many as eight specific computers and as few as one computer on the network.

LOGON TO

By default, all users can log on to any workstation in the network. In Chapter 8, "Managing Files and Directories," you see that the resources available to a user remotely, or over a network, can be different from those available when logging on locally.

In planning, you may find a need to restrict which computers a user can use. This option is particularly helpful when you need to restrict users to using only specific computers in your network as shown in Figure 7.6.

ACCOUNT

This area is useful when creating temporary user accounts. By specifying an expiration date on the account, you can ensure that tem-

Figure 7.7 Use this dialog box to designate an account as local or global and to assign an expiration date to an account.

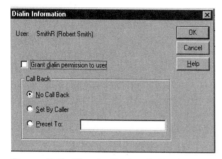

Figure 7.8 Use the Dialin dialog box to configure dial-in options for that user.

porary employees are restricted from accessing the network after their employment is over.

If an account expires, you can reinstate it by changing the date, changing the account to `never`, or by removing the check mark in `Account Locked Out` on the user's main screen (see Figure 7.7).

This dialog box also is where Account Types, either global or local, are configured for the users needing access to other domains. Groups are discussed later in this chapter in more detail.

DIALIN

The Dialin option as shown in Figure 7.8 enables two things:

- Network Logon using RAS
- Call Back options

A user can have Call Back rights without having Dialin permission and vice versa.

The purpose of Dialin is two-fold. An understanding of Dialin, along with RAS, is part of the requirements of the MCSE Connec-tivity sections. First, Dialin allows access to a network when a user cannot connect via traditional methods, namely a WAN or LAN. Using a modem, Dialin can help a user access their organizational network from any location with a telephone line.

Allowing Dialin presents several issues of security. Mostly because of the threat of hackers, Dialin must be configured with the proper security features to prevent unauthorized intrusions.

For this reason, the Call Back permissions granted to a user are very important considerations.

In the preceding figure, you can see that three options are avail-able for Call Back. The MCSE test may ask about these configura-tions, so it is worth understanding their features:

- **No Call Back**—This option is the default setting. The user con-nects, stays connected, and pays the connection charges.

- **Set By Caller**—This option enables the user to specify a number where the Dialin utility can call back and reach them. This fea-ture is great for remote callers who are constantly changing loca-tions and is a great way to reduce access charges. The company can contract for reduced rates based on volume.

- **Preset To**—This feature enables the highest degree of security for Dialin. Preset To requires that a telephone number be entered and that the user must be called back at that number only.

Logon Scripts

The logon script creates a way for these users to establish a network and/or printer connection. Written as a batch file, the scripts are invoked at logon.

Logon scripts do not have anything to do with the user's desktop configuration. Profiles, on the other hand, have everything to do with a desktop. (See Chapter 9, "Policies and Profiles.")

Groups

Understanding the concept of groups is not difficult. However, they are more complex than they appear on the surface. You must have a thorough understanding of the basics. For the exams, you need to understand how groups interact with each other.

The two types of groups in Windows NT are local and global. What is unusual is the concept of how groups work within domains, which is discussed in Chapter 2. Local groups exist in the SAM of the computer controlling the resource and are used to grant access to these resources.

For purposes of the MCSE exam and for your future as a Windows NT system administrator, never forget the importance of planning. Groups can become overwhelming without planning, and the exams will slam you on planning.

For example, questions are asked about groups in Paris and Sydney, where they should be created, and how they should be created. Read each question thoroughly before answering.

If you plan your groups well, you will not need to *delete* groups. Deleting groups is a scary thing. You can't recover a group after you've deleted it. A group contains users and rights, including all of those modified rights you labored over for the last year. Be very sure you want to delete a group!

Local Groups

A local group gives an individual user or the members of a global group the permission to do something with the resources on the network. These permissions can include accessing a printer or folder or permission to administer different functions on the network. To visualize this, look at the diagram in Figure 7.9

When you are thinking about Local groups, think of them as the *power group*. Not only do they enable you to do something, but they include users and/or global groups. *This is very important to remember.*

Windows NT creates default local groups when installed. These groups are covered in the section, "Default Groups."

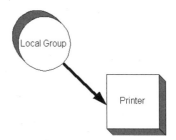

Figure 7.9 Local groups are used to grant access to resources, such as printers.

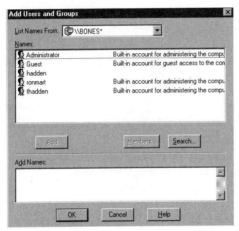

Figure 7.10 Add Users and Groups screen is displayed when you click the Add button from the Create Local Groups dialog box.

Although you will review the procedures for creating local groups later in this discussion, for now reviewing the actual place where the groups are created is the most important. In Figure 7.10, you see a screen called Add Users and Groups.

- List Names—Shows the domain you are currently working in
- Names—Shows the global groups and users that can be added to this local group
- Add Names—Shows the names that already have been added to the new local group

Remember that local groups are restricted to the computer controlling the resource.

TIP
If you create a local group on the PDC, that group exists on all domain controllers because the SAM located on the PDC is copied to all BDCs. However, if you create a local group on a member server, that group exists only on that computer and can be used to manage permissions for any resource controlled by that computer.

TIP
Local Groups depend solely on the "need to have access" to resources.

Global Groups

You may be asking, "Why even have global groups if they can't do anything?" You use the global group to organize users. In small organizations of 15, 20, or even 100 employees, this practice may not seem sensible. However, consider a company of 10,000 with 500 accountants: Wouldn't organizing all of the accountants, all performing the same functions, into one logical grouping make sense? Well, that is what the global group is for: to organize users by function or geography.

This organization is especially helpful in multiple domain models. Global groups can cross domains to access resources in other domains. Placing one global group into a local group is easier than adding 500 users to that local group.

When it comes to global groups, you'll want to spend a lot of time planning how to set them up. And, as you've already read, the MCSE test questions will ask you in subtle ways about this.

You use the screen in Figure 7.11 to add users to a new global group. Keep the strategy for planning global groups simple by remembering to keep groupings logical:

- Group users by their need to access a resource.

- Group users by locations, either geographic or department.

Putting It All Together—Global and Local Groups

Understanding the concept of groups is vital to passing the MCSE exams. Figure 7.12 is a simplistic yet realistic depiction of how these groups work. Remember, local groups have permission to access

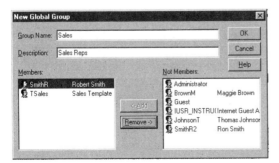

Figure 7.11 Adding users to a new global group.

Figure 7.12 Global groups are put in local groups to gain access to resources.

resources, and therefore are *powerful*. Global groups organize the users.

Although you can add users to local groups, it is not wise. This practice results in additional work for the administrator managing access to resources, especially as users change job functions or leave the organization.

Instead, you create a global group, which you then add to the local group. For example, this structure gives the members of the global group access to the printer as shown in the figure. The added convenience is that if you ever need to remove the global group, you can easily do so.

Questions throughout the MCSE exam will ask about placing a global group in a local group. You may be asked about putting a local group in another domain's local group. The exam also may attempt to trick you by asking about global group permissions. Read all of these questions carefully. They are very tricky.

In the perfect Microsoft world, which exists on these exams, you are expected to follow the rules strictly, which means the following (see Table 7.2):

- Users are assigned only to global groups.
- Individual users are *not* assigned to local groups.
- Permissions are granted only to local groups.
- Only local groups can access resources.
- Global groups are added to local groups.

For purposes of the MCSE exam, remember that you create global groups on the PDC, using Windows NT Server and User Manager for Domains.

TIP

For the MCSE exam, memorize this sentence: "Global groups are put into local groups, and local groups access local resources." This statement will help you sort through difficult and confusing test questions.

Table 7.2 Recapping Global versus Local Groups

Global	Local
Individual users only from the global group's domain	Individual users and/or global groups from any domain
Cannot include local or other global groups	Can include global groups
Used to organize users	Used to grant access to resources in a logical manner
NEVER assigned a permission	Has the power or the permission to do something with the resources in a domain
Cannot be created with NT Workstation (User Manager)	Rights are restricted to resources on the computer on which the local group is created.
Global groups can be added to local groups in other domains	Local groups are restricted to their domain
Default global groups	Default local groups

Default Groups

When a user account is created, the account automatically is placed in the default DOMAIN USERS global group. Windows NT Server does not allow you to remove users from this group or to remove this group. In fact, Windows NT builds in several groups, none of which can be deleted or renamed. Table 7.3 is a list of the default groups. You can modify the default rights given to these groups:

```
START | PROGRAMS | ADMINISTRATIVE TOOLS | USER MANAGER FOR
DOMAINS | POLICIES | USER RIGHTS
```

User rights establish what a group can do on the network. You will not need to know all of the different permissions for each group, but you should familiarize yourself with the built-in groups.

The special groups listed are unlike a global group or local group; they exist for special reasons. About all you will need to know for the Windows NT Server test follows:

Table 7.3 Default Groups

Special Groups	Local	Global (PDC/BDC only)
EVERYONE (all users including guests and anonymous)	ACCOUNT OPERATORS	DOMAIN ADMINS
GUESTS	ADMINISTRATORS	DOMAIN USERS
CREATOR OWNER	BACKUP OPERATORS	DOMAIN GUESTS
	GUESTS	
	PRINT OPERATORS	
	REPLICATOR	
	SERVER OPERATOR	
	USERS	

- Special groups are on all Windows NT computers.
- Everyone is a member by default, and it can't be changed.
- The group's permissions can be modified.

Of the eight default local groups listed, you need to become very familiar with five of them: USERS, ADMINISTRATORS, GUESTS, BACKUP OPERATORS, and REPLICATOR. Of these five, remember that the GUESTS group doesn't have the right to change its desktop environment.

You also know should that BACKUP OPERATORS can start the backup and restore the backup on Windows NT computers.

Also, remember that the ADMINISTRATORS can do whatever they want on the network when logged onto the domain, but when logged onto a local computer that is not a domain controller, they are limited to administering the local computer.

A good trick to use to remember the three default local groups located only on domain controllers is to think of the *three Os*, or the three operators:

- Account Operators—Manage users, global groups, and local groups, except for the ADMINISTRATORS and SERVER OPERA-TORS groups.

- Server Operators—For the test, remember this group creates shares as well as backing up and restoring files.
- Printer Operators—This group creates and manages printers.

Likewise, you can remember the three default global groups installed on the domain controller by remembering,the *three Ds*, or the three domains:

- Domain Users
- Domain Admins
- Domain Guests

Creating Groups

Members of the Administrators or Account Operators local groups are granted the right, by default, to create groups on Windows NT Server with User Manager for Domains. For the exam, just remember that you cannot do this by default from Windows NT Workstation. However, you should know that you can add the Administrator Tools (see Chapter 11, "Remote Administration") to the workstation and map a drive to the server.

Additionally, whenever you create a group, as the administrator, you can assign the right to create groups. For the MCSE exams, you need to remember who can create groups by default.

Global Groups	Local Groups
Maximum of 20 characters	Maximum of 256 characters
Can't use / \ [ ] ; : | = , + ? < >	Can't use \

Here are the rules you need to know for creating both local and global groups:

- You must be a member of the administrators or account operators local groups.
- You can create the global group on the PDC, either by sitting at the PDC or from a remote computer running User Manager for Domains

- Unique names are required for groups in a domain. The names shouldn't be duplicates of either a domain or user name (always make group names original and meaningful, regardless of domains).

For Review

- User Manager for Domains is installed on Windows NT 4.0 Server; User Manager is installed on Windows NT 4.0 Workstation.

- The purpose of directory services is to organize your network and validate, or authenticate, each user through a single user logon.

- When you install Windows NT 4.0 Server, two accounts are created by default, ADMINISTRATOR and GUEST.

- On the MCSE test, a focus is placed on a best policy strategy.

- Identical usernames cannot be in the same domain.

- Basic rules for creating user account names are as follows:

  - Maximum of 20 characters, upper- or lowercase

  - The following are illegal characters:

    / \ [ ] : ; | = , + * ? < >

- Use User Manager for Domains for creating, renaming, and deleting user accounts.

- Create templates and only use the defaults. Don't copy individual user accounts.

- A default user profile is created when a user logs onto Windows NT for the first time.

- The three types of profiles are roaming, mandatory, and personal.

- For the MCSE exams, you need to understand the concept of Home Folders thoroughly.

- Three options are available for Call Back. The MCSE test may ask about these configurations: No Call Back, Set By Caller, and Preset To.

- The two types of groups in Windows NT are local and global. A local group gives an individual user or global group the permission to do something with the resources on the network. The global group is used to organize users by function or geography.

- BACKUP OPERATORS can start the backup and restore the backup on Windows NT computers.

From Here

Refer to Chapter 2, "Microsoft NT 4.0 Directory Services," for information on directory services and domain administration. "Policies and Profiles" are covered in Chapter 9. For more information on managing resources, see Chapter 8, "Managing Files and Directories," and 11, "Remote Administration." Installation is covered in Chapter 4, "Windows NT 4.0 Installation."

CHAPTER 8

Managing Files and Directories

The exam for Windows NT 4.0 Server in the Enterprise will test you extensively on managing resources, especially files and directories. The following is a summary of the topics covered in this chapter:

- Windows NT directory services
- Local versus domain logons
- Account policies
- Passwords
- Shared folder permissions
- NTFS file permissions
- Mapping a network drive
- Copying and moving NTFS files
- Auditing

Windows NT Directory Services

In a peer-to-peer network, a separate database directory of users is maintained on each computer in the network. However, a domain, which has only one PDC, maintains the primary user database directory on the PDC. You might think of this database as a telephone directory, which centralizes the domain's users and groups. This directory provides a single location for the user name and password of each user.

The purpose of directory services is to organize the network and its resources. User authentication allows access to the network's resources.

Local versus Domain

One of the most important concepts that you need to know for the MCSE exam is how a local account differs from a domain account. Although you may never be questioned directly about this subject, references to local and domain accounts surface rather consistently throughout the exams.

A *local logon* occurs when you are validated by the SAM of that computer, allowing access to the resources of the computer you are using; a *remote* or *domain logon* is when you are validated by the SAM on the domain controller, allowing access to resources over the network. The primary difference is that the remote logon is through the PDC or a BDC.

NOTE
A remote logon also occurs when accessing resources on a stand-alone server or a workstation over the network. In this case, the SAM of the computer containing the resource you are accessing is authenticating you.

Account Policies

Perhaps no other feature is of greater value and greater risk than the way that passwords are used on a network. For *full control*, the administrator determines all passwords. For *no control*, the administrator turns over control to the user. Most networks actually have a policy somewhere in between full control and no control.

Account policies, which could be more appropriately referred to as password policies, apply to the entire domain. You should know *everything* about account policies for the exams.

 By default, the only password rule in effect is that *every new user must change their password the first time they log on*. After that, no set rules govern how the policy must be set. The policy is as individual as the organization. Therefore, plan-

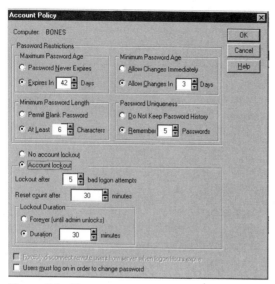

Figure 8.1 The various options that may be applied to passwords are configured using the Account Policy dialog box.

ning, again, is crucial in determining the password policy. The Account Policy dialog box is shown in Figure 8.1.

The first consideration regarding the password account policy is who creates the password—the user or the administrator? By configuring the account policy, you are determining who creates the passwords. This determination can be a time-consuming process for the administrator. Every password must be recorded and kept in a safe place. Allowing the user to create the password is much simpler.

If a password is forgotten, an administrator can unlock the account or change the password for the user through User Manager for Domains. You need to know that you can turn over password control to the user. Do this by checking the following options:

- Password Never Expires
- Permit Blank Password
- Allow Changes Immediately
- Do Not Keep Password History
- No account lockout
- Password size—You set minimum and maximum lengths. You want to create longer passwords in high security settings.

- Life of a Password—The password age can be from 1 to 999 days. Requiring users to change their passwords often can result in many forgotten passwords. Think out the usage of this function carefully before implementing it.

NOTE
Keep in mind that if you check Password Never Expires on the main User screen, this option overrides Minimum Password Age.

- The minimum password length can be from 1 to 14 characters. Forbidding the use of blank passwords on a network is very important.

- Password Uniqueness—This option enables you to specify that a password cannot be the same as a previous password for a certain length of time. Windows NT monitors this restriction by maintaining a history file on the user passwords. You can allow the history file to maintain a record of from 1 to 24 passwords.

- Account lockout—When password attempts are unsuccessful, this setting determines whether or not an account is locked out.

This setting is a very good way to maintain a secure network. You can keep the hackers and others from any unauthorized access to the network and its resources by using this function.

In particular, pay attention to the number of attempts allowed, which is from 1 to 999. Notice that you also can specify a lockout duration time. Specify the time allowed in minutes.

Notice also that you can specify whether an account is locked out *forever*, requiring the administrator or account operator to unlock the account.

TIP
An account cannot be locked out by an administrator but results from unsuccessful logon attempts. An administrator, however, can disable an account.

- Lockout After Hours—Do you recall that you can specify a specific timeframe for users to be on the network? The Account Policy dialog box is where you specify whether users are cut off if they go over the time or whether they can remain on the network if they're already logged on. Regardless, no new connections are allowed if this option is checked.

- Users must log on in order to change password means that the administrator cannot require the user to change his password the first time he logs on. In addition, the administrator has to change an expired password.

Shared Folders and Share Permissions

Saying that sharing is a way to secure a network sounds contradictory; however, this statement is true, and it works. The MCSE test will give you a scenario question, generally a paragraph or two. You will be told what permissions are assigned to a resource and then you will be asked what the user's effective rights are to that resource.

First, you must understand that *sharing* a folder is the only way to secure the folder on a FAT partition. If you try to access an unshared folder over a network, you cannot get in. Sharing applies only to network access. If a user logs on to a computer, and they have the Log on Locally user right, the shares and share permissions do not apply.

By sharing a folder, you grant the right for this folder to be accessed over the network. You also control how users or groups access a folder by assigning *shared folder permissions*.

By default, the Windows NT Server groups that can share a folder are shown in Table 8.1.

Table 8.1 Windows NT Server Groups That Share Folders

	PDC/BDC only	Member Servers	NT Workstation
Administrators	x	x	x
Server Operators	x		
Power Users		x	x

TIP
You can give a user the right to create shares by granting the List permission on an NTFS partition.

You should remember two rules about share names:

- MS-DOS and Windows 3.x clients can read only 8.3 filenames.

- The $ is used at the end of a share name to designate a hidden share. The system root is designated as ADMIN$. It is a default administrative share and a hidden directory, and it does not appear in network neighborhood. By default, at setup, each partition is shared as a hidden share designated <drive letter>$.

Figure 8.2 shows the dialog box used to manage shares.

 For the MCSE exam, you should remember the following:

- A share name is required when you select Shared As.
- Server allows an unlimited number of shares.
- Review the permissions because the Everyone group gets full control by default.

Note the button for NEW SHARE. You can share a folder more than once.

When sharing a folder, you also want to consider system performance. For example, if you share a folder with the maximum allowed connections, how will that share affect the server's performance and network traffic? Is this a popular folder that people will be accessing frequently? If so, you'll want to consider putting this folder on a special data volume or perhaps limiting the number of connections available at any one time.

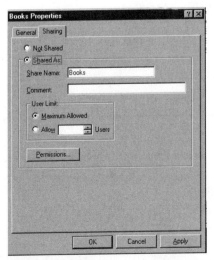

Figure 8.2   When creating a share, a share name must be assigned. Use the $ as the last character of the share name to make it a hidden share.

Permissions for a share are as follows:

- Full Control
- Change
- Read
- No Access

Table 8.2 shows what tasks require what level of access.

Table 8.2 Access Levels

	Full Control*	**Change**	**Read**	**No Access**
Access Denied				x
Run Program Files	x	x	x	
View Subfolders	x	x	x	
View Data and File Attributes	x	x	x	
View Folder and File Names	x	x	x	
Delete Files and Folders	x	x		
Change File Attributes	x	x		
Change File Data	x	x		
Create Folders	x	x		
Add Files	x	x		

*Full Control is the default permission assigned to the EVERYONE group.

Permissions can become very tricky, however. Users can be assigned permissions as individual users and as members of multiple groups, each of which may have different levels of access assigned. Because of this, restricting access and ensuring that users actually can access the files they need can become quite difficult.

Because of this, multiple permissions to the share are summed resulting in the least restrictive access, and the user is allowed access only after this summation takes place. When this happens, the least restrictive permission is given to the user, unless No Access is one of the permissions. In this case, No Access overrides all other permissions and the user is denied access.

Examine Figure 8.3 for a diagram of how this takes place.

In example 1, a user is attempting to access a folder that the user has been assigned permission to as both an individual user and as a member of Group 1. When the permissions are combined, Full Control, the least restrictive of the two permissions, is granted to the user.

In example 2, the same user has been added to Group 2 and is attempting to access the same folder. However, Group 2, of which the user is a member, has No Access permission for the shared folder. Therefore, access is denied.

One interesting fact about a share is that it flows down, but not up. In other words, in the preceding example, subdirectories of the shared folder can be accessed. However, directories higher in the directory are not accessible.

TIP

When permissions conflict, the least restrictive or more permissive is given. The exception is No Access, which overrides all permissions.

 As with all things in Windows NT, planning is crucial to ensure that your resources are secured and accessed properly. So, make sure that you give permissions to users and groups who need it and to the extent they need.

Microsoft stresses using groups rather than individual user accounts. In other words, assign the users to global groups, the global groups to local groups, and assign the permissions only to the

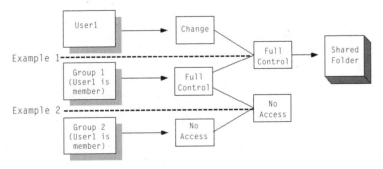

Figure 8.3 When a user has multiple access levels due to permissions assigned to the user as an individual and through group memberships, the permissions are summed.

local groups. In this way, you can better track who has permission to shares on the network. Assigning permissions carelessly results in a patchwork of irretrievable chaos on your network.

One very important thing to remember, however, is that the Everyone group is assigned to every shared folder. And, Full Control also is assigned. Make it a habit to *always remove the Everyone group*. Leave the Full Control permission if you want; however, if not, change it immediately. Assign permissions to another group; the Users group is suggested.

NTFS Permissions (Local Permissions)

The key to remembering NTFS permissions is that no other operating systems besides Windows NT can read them. So, if you are ever troubleshooting a local access problem on a dual boot system, or if you have a test question about it, check to ensure that Windows 95 or DOS is not trying to read the NTFS.

The great thing about NTFS is that it creates a greater level of security than a share because NTFS secures files as well as folders. Also, NTFS permissions do apply locally as well as remotely, unlike a share on a FAT volume.

As the system administrator, you need to educate your network users about the functions of NTFS permissions, because users become creator/owners of files and folders they create.

The Everyone group is assigned to any NTFS partition when it is created. Full Control also is assigned. Because this permission is assigned to the entire partition, everything on that partition is given the same permission by default—every file and folder. If you have files on the partition, make it a habit to always remove the Everyone group.

TIP
This recommendation applies to nonsystem partitions. If you change the permissions on a system partition, you may end up with a nonbootable system.

Table 8.3 gives the details of NTFS permissions. As you can see, they are much more extensive. Also, as you review the chart, note that permissions compound; that is, they build upon each other.

As you encounter NTFS permissions, note abbreviations for each of the permissions. Remember these abbreviations.

NTFS, however, is more complicated than shares and enables permissions to be combined. In an effort to alleviate some of the complications, Windows NT created standard permissions that can be used on folders, which apply to files in the folders.

Table 8.3 NTFS Permissions

Read	Displays folders' and files' data, names, attributes, and permissions
Write	Displays folders' and files' data, names, attributes, and permissions
	Changes folders and files, data, names, and attributes
	Adds files and folders
Execute	Displays folders' and files' data, names, attributes, and permissions
	Changes folders' and files' data, names, and attributes
	Adds files and folders
	Runs executable files within a file
Delete	Deletes a file or folder
Change Permission	Changes a file's or folder's permissions
Take Ownership	Takes ownership of a file or folder

But, first you need to understand how standard permissions are created. In Table 8.4, the column on the left represents the NTFS permissions you reviewed previously. The letter next to each represents the code for this permission. The row across the top of the table represents the standard permissions. The code letters placed in each column below each standard permission represents how regular NTFS permissions are combined. These letters also represent how you will see these various permissions represented on the MCSE exams.

For the MCSE exam, this information is the extent of what you'll need to know. Be sure, however, that you understand how the permissions are combined and what the code letters represent.

You apply NTFS permissions in the same manner as you applied share permissions. A crucial difference is displayed in Figure 8.4.

Table 8.4 Standard Permissions' Abbreviations

	No Access	List	Read	Add	Add and Read	Change	Full Control
READ (R)		RX	RX				
WRITE (W)				WX	RWX		
EXECUTE (X)		X					
DELETE (D)						RWXD	
CHANGE PERMISSION (P)							
TAKE OWNERSHIP (O)							RWXDOP

When a user is the member of multiple groups, the combination of shares and permissions can get rather bizarre. What you must remember for the test, however, is when combining share and NTFS permissions, the most restrictive applies. And, when combining NTFS versus NTFS, the user gets the better of the permissions, unless No Access is one of the NTFS permissions.

In the example, the user is denied access to the Shared folder because No Access is specified. Why? Whenever the NTFS permission

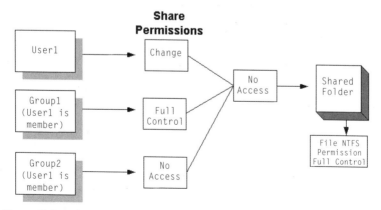

Figure 8.4 When determining a user's effective permission, sum the share permissions and then sum the NTFS permissions. The user receives the most restrictive of the two.

is compared with a share permission, the most restrictive permission is granted. For purposes of securing network resources, this method is effective.

TIP

Remember, share permissions apply only when accessing a resource via the network. If a user attempts to access a resource located on the computer he is using, only the NTFS permissions apply.

The user does have permission to access the NTFS file, which is a member of that shared folder. Although the user is denied access through Network Neighborhood, typing the UNC path to the file opens the file to the user.

For the MCSE exams, use Table 8.5 as a guideline for remembering.

Table 8.5 Local versus Remote Access

	Share	**NTFS**	**NTFS and Share**
Local Access	No Restrictions	Least Restrictive Permission	Most Restrictive Permission
Remote Access	Least Restrictive Permission	Least Restrictive Permission	Most Restrictive Permission

Because a share protects downward into a directory, you create the most protection for a volume by securing folders as high in the directory tree as possible. This is demonstrated in Figure 8.5. By assigning Folder A No Access permission, Folders A-1 and A-2 are protected. Conversely, by assigning Folder B-1 No Access does not provide any protection to Folder B, which is above it in the directory hierarchy.

In some instances, using the method outlined for Folder B is desired. In this way, you can secure the Home Folders you create for users on your network. Create a directory on the server for the Home Folders but don't share it. You then create a folder for each user, assigning each user Full Control to their Home Folder.

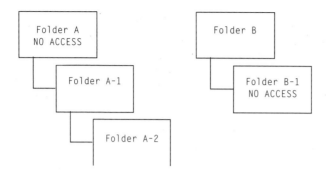

Figure 8.5 When creating a share, remember that any subdirectories receive the same access permissions.

Take Ownership Permission

Numerous reasons exist for taking ownership of a folder. Most importantly, after an employee leaves a company, the administrator can *take ownership* of the ex-employee's files by exercising this permission. By default, the administrator has the right to do this.

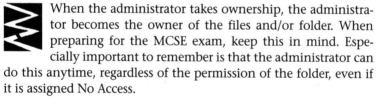

When the administrator takes ownership, the administrator becomes the owner of the files and/or folder. When preparing for the MCSE exam, keep this in mind. Especially important to remember is that the administrator can do this anytime, regardless of the permission of the folder, even if it is assigned No Access.

Remember that the owner of the resource can assign the Take Ownership permission to other users.

Map Network Drive to a Share

You may map a network drive for various reasons in Windows NT Server. Mapping is a convenient way to access a resource, such as a file or folder, quickly. To map a network drive, right-click the My Computer button on your desktop and select Map Network Drive.

From here, either browse to the desired network share or type the UNC path in the *Path* text box. This dialog box is shown in Figure 8.6.

You should be aware of the options available to you from the Map Network Drive dialog box in case something gets sneaked into the test:

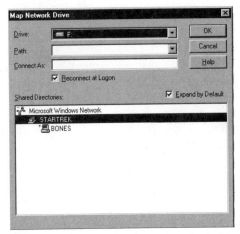

Figure 8.6 Either type the UNC in the Path text box or browse to the desired network share.

- Drive—Assign a letter here, and the shared network drive can behave like a local drive.
- Path—Enter the UNC path to the folder.
- Connect As—Enter the Domain Name\User Name.
- Reconnect at logon—If you check this option, the path to the share is established every time you log onto the network. Keep in mind that the Run command will suffice if you don't want or need to bother with mapping a network drive. This option is especially important if this is a one-time or occasional mapping.

Copying and Moving NTFS Files

Special rules apply to the permissions of files and folders when they are moved or copied:

- When copying a file, the permissions are inherited from the destination folder.
- Whoever does the copying becomes the owner of the file they copy.
- NTFS permissions are lost when they go to a Fat volume.

Memorize Table 8.6. When *permissions change* is stated, this means that the permissions of the destination folder replace the existing permissions.

Table 8.6 Copying and Moving NTFS Files

	To Same NTFS Partition	To Another NTFS Partition
Copy	Permissions change	Permissions change
Move	Permissions stay the same	Permissions change

Remembering the information in this table is very important. Notice that Moving to the Same Partition, is the only way to keep the permissions intact.

TIP
Using the *scopy* utility from the resource kit enables you to copy files while retaining their permissions.

Auditing

Some key points to remember about auditing are as follow:

- You can audit only an NTFS partition.
- Only administrators can start auditing.
- You must enable auditing on the computer that has events you want to audit using User Manager for Domains.
- Auditing is a great way to see what's working, what's not, and who's doing it.
- Auditing records activities in the Security Log.
- You can review the audit logs from any computer remotely using the Event Viewer.
- Auditing puts a load on system resources, so discretion is important.

Auditing is an important consideration for any organization. Planning is crucial. The needs of the company determine the auditing, if any, that must be initiated. Primarily, however, is the need for security.

To set up auditing, select Start | Programs | Administrative Tools | User Manager for Domains | Policies | Audit.

The Audit Policy dialog box is shown in Figure 8.7.

Auditing is covered on the MCSE test extensively. To be specific, you are asked about how to audit certain events, such as *File and*

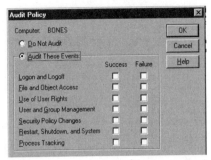

Figure 8.7 Auditing must be enabled via the Audit Policy dialog box before it will work.

Object Access. You can audit whether a printer is accessed and whether the access was a success or failure.

TIP
The most frequent cause of auditing failing is that auditing has not been enabled on the computer where the events occur.

Keep in mind that each object, in this instance, the printer, must be set up for auditing. To do this, select the printer, or any object being audited, and select Properties | Security | Auditing. The features you can set up to audit are shown in Table 8.7.

Table 8.7 Features to Audit

	Files and Directories	**Printers**
Read	x	
Write	x	
Execute	x	
Delete	x	x (delete jobs)
Change Permissions	x	x
Take Ownership	x	x
Print		x
Full Control		x

Become familiar with the properties of each audit event:

- Logon and Logoff—Success or failure of being authenticated by either the local or domain SAM

- File and Object Access—Success or failure of access to resources located either locally or on the network

- Use of User Rights—Success or failure of a user's implementation of his individual rights

- User and Group Management—Success or failure of user and/or group management

- Security Policy Changes—Success or failure of changes made to the security features of the network (i.e., auditing and user rights)

- Restart, Shutdown, and System—Success or failure of computer restarting as well as event log entries

- Process Tracking—Success or failure of things such as starting applications, etc.

TIP
Establishing an audit policy is the responsibility of the administrator and *only* members of the Administrator group can initiate an audit policy.

SECURITY LOGS

For the MCSE test, you need to be familiar with the following options as displayed in Figure 8.8:

- Overwrite Events as Needed—Because the default log size is 512K, selecting this option overwrites the log when it is full.

- Overwrite Events Older than ____ Days

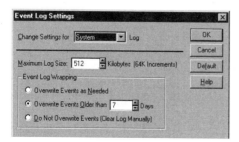

Figure 8.8 Three options on the Event Log Settings dialog box refer to how the size of the logs is managed.

- Do Not Overwrite Events (Clear Log Manually)—This choice is important to consider. You must archive the logs manually if you select this option. Otherwise, the log becomes large and unmanageable.

These settings must be set for each of the three event logs: System, Security, and Application.

TIP

If the event logs are configured to be manually cleared and become full, the computer cannot boot properly until an administrator clears the log. If you choose to configure your computer this way, be sure and establish a routine for viewing and clearing the logs.

Managing access to files and directories is a major part of managing your network. As such, expect to see several questions on the exam relating to this task.

For Review

- A *local logon* occurs when you are being authenticated by the SAM of the computer you are using; a remote or domain logon is when you are authenticated by the remote SAM, such as on a domain controller. The primary difference is that the remote logon is through the SAM that resides on a different computer.
- *Account Policies* apply to the entire domain.
- When you *share* a folder, you also assign permissions to the folder or share.
- Share permissions do not apply when accessing a resource interactively (locally).
- NTFS permissions do apply whether accessing a resource interactively or via the network.
- When permissions conflict, the least restrictive is given. The exception is No Access, which overrides all permissions.
- When accessing a resource via the network, the sum of the Share permissions is compared to the sum of the NTFS permissions. The effective permission is the most restrictive of the two.
- The $ is used to designate a hidden share.
- NTFS volumes have the following permissions assigned by default: Everyone group with Full Control.

- New NTFS files and folders acquire the permissions of the parent folder.

- Shares may be created on FAT or NTFS partitions.

- Consider creating a second administrator account. Use a different name and password, restricting the rights to functions that don't compromise security (i.e., backups, creating user accounts, etc.).

- Don't use the Guest account; instead create a separate account for each user.

- You may not want all users to be able to log onto all computers. If so, restrict workstation access using User Manager for Domains.

From Here

For more information on managing resources see Chapter 7, "User Manager for Domains." Other security issues may be found in Chapter 9, "Policies and Profiles."

CHAPTER 9

Policies and Profiles

The exam for Windows NT 4.0 Server in the Enterprise tests you extensively on policies and profiles. The following is a summary of the topics covered in this chapter:

- System policies
- Default policies
- Roaming profiles
- Mandatory profiles
- Personal profiles
- Local profiles
- Logon scripts
- Directory replication

Profiles

When a new user logs onto Windows NT for the first time, a user profile is created for that user. This profile is created by combining the Default User and All Users profiles on that computer. This profile is associated with that user and is stored in the `%SYSTEMROOT%\ Profiles\%USERNAME%` directory.

Basic configurations such as the desktop setup, network configuration, and a directory for personal files are included in the profile. Without this step, the user would not have access to the computer. After logon, the user or the administrator can reconfigure the settings included in the profile.

Three types of profiles are available:

- Roaming—Follows the user from computer to computer in a network.

- Mandatory—This profile is a special type of roaming profile. Any changes made by the user are not saved when s/he logs off.

- Local—This profile stays on a single computer and never follows the user from computer to computer.

Although user profiles are stored locally by default, the path to their directory can be configured in User Manager for Domains using the PROFILE button, which brings up the screen shown in Figure 9.1.

Notice that the path for a logon script, discussed later in this chapter, is also entered here.

By specifying a path for a user profile, you are telling the network that this is a Roaming profile. Doing so benefits the network administrator who needs to control profiles in the organization by centralizing administration. However, you also must create a folder on the server for the profiles, and that folder must match the path you specify for the user in the User Environment Profile dialog box.

To create a roaming profile, copy a local profile to the server using the System Applet | User Profiles:

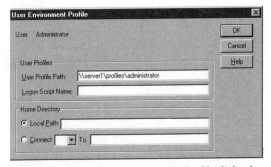

Figure 9.1   The User Environment Profile dialog box is used to set the path to a roaming or mandatory profile.

1. Make sure that a folder is created for the profiles on the destination server. Generally, this folder is called Profiles. This folder must be shared.

2. Determine which local user's profile you want to copy.

3. Log on as the administrator on the *local* computer.

4. Go to Control Panel | System | User Profiles.

5. Select the profile for the local user you will be using for the roaming profile.

6. Press the *Copy To* button and enter the network path in the Copy Profile To dialog box using its UNC name, `\\servername\ sharename\%USERNAME%`. If the profile is to be a mandatory one used by multiple users, then the path may look like `\\servername\ Profiles\directoryname`.

7. Next, select Change to modify Permitted To Use.

8. Add the user or users that will use this profile and select OK.

9. Don't forget that if you are creating a mandatory profile on the server, you must remember to rename the file's extension to MAN (.man = mandatory).

10. Finally, while still logged on as the administrator, go to User Manager for Domains | User screen | Profiles and enter the path to the profile (i.e., `\\servername\Profiles\%USERNAME%`.

Creating a mandatory profile is similar to creating a roaming profile. The difference is that you first create a profile template for the users by creating a new user or by using an existing one. Log on as that user and modify the desktop and network configurations appropriately.

For the MCSE exam, you need to know the differences between roaming and mandatory profiles and their extensions which distinguish them.

The mandatory roaming profile has the following characteristics:

- The profile has the extension MAN.

- Changes made by the user are not saved.

- A single mandatory profile can be applied to multiple users.

The personal roaming profile has the following characteristics:

- The profile has the extension DAT.

- The profile can be changed by the user, and the changes can be saved.
- The personal profile is unique to each user.

NOTE
Changing an existing profile type is as easy as using Rename to change the extension on the profile. You also can specify that the entire Profiles folder on the server be either mandatory or personal by changing its extension.

Remember that the network acknowledges the importance of profiles and policies in a particular order. When a user firsts logs on, the appropriate profile is applied. Next, policies are applied.

Policies

Policies are useful in every organization, but especially so in the larger organization. Implementing policies enables administrators to control the computer work areas and to maintain consistency.

When assessing policies and profiles, a hierarchy determines which takes precedence over the other. You should memorize the following list, which shows that order:

1. Individual system policy
2. Group system policy
3. Individual computer policy
4. Default computer policy
5. Mandatory user profile
6. Personal user profile
7. Default user profile

Policies Override Profiles

Individual system policies have greater priority over the group system policy, and so forth. Within profiles, *mandatory* has priority over *personal*.

System policies are not installed by default. To create a System Policy, use the System Policy Editor by choosing Start | Programs | Administrative Tools | System Policy Editor. Figure 9.2 shows the System Policy Editor.

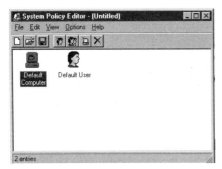

Figure 9.2   The System Policy Editor is used to create and manage policies.

On the System Policy Editor two default policies are created when creating a new System Policy— Default Computer and Default User.

Both of these policies could be sufficient for setting policies for any organization. You can tailor these two policies to the needs of the organization. You also can create entirely new system policy configurations. Regardless, remember for the test that a policy can apply to the whole domain or to as few as one or two users.

During logon, several dynamics are at work in the background checking the various policies and the profile, deciding which one has priority over the other. For the exam, you need to know how this takes place. The diagram illustrated in Figure 9.3 gives a visual aid for understanding how this takes place.

In viewing this diagram, focus on how profiles and policies (user, group, and computer), interact:

- After the user is authenticated by the SAM, the user profile is applied.

- Next, the Ntconfig.pol file is consulted to see whether a user policy exists. If one exists, it is applied.

- If an individual user policy does not exist, group policies for any groups the user is a member of are applied in their order of priority.

- Next, the individual computer policy is applied. If no policy exists, the default computer policy is applied.

TIP

If a user has an individual user policy defined, the appropriate group policies will not be applied. If no user policy exists, the group policies are applied in the order of their priority.

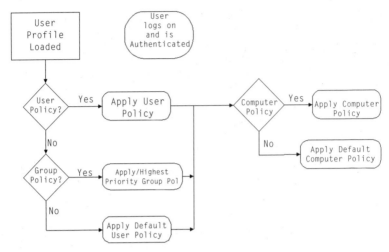

Figure 9.3 Both the user's profile and any system policies are applied during the logon process.

Whenever a logon occurs, this process repeats itself, recreating the current user and local machine settings in the registry.

The MCSE exam covers the subject of policies by including it in the scope of other questions, especially in relation to troubleshooting. To prepare yourself for these questions, know the following:

- Server-based—System policies are created and managed on the server.

- Used to create new system profiles—Using the system policy editor, new policies can be created at any time.

- Used to manage the default system profiles—Default profiles can be modified to suit the needs of the organization or kept as is.

- The policy files are saved in the \winnt\system32\repl\import\ scripts\ directory—This placement enables the NETLOGON service to find the policy files during logon.

- Changes made to policy go into effect only after logoff/logon—This concept is *very important* and may involve a test question. You must have users log off and back on to the system before any new policies go into effect.

- System Policies must be replicated if more than one domain controller exists—See "Replication" later in this chapter.

- Multiple copies of policies can exist to ensure implementation no matter which domain controller authenticates the user at logon. —Multiple copies are achieved through replication.

- Because policies can apply to individuals, they can exist on any Windows NT computer.—System policies and user policies may be created on stand-alone machines.

Windows 95 Policies

Finally, remember that Windows 95 policies are stored in a file called `config.pol`, although Windows NT policies are stored in the `ntconfig.pol` file. Save both `config.pol` and `ntconfig.pol` to the NETLOGON share on all domain controllers to be sure that they are consistently applied. Users who access a Windows NT network using both Windows 95 and Windows NT require *both* a Windows NT policy and a Windows 95 policy.

TIP

Windows 95 policies must be created using the Windows 95 policy editor. Windows NT policies must be created using the Windows NT policy editor.

The following are a few of the default policy options that you should know:

- Control Panel—Controls the display of the Control Panel and may forbid user access

- Desktop—Used for configuring colors and wallpapers

- Shell—Control of what appears on-screen, such as the Run command

- System—For configuring user access to the Registry and Registry Editor

- Windows NT Shell—For configuring desktop shortcuts

- Windows NT System—For creating an environment comprised of various system variables

When users begin having multiple profiles and are members of multiple groups, a pattern emerges as to how the profile and any policies are applied. This pattern is hierarchical, and the precedence is as follows:

1. Individual system policy
2. Group system policy
3. Individual computer policy
4. Default computer policy
5. Mandatory user profile
6. Personal user profile
7. Default user profile

Logon Scripts

Logon Scripts may be used to ensure that network drives are mapped and that printer connections are made automatically when a user logs on. This is especially beneficial when a non-Windows NT client, or for that matter, a non-Windows client needs to log onto Windows NT.

 Logon scripts are written as a batch file and may be created using any text editor. Use the User Manager for Domains to enter the name of the logon script to be run as shown in Figure 9.4. The scripts are saved to the NETLOGON share and are invoked at startup.

Although drive mappings and printer connections can be configured by either a logon script or a profile, you need to understand the distinction between the two. Logon scripts do not have anything to do with the users' desktop configurations. Profiles have everything to do with the desktop configuration.

Figure 9.4 Enter the name only, not the path, of the logon script to be run upon logon.

Replication

Before beginning a discussion of replication, one key point to remember for the MCSE test is that *replication is one-way*. Remembering this essential point is important to a clear understanding of this process.

What replication does best is free you up from maintaining copies of a file or files on multiple servers across the network. Therefore, you need to update the master copy of a file. Replication does the rest by copying the newer version of a file to its multiple locations on a network.

The Windows NT replicator is managed with Server Manager. When the Master Account Database is changed on the Export Server, the replicator service copies the changed file to its copies on the import computer. This replication obviously saves you, as the system administrator, a lot of time.

This process also is the basis for the statement that replication is one-way. Changes go from the export server throughout the network. Changes made on the import computer are not replicated to the export server.

The process is straightforward. After setting up the export server and import computers, the process begins. If a change is made to a file on the export server, notification of the change is sent to the import computer. However, before the change is sent, a broadcast is made to notify import computers that changes are available. The import computer looks at the directories of the export server and copies the changes. Because the import computer maintains an identical copy of the files, it also compares the directories and deletes files no longer needed.

 Any type of data can be replicated. You can create a phone book for your organization and replicate the phone book across the organization. The only requirement is that the phone book be kept and updated on the export server.

The most common use of replication is to ensure that system policies and logon scripts are applied consistently. Throughout the MCSE exam, you will be asked scenario questions about system policies not being consistently applied. This inconsistency is corrected by using replication so that a copy of the system policy is available on every domain controller.

Although user profiles also may be replicated, generally this is not a good idea. Profiles, which consist of multiple subdirectories, can grow quite large. Replicating this much data can result in a significant decrease in network performance.

The replication service requires that a Windows NT Server be the export server. To receive the updates, only computers running Windows NT or Microsoft LAN Manager for OS/2 Server can be import computers.

The path for outgoing replication files is `%SYSTEMROOT%\system32\ Repl\Export`; the path for incoming replication files is `%SYSTEMROOT%\ system32\Repl\Import`.

TIP
Do not place your replication files directly in the Export directory. You must create subdirectories in the Export directory, or replication will fail.

Also, for the exam, you should know how to configure the *interval*, that is, the time between the checks that the export server looks for changes to the directories. This must be done in the Registry:

```
HKEY_LOCAL_MACHINE\SYSTEM\CurrentControl Set\Services\
Replicator\Parameters
```

The default is five minutes and may range from 1 to 60 minutes. See the "Directory Replication" section in Chapter 6 for more details on this and other registry entries used to configure replication.

 The process for creating the export server is very specific:

- With User Manager for Domains, create a User Account configured as follows:
  - Logon hours should be set to All.
  - The account must be a member of the Backup Operators and Replicator groups.
  - User Must Change Password at Next Logon is not checked.
  - Password Never Expires is checked.
- Configure the Directory Replicator service on the export server by going to Control Panel | Services |. Set the Directory Replicator Service to start automatically and to log on as the newly created user account.
- Create the subdirectories in the export folder on the server.
- Use Server Manager on the export server to specify which directories to export and the import computers.

- If the import computer is in another domain, create an identical user account on the import computer.

- On the import computer, select Control Panel | Services | Server Manger.

  Set the Directory Replicator Service to start automatically and to use the newly created user account.

- You do not need to create the subdirectories in the import folder on the import computer, because the Directory Replicator Service will create them.

- Use Server Manager to configure the import computer to specify which directory to import to as well as the export server.

All events relating to replication are written to the Application Log, which is viewed using the Event Viewer.

For Review

- Memorize the following order of consideration for policies and profiles:

  1. Individual system policy
  2. Group system policy
  3. Individual computer policy
  4. Default computer policy
  5. Mandatory user profile
  6. Personal user profile
  7. Default user profile

- Policies override profiles

- Two default policies are created as part of a new system policy: Default Computer and Default User.

- The policy file is saved in the NETLOGON share as `ntconfig.pol`.

- Windows 95 policies are stored in the `Config.pol` file, and Windows NT policies are stored in the `Ntconfig.pol` file.

- You should know the following default policy options: Control Panel, Desktop, Shell, System, Windows NT Shell, and Windows NT System.

- Three types of profiles are available:

  - *Roaming*—This profile has the extension DAT; changes made by the user can be saved; and the Personal profile is unique to each user.

  - *Mandatory*—With this profile, changes made by the user are not saved; it has the extension MAN; and a single Mandatory profile can be applied to multiple users.

  - *Local*

- Changing a Roaming profile to a Mandatory profile is as easy as using Rename to change the extension on the profile. You also can specify that the entire Profiles folder on the server be either mandatory or personal by changing its extension.

- *Replication is one-way.* Changes go from the export server throughout the network. Changes made on the import computer are not replicated to the export server.

From Here

Windows directory services are covered in Chapter 2, "Microsoft NT 4.0 Directory Services." For more detailed information on managing directory replication, see Chapter 6, "Network Services."

CHAPTER 10

Printing

This chapter introduces printing in Windows NT Server in the Enterprise. You will have an opportunity to see the variety of printers and the numerous configurations supported. The Windows NT printing environment is a robust component of Windows NT 4.0, and configuring printing is not difficult. You can handle configurations locally or remotely, as well as across other operating systems. For the Enterprise environment, trust relationships play a pivotal role in determining access to resources across domains. For a complete review of trusts, read Chapter 2, "Microsoft NT 4.0 Directory Services."

The topics in this chapter include the following:

- Printers
- Printing devices
- Printer pools
- Network printers
- Network print devices
- NetWare printers
- Sharing printers
- Sharing printers in the Enterprise

- Spoolers
- Print monitors
- Local printers
- Print management
- Non-Windows printing
- Troubleshooting common print problems

Before You Begin . . .

You may want to review Chapter 4, "Windows NT 4.0 Installation," to reacquaint yourself with the *Hardware Compatibility List* (HCL). You need to research your printer hardware as you would any other hardware you plan to install in Windows NT. Because Windows NT 4.0 is not plug-and-play, attaching anything to a Windows NT 4.0 computer that is not on the HCL is *at your own risk*.

In the case of printing, print drivers, the software that interfaces to the operating system, may present the most problems. The bottom line is that you should check the HCL before making printer purchases.

You must understand the differences between the two most basic components of any Microsoft printing environment:

- *Printers*—In a Microsoft world, the printer is the driver, or software that runs the print devices attached to a computer or network. Although referring to the hardware as the printer is common, for the MCSE exam, it is imperative that you make this distinction.

  Think of the printer as the "middle-person," negotiating the communication and printing requirements of the application with the physical capabilities of the hardware. In this case, the hardware and application never communicate directly with each other but use the printer (driver) as an intermediary.

- *Print Devices*—A print device is the actual physical print device, such as the Hewlett Packard Deskjet or the Epson Bubble Jet. The print device creates the printed output pages and is the place where you add paper, change the ribbon or ink cartridge, and so forth.

The term *printer* is so familiar that you should not assume this distinction is easy to remember. Caution is definitely the watchword for dealing with *printers* on the exam, because familiarity may give you false confidence.

TIP
The hardware is a *print device*, and the *printer* is the printer driver, or software.

Windows Print Architecture

A modest portion of the Windows NT 4.0 Server in the Enterprise print architecture is relevant to the MCSE exams. The balance of the architecture is also worth knowing.

In fact, the interfacing, or modularity, distinguishes the Windows NT Print architecture. Each component has a specific function, yet it is not so isolated that it ignores the rest of the system.

Take some time to review the following components:

- Print monitor—Sends the print job to the print device.

- *Graphics Device Interface* (GDI)—Helps translate the graphic portion of a print job into something the printer and print device can understand and print.

- Printer—The actual software that translates the print job request to the printer device. More detail on this component is provided in the next section.

- Router—Sends the print requests to the spooler.

- Spooler—A spooler, or *print provider*, can intercept print jobs for local or remote print devices. If local, the spooler holds the job until the print device is free to print the job. If acting like a remote spooler, it intercepts and then sends the print request to the appropriate local spooler, where the job is printed. The default folder for the spooler is \Winnt\Spool.

- Print Processor—The print processor is the last stop for the print job, where the print job is processed before going to the print monitor.

Printers or Printer Drivers

Now, we focus on the printer aspect of the preceding section. Understanding the concept of the printer as software is often the biggest hurdle for test-takers. For you to overcome this obstacle, you need to forget the slang you've learned in the real world.

Pretend everything you already know about printers is now wrong.

You must remember two other concepts about printers:

- A print device (hardware) can interface with multiple printers (software).

- A printer (software) can interface with multiple printing devices (hardware).

Let's review these two statements in more detail.

A Printer Can Interface with Multiple Print Devices

Many organizations do enough printing to need multiple print devices (hardware) to handle the printing volume. In this case, only one printer, or driver, may determine which print device receives a particular print job. The process of managing multiple print devices is known as *pooling*. When multiple print devices are combined, they form a *printer pool*.

The primary requirement of a printer pool is that all printers in the printer pool must be able to use the same print driver. All of the print devices must be very similar. Identical print devices, or print devices all emulating the same type of print device, must be pooled together.

For example, you can have a Hewlett-Packard printer pool or an Epson printer pool; thereby creating a printer pool according to printer manufacturers of similar or identical print devices. Another method of organizing printers is also by type (i.e., all laser printers, all inkjets, etc.). This method, however, can create compatibility problems. Generally, combining different manufacturers in a printer pool, regardless of the printer type, is not recommended.

Enable printer pools by doing to the following:

1. Start | Settings | Printers

2. Select a printer to configure.

3. Select Properties.

4. Select Ports.

5. Check the Enable Printer Pooling box.

6. Select each port you want to be part of the pool.

An example of the dialog box used to configure a printer pool is shown in Figure 10.1.

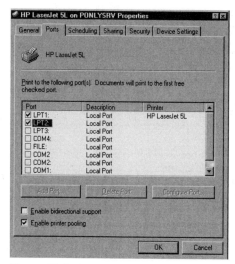

Figure 10.1   Enable printer pooling from the Ports tab in Printer Properties.

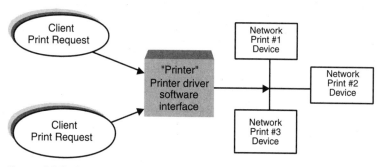

Figure 10.2   Printers (software).

In the example in Figure 10.2, client computers send their print requests to the printer. The printer then polls the network print devices, to see which one is free to accept a print job. If all are free, the print job goes to the default system print device. If none are free, the print job is sent to the print queue. The queue holds the print job until it is printed or canceled.

NOTE
If you work with NetWare Networks or OS/2, keep in mind that other manufacturers refer to a printer as a *print queue*, as shown in Table 10.1. Windows NT users submit print jobs to a printer, and OS/2 and NetWare users submit print jobs to a print queue.

Table 10.1 Novell terminology calls printers queues.

Microsoft Terminology	Novell NetWare Terminology
Printer	Print queue
Printers	Print queues

The Printer can reside almost anywhere on the network. On a larger network, where printing demands are large, a dedicated print server is common. On a smaller network, even a Windows 95 peer-to-peer network, a printer can reside on the client computer where you attach the print device. In addition, some print devices do not require a client computer connection; instead, they attach directly to the network with their own network card. In multiple domains, you must configure trusts, discussed later.

Print Devices Can Interface with Multiple Printers

Sophisticated printers (the printing software interface) can support multiple printing languages. Although interfacing with a single print device, multiple print icons reside in the Printers applet. When multiple printers are created corresponding to the same print device, and the print device is connected to a computer rather than directly to the network, then the printers are installed from the computer locally to the print device.

Figure 10.3 shows a single print device configured for multiple printers. Note that two requirements must be met to enable one print device for multiple printers.

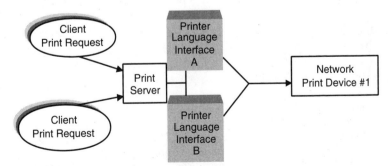

Figure 10.3 Print servers may contain more than one printer.

- One print server contains all involved printers.
- One port is configured for a single print device.

For the time being, the preceding explanation is enough; however, you should review a Printer Properties page for further explanation of ports.

Before a client computer can interface with the printer, the printer driver software must be loaded on the client computer. For example, a client computer with only Language A, as shown in Figure 10.3, cannot print to the Language B interface because that client computer does not have the Language B software loaded.

In this example, the client computer sends the print request to the appropriate alternate printer by selecting the appropriate printer from those available. Each available printer is represented as an icon in the Printers applet of the Control Panel, as shown in Figure 10.4.

Configuring all print jobs to a specific printer by default also is possible. Just select the printer icon as shown in Figure 10.4, right-click on the icon, and select the Set As Default option.

The MCSE exam contains many references to *printers, print devices,* and *printer pools.* Therefore, you must have a clear understanding of these foundation principles before the exam.

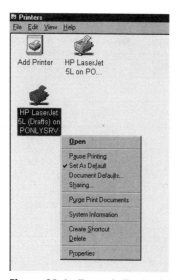

Figure 10.4   To send all print jobs to a specific printer, set the printer as default.

Sharing

Applications interface with the *printer* not the *print device*. Therefore, where the print device is located and what the print device is attached to is inconsequential. This situation is ideal for purposes of running a network because it enables sharing of print devices. See the next section for information on sharing resources in multiple domains in the Enterprise environment.

The network operating system is responsible for sending print jobs to the right place. The advantage to this is that a network can facilitate and serve many different clients running many different operating systems. Best of all, they can share a single printer and print device.

For the specifics of how to share a printer on a network, see "Printer Properties" later in this chapter.

For the MCSE exam, you need to understand the overview of the select print permissions shown in Table 10.2. If a user has one of the permissions across the top of Table 10.2, the consequent powers are indicated in the table with "Yes."

Other assignments also can be given to printer permissions; however, these are the ones you will need to know for the exams.

Table 10.2 User or Group Print Permissions

User or Group Print Permissions	No Access	Print	Manage Documents	Full Control
Print All Documents		Yes	Yes	Yes
Pause All Documents			Yes	Yes
Pause Own Documents		Yes	Yes	Yes
Delete All Documents			Yes	Yes
Delete Own Documents		Yes	Yes	Yes
Restart All Documents			Yes	Yes
Restart Own Documents		Yes	Yes	Yes
Resume All Documents			Yes	Yes
Resume Own Documents		Yes	Yes	Yes

User or Group Print Permissions	No Access	Print	Manage Documents	Full Control
Change Permissions				Yes
Delete a Printer				Yes
Share a Printer				Yes

Go back and review Table 10.2 again. Note the difference between the *Print* permission and the *Manage Documents* permissions. By default, the Print permission is assigned to all users through the Everyone group. Full Control is assigned to the Administrators group by default, giving them the ability to administer printing on any Windows NT computer.

Default Full Control permissions are assigned to Administrators, Server Operators, and Print Operators. No Access permission, if assigned, of course, overrides all other print permissions.

Because permissions are domain-specific, multiple domains require trusts. Otherwise, administrators administer each domain independently. For the MCSE test, you should understand the default permissions of these groups (Administrators, Server Operators, and Print Operators).

Administrators can change the permissions for these groups, other groups, and individual users by going to the Printer Permissions screen, shown in Figure 10.5. To get there, go to Start | Settings | Printers | File | Printer Properties | Security | Permissions | Add.

For an in-depth review of changing Windows NT group permissions, see Chapter 8, "Managing Files and Directories," and Chapter

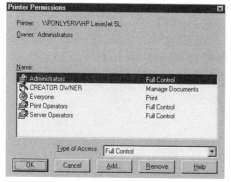

Figure 10.5 Administer Printer Permissions from this dialog box.

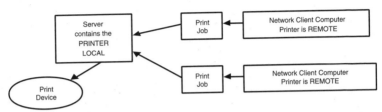

Figure 10.6   Remote printers are not connected to the computer you are using.

9, "Policies and Profiles." As you review Chapters 8 and 9, remember print permissions are *not* the same as Share and NTFS permissions.

Remote versus Local Printers

In any discussion of printing on a Windows NT enterprise network, you must distinguish between the *remote* and the *local* printer. For example, if the printer resides on a computer, the printer becomes *local* to that computer. Therefore, to any client computer on the network, that printer becomes a remote computer because it is not attached to their computer.

To put it another way, a remote printer does not reside on the computer you are using. Therefore, when you have a print job, you must send the request to the remote printer, where the request is spooled and sent to the print device. Your perspective of what is remote and what is local determines everything. As seen in Figure 10.6, the perspective of the print device is noted relative to which computer the print device is connected.

Please note in Figure 10.6, the server printer that spools the print jobs must be shared to enable network clients to use it. If other domains are using the spooler, the proper trusts also must be in place.

Putting It Together—Sharing Printers in the Enterprise

When printers exist in a single domain, you need to assign users the proper rights to access the resources. However, when multiple domains are present, each requiring access to resources across the enterprise, you also must configure *trust relationships*. What follows is a synopsis of printers in the Enterprise environment. For a review of trusts, see Chapter 2, "Microsoft NT 4.0 Directory Services," which explains the fundamentals in detail.

 The *rule* for printer trust relationships has several versions, but says, in essence:

The resource, or printer, trusts the user.

Some other versions of the same principle are as follows:

- The printer gives a user permission to use it.
- The user is trusted.

Rather than memorize this concept *verbatim*, develop an understanding of the concept, then create a version of your own. On the MCSE exams are several questions on trust relationships. Having a clear understanding of the resource domain and giving permission to users is crucial.

Creating a trust establishes a link to the printer across domains but conveys no rights to the user. Assume that you are administering two domains. Each domain has a printer, or resource. Your goal is to give the second domain, Domain B, access to both printers. Look at Figure 10.7 for a visual depiction of how to do this.

In this example of a *one-way trust*, Domain A *trusts* Domain B. (Remember that the arrow always points away from the trusting domain.) The essence of a one-way trust is that one of the domains has access to resources, and the other domain is restricted. The relationship in Figure 10.7 gives the users in Domain B access to the printers in Domains A and B.

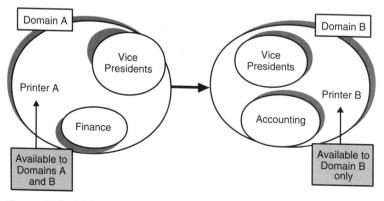

Figure 10.7 Multiple domain trust relationships are always covered on the Windows NT Server in the Enterprise exam.

The users in Domain A are restricted to using Printer A because they have no access to the resources in Domain B. (The arrow would have to point the other way—Domain B trusting Domain A —for this trust to exist.)

Single domain models require users to have permissions to resources, which you give through membership in local groups. The same rule applies to *multiple domains*. To access the printer in Domain A (see Figure 10.7), you must add groups from Domain B to groups in Domain A.

If you want to give both domains equal access to each other's resources, you can configure a two-way trust, as shown in Figure 10.8.

By creating a two-way trust, both domains trust each other, sharing resources equally. Again, the rules of groups and sharing still apply. The users from the trusted domain must be in the appropriate local and/or global groups in the resource domain.

Remember that trusts are *independent*. Consider the example in Figure 10.9.

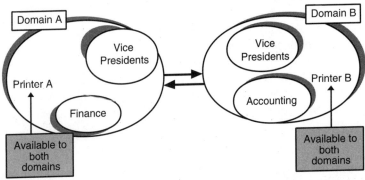

Figure 10.8 Create two one-way trusts to enable a two-way trust relationship.

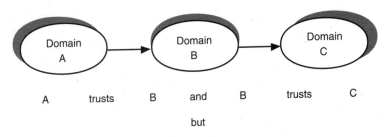

Figure 10.9 Independent trusts and printer resources.

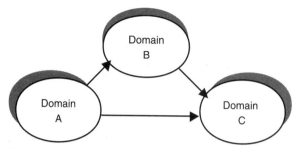

Figure 10.10   Resources always flow in the direction of the arrow, from the trusting domain to the trusted domain.

A trust exists mutually between two domains. For three domains to have interdependent trusts, a minimum of two trusts must exist. In Figure 10.9, Domain C cannot access the resources of Domain A, because the trust between Domain A and B does not imply a trust between A and C. The only way to create a trust relationship between Domains A and C is as shown in Figure 10.10.

In Figure 10.10, Domain A now trusts Domains B and C, allowing access to Domain A printer resources by both Domains B and C.

Trusts are a simple concept that can become complex. Understanding these basic concepts will enable your success on the MCSE exams; however, several reviews of the principles are recommended.

Attaching the Print Device

By now, having distinguished between a printer and a print device, you realize you cannot just attach a print device to a computer and expect it to print from Windows NT. However, the process of creating a local printer is not difficult. Microsoft has supplied an Add Printer Wizard, shown in Figure 10.11 to facilitate this process. You can find this wizard in two ways:

■ Start | Settings | Printers | Add Printer

■ My Computer | Control Panel | Printers | Add Printer

To configure the print device, you need the CD-ROM or floppy disk that came with the print device. During the setup of the printer using the wizard, you are asked for the following information:

1. Local (my computer) or remote printer (network printer server)
2. Manufacturer name or generic
3. Printer device type or model
4. Printer port, usually LPT1 or LPT2
5. Printer name
6. Whether the printer will be the default printer
7. Whether you want to print a test page

If you specify a remote printer, you are asked for additional information, including the following:

- Shared or not shared
- If shared, the share name
- Operating system(s) of computers accessing the printer

When connecting to a remote printer, you will see the dialog box shown in Figure 10.12. Using this screen, you can browse the network to locate and add a printer. This is not only useful to the client computer adding a remote printer, but also to the administrator of a large network. The ability to browse a network to see the UNC path of printers eases administration.

If the remote printer exists on another domain, you need to configure a trust between the domains before continuing.

If you did not specify the printer as a network printer when setting it up, you can modify this property later by going to My Computer | Control Panel | Printers | select the printer | right-click | Sharing.

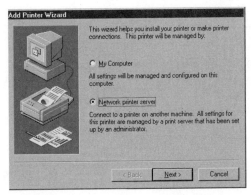

Figure 10.11 Add a printer by using Windows NT Add Printer Wizard.

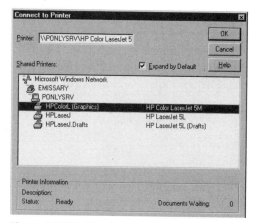

Figure 10.12 Use the Connect to Printer screen to add a remote printer.

From here, you enter the share name and password. You also can reach the sharing option through the Printer Properties page of the printer.

Printer Properties

You can configure the properties for the print device during the installation or later. Regardless, the procedure is the same.

You reach the Printer Properties page of the printer, shown in Figure 10.13, using the following method:

```
My Computer | Control Panel | Printers | select the printer |
right-click | Printer Properties
```

The properties page has most of the settings you made during the setup procedure. If you use the properties at all during the setup process, it will be to take advantage of the additional options you can configure, or because you're troubleshooting a printer setup problem. Some of those properties you'll need to know for the MCSE test are covered in the next few sections.

GENERAL TAB, PROPERTIES PAGE; PRINT A SEPARATOR PAGE

This option enables you to configure a blank page to be printed between print jobs. The two types of separator pages are as follow:

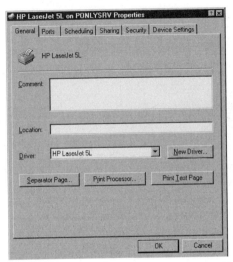

Figure 10.13 The Printer Properties page offers many tabs and options.

- Sysprint.sep—Separates each print job with a blank page.
- Pcl.sep—Separates each print job with a blank page and puts the printer in PCL mode for HP print devices.

The Pscript.sep option doesn't print a blank page between print jobs but does switch to PostScript for HP print devices.

JOB SCHEDULING TAB, PROPERTIES PAGE

Think of this as a way of restricting the print device, much as you can control the logon hours of users. Scheduling enables you to control *when* the print device is in use and controls the queue of print jobs to the print device, giving priority to users or groups as specified. Several questions on the MCSE test are about scheduling print jobs on network print devices.

One terrific feature of scheduling, which you should know for the exam, is that you can create multiple icons for the same printer, assigning different properties for each icon. For example, you can create an icon for vice presidents, sharing it only to the Vice-Presidents group. By doing this, you can assign a higher priority to that printer, which enables the vice presidents' print jobs to print ahead of other groups.

Alternatively, you can create a printer icon for large print jobs, configuring it to print only after business hours. By doing this, the large print jobs do not print during the day, freeing up the print device for other uses.

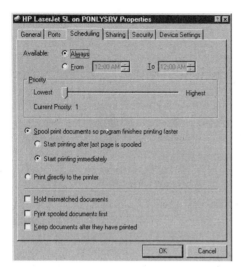

Figure 10.14 Schedule printer times and set printer priority from this dialog box.

Remember each icon you create for the same print device is a *logical printer*.

Review the screen in Figure 10.14 and the options to understand this more fully.

■ Available—You can exercise great control over the availability of the print device by making it available:

Always—making a printer available all the time can cause traffic jams at the print spooler. Only use this option if you have low print volume on your network.

From—Specify times in the From and To areas to restrict print times. You could create a LARGE JOBS printer icon, specifying print jobs sent through it to spool during the day and print after normal business hours. This makes excellent use of the printer's time.

■ Priority—Each logical printer you configure can have a different priority setting. The default priority is 1, which is the lowest priority. The highest priority is 99. A priority 99 job will take precedence over a print job with a priority of 1.

■ Spool Settings—You'll want to consider these options carefully:

`Spool print documents so program finishes printing faster`—The following two choices are important to consider. Before deciding on one or the other, assess your network printing volume.

- `Start printing after last page is spooled`—If you choose this option, print jobs start printing only after the last page of the job is spooled. This option is good to choose for large print jobs, so the printer is not tied up while the spooling is taking place.

- `Start printing immediately`—With this option, print jobs start printing after the first page is spooled. Choose this option if the printer is used primarily for smaller print jobs.

Notice that last statement, "if the printer is designated for smaller print jobs." *Planning* (there is that word again) a print strategy for your network is important. If you find large print jobs are tying up your printers, consider having two printer devices. Designate one printer for large print jobs and one for smaller and quicker print jobs.

- `Print directly to the printer`—Although the print job goes through the spooler, it does not spool, instead going directly to the print device.

You should be aware of three other options in the Scheduling section for the exams:

- `Hold mismatched documents`—When the print job and printer settings are not compatible.

- `Print spooled documents first`—Documents already spooled and waiting in the queue are given priority.

- `Keep documents after they have printed`—Saves a copy of all print jobs to a file on the disk.

SHARING TAB, PROPERTIES PAGE

You may configure and modify sharing in the Printer Properties page. You also can restrict the printer from network access by selecting the Not Shared option.

 When printer drivers are loaded on the server, you can automatically download them to a client computer needing access to a print device. *This feature is supported only by Windows 95, Windows NT Workstation, and Windows NT Server.*

The MCSE exams may ask about downloading print drivers. Specifically, questions focus on how to distribute print drivers to client computers. You must understand the concept of sharing a printer, as well as how sharing enables automatic downloading of drivers to client computers.

You also must remember that clients can download *updates* of printer drivers to clients in the same way. If, for example, you update a print driver on the server, the clients who have previously downloaded the older version automatically receive the updated version the next time they access that printer driver on the server.

SECURITY TAB, PROPERTIES PAGE

If configured correctly, one of the most powerful features of the Printer Property page is the Security section. You must know the three configurations shown in Figure 10.15.

- *Permissions*—From this screen, you can determine which users have print and print/manage print jobs. You must know this for the exams. Review the next section, "Print Management," which covers this topic in more detail. To configure users rights in this area, do the following:

1. Start | Settings | Printers

2. Select a printer from the screen.

3. Then select File | Printer Properties | Security | Permissions.

4. You use this selection not only to give rights but also to restrict users.

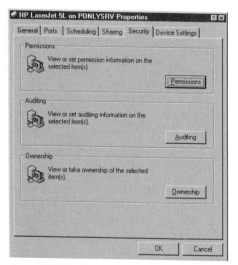

Figure 10.15 The Security tab offers Permission, Auditing, and Ownership options.

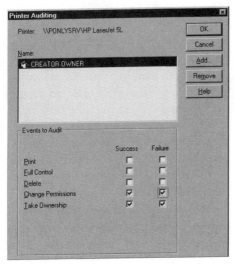

Figure 10.16   Set up printer auditing from this dialog box.

- *Auditing*—The auditing option displays the screen shown in Figure 10.16.

Auditing a printer enables you to track printer access as well as user and/or group access of a printer. A trust must exist to audit printers on other domains.

- *Ownership*—Literally, ownership is what it implies. You can take ownership of the printer. Remember taking ownership requires you have the appropriate user rights. The Administrator group has the Take Ownership by default.

Review the concept of Take Ownership. Samples of the new adaptive tests for the MCSE, which you can download from the Microsoft Web site, refer to this subject. If a sample question is about this subject, assume that Microsoft deems it a fitting subject for a future MCSE test question. Here are some other key points about ownership:

- The ownership of a printer is assigned to whomever installs it. In most cases, this is the Administrators group, but not always. Ownership also could be established by the Print Operators, Server Operators, or anyone assigned Full Control.

- Assigning ownership rights is a bit tricky. Remember the owner of something cannot give ownership to someone else. To do this, someone with the rights of Full Control must reassign ownership.

- In short, don't do it. For the test, you should know what it is, who can do it to whom, and who can't do it.

DEVICE OPTIONS TAB, PROPERTIES PAGE

The Devices Options page acts as a "catch-all" page for all of the miscellaneous printer configurations.

You can configure the orientation of the paper as follows:

- Landscape or portrait
- Paper size and type

You also can configure the fonts and the paper trays used for printing.

Print Management

You can control each logical printer individually. Therefore, you should review and understand each of the options available to you in the drop-down boxes as shown in Figures 10.17 and 10.18.

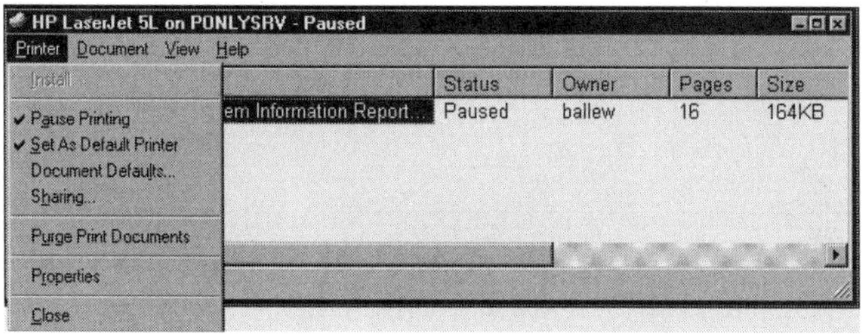

Figure 10.17   This Printer drop-down box shows that the print job has been paused.

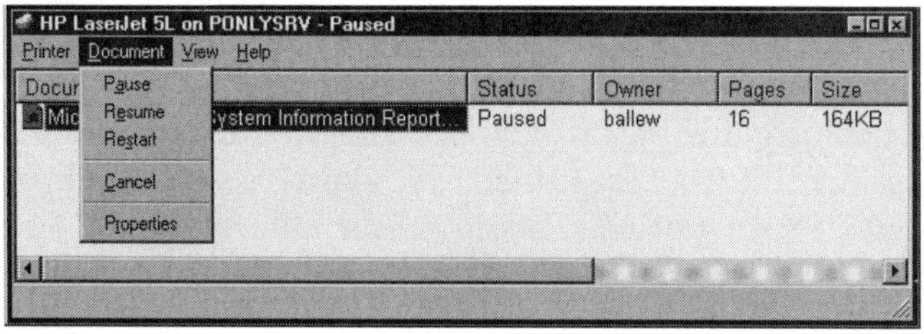

Figure 10.18   The Document drop-down box offers additional options for the selected document.

The first item that you should note about these screens is that one print job is in the print queue. (The status of the print job is noted in the lower left corner of the print window; however, that portion of the screen is not visible in Figures 10.17 or 10.18.) Also, note that the document is paused.

 One of the best features of printing with Windows NT is that you can stop, or *pause* document printing. You should remember this for the MCSE exams. At least one test question asks what to do with a print device that has jammed. The scenario asks you to consider the following facts:

- A document is jammed.
- The document cannot be resent to the printer.

In this case, you'll want to remember that you can pause a printer using the drop-down menu, clear the jammed print device, and resume printing by clicking on Resume or Restart. These options, which are alternatives to reclicking Pause Printing to resume printing, are as follow:

- Resume—Use this option to start printing documents after pausing. For instance, if you paused the printer after printing page 18 of a document, Resume would start printing at page 19.
- Restart—Regardless of where the document was paused, you can use this option to start printing a document from page 1 of the document.

You also can pause printing when no documents are in the print queue. This option enables you to retain documents in the print queue until you are ready to print them.

Numerous reasons for wanting to do this. For example, suppose that the default paper in the print device is 8 1/2 × 11. But, you are printing legal-size documents on 8 1/2 × 14 paper. By *pausing* the printer, you can change the paper and resume printing. Documents can be paused individually, as a whole (all documents), or as a group (select documents).

To pause all documents, do not highlight any documents and select Pause Printing from the Printer drop-down menu. When you want to pause several documents at the same time but not all documents, do the following:

- When the documents are in consecutive order, highlight the first document to be paused, hold down the Shift key, and highlight the last document to be paused. Select Pause Printing from the Printer drop-down menu.

- When the documents are not in consecutive order, highlight the first document to be paused, hold down the Ctrl key, and highlight each document you want to pause. Select Pause Printing from the Printer drop-down menu.

 Notice that you can set the printer as the default printer with he Set As Default option on the Printer menu. You can designate a printer as the default printer so that all print jobs sent from a client computer always go to that computer.

Finally, notice that you can cancel a print job and purge print documents. The difference between the two is that Cancel is for canceling single documents in queue. To do this, select the document and then select Cancel. Cancel a document is only offered in the Document drop-down menu.

Purge Print Documents removes *all* documents from the queue. Purge is available only in the Printer drop-down menu.

In large organizations, it is common to have users sending print jobs to printers regularly. Because these users cannot know whether the print devices are working or not, problems can occur when the print devices break down. Print jobs sit in the queues of print servers, backlogging the computer and filling the memory. If enough print jobs are waiting, this can slow network performance.

In cases like this, if multiple printers are available, consider sending the print jobs to other print devices, using a process called *redirecting*, while you repair the broken machines.

To send print jobs to other printers, use the following method:

1. Go to Start | Settings | Printers.

2. Select the printer that is not working.

3. Select File | Properties.

4. Select Ports | Add Port.

5. Select Local Port.

6. Select New Port.

7. Enter the UNC path to the printer you want to use temporarily, for example, `\\computername\hp9`.

When you want to revert to the default printer, remove the new port you added. The MCSE exam may ask you about redirecting print jobs across networks to remote printers, so make a mental note about this short routine.

Non-Windows Printing

APPLE

Apple computers, specifically, but not limited to the Macintosh, require the AppleTalk protocol to interface with Windows NT print networks. To enable this interface, you must install *Services for Macintosh*, which comes with the services utilities on Windows NT Server.

Services for Macintosh enables two things:

- Apple computers to access printers attached to Windows NT clients
- Windows NT computers to access Apple printers

Novell NetWare

You can use a printer on a Novell network by installing *Gateway Services for NetWare* (GSNW) on your Windows NT server. Full details for installing GSNW can be found in Chapter 16, "Network Connectivity."

UNIX

To connect a computer with a Unix operating system to a Windows print environment, you first must create a share on the computer and install the *TCP/IP Printing Services*. The *Line Printer Daemon* (LPD) service then is installed, enabling Unix clients to connect using the LPR command. Also know the IP address for the Unix computer, so TCP/IP knows where to send the print job.

To install TCP/IP Printing Services, go to

```
Start | Settings | Control Panel | Network | Services | Add |
Microsoft TCP/IP Printing
```

Each Unix client computer must install the appropriate printer driver software. This also applies to other non-NT compatible clients such as MS-DOS, OS/2, Windows 3.1, and Windows for Workgroups 3.11.

LAN MANAGER 2.X

LAN Manager also requires that each client computer installs the printer software. As a non-Windows NT system, LAN Manager can access Windows NT network printers using the net use command.

DLC

You should remember that DLC is a special communication protocol used by network print devices with their own network interface cards directly connected to the network and for mainframe connections. Some HP print devices with their own network interface cards, particularly those called Jet Direct print devices, require DLC. Lexmark also has print devices and other devices that require the DLC protocol.

Troubleshooting Common Print Problems

When troubleshooting the print process, you can be certain the failure will originate in one of the three areas shown in Figure 10.19. Somewhere along the path from the request to the logical printer interface to the actual hardware of the print device a problem exists.

 Here are some recommendations for troubleshooting your printer network:

- *Check the cables*—Make sure that the cables connecting the hardware are firmly attached. If possible, check the integrity of the entire cable by examining the length of it. Cuts in the cable can disable the communication process.

- *Drivers*—The software driver may become corrupt. In this case, you need to reinstall it. Doing this probably will not affect the system, so go ahead and do it if you're not sure of the nature of your problem. Remember to reboot after installation.

- *Check the printer*—Any lights blinking on the print device? Consider turning the machine off and back on again. Sometimes a solution as simple as power-cycling the device will solve what seems to be a complex problem.

- *Printer Diagnostics*—Some printers have their own diagnostics programs that enable you to investigate problems.

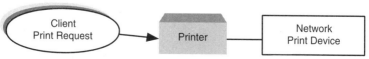

Figure 10.19 Troubleshoot printer problems with this schematic in mind.

- *System Properties*—Don't forget to check the Start | Programs | Administrative Tools | Windows NT Diagnostics | Resources to see whether an IRQ or I/O conflict with the printer exists.

- *Are you using the correct printer?*—Has a network printer been changed recently? If so, you will need to use the Add Printer Wizard to add the printer to your computer.

- *Is the spooler confused?*—Sometimes, due to a variety of networking factors, the spooler needs to be reset. You can stop and start the spooler service as the first course of action. If that doesn't fix the problem, try deleting the print job in progress to see whether that particular print job is causing the problem. (You will need to resend the print job.) To reset the spooler, select the following:

  ```
  Start | Settings | Control Panel | Services | Spooler | select Stop |
  then select Start
  ```

- *Is the printer or print job paused?*—Have you recently paused the printer? If so, it will not print until you resume the printer.

- *What's the priority of the printer?*—If your print job is not printing, yet other clients' print jobs are, you might consider the priority. Perhaps your printer has a low priority.

- *Is the printer accessible during the day?*—If your printer has been configured for specific operating hours, you should check to make sure that you're not attempting to print illegally.

- *Are you having problems accessing printers on another domain?*—You will want to ensure that trust relationships are in place. Additionally, make sure that the trust is configured correctly, with the resource trusting the user.

- *Application problems*—Don't assume the printer or the hardware is always the problem. Try printing from a different program. If it works, the problem is that particular software application.

- *Is the printer out of control?*—Turn it off. There is no better way to test a printer problem than to simply turn it off, wait, and turn it back on. Alternatively, try selecting a pause button on the printer device (if there is one.)

- *Reboot*—If everything else fails, sometimes rebooting is another solution. In addition to clearing the cache, rebooting sets the system back to a proper environment.

For Review

- Know the distinction between a printer and a print device:

- The *printer* is the *driver* or software that runs the print devices attached to a computer or network.

- The *print device* is where the printing paper goes, the Hewlett Packard DeskJet printer or the Epson Bubble Jet printer. The print device is where you change the ribbon or ink cartridges.

- The term *printer* is so familiar to us you should not assume this distinction would be easy to remember. Caution is definitely the word here, as your familiarity may prove to be false confidence.

- A spooler, or print provider, can intercept print jobs for local or remote print devices. If local, it holds the job until the print device is free to print it. If the spooler is acting like a remote spooler, it intercepts and sends the print request to the appropriate local spooler, where the job is printed. The default directory for the spooler is Winnt\Spool.

- Where multiple print devices are used, there is a *printer pool*. The only requirement of a printer pool is that all of the print devices must be similar.

- Before a client computer can interface with the printer, the printer driver software must be loaded on the client computer.

- Because an application interfaces with the printer and not the print device, where the print device is located and what it is attached to are inconsequential. This situation is ideal for purposes of sharing print devices on a network.

- For the MCSE exam, you need to understand print permissions. By default, the Print permission is assigned to all users through the Everyone group. Full Control is assigned to the Administrators group by default, giving them the ability to administer printing on any Windows NT computer.

- In any discussion of printing on a Windows NT network, you must distinguish between the *remote* and the *local* printer. For example, if the printer resides on a computer, the printer becomes *local* to that machine. Consequently, to any client computer on the network, that printer is *remote*. If the remote printer is on a different domain, a trust relationship must exist.

- You should know three types of separator pages for the MCSE exams:

  Sysprint.sep—Separates each print job with a blank page.

  Pcl.sep—Separates each print job with a blank page and puts the printer in PCL mode for HP print devices.

`Pscript.sep`—Does not print a blank page between print jobs but does switch to PostScript for HP print devices.

- One terrific feature of scheduling, which you should know for the exam, is that you can create multiple icons for the same printer, assigning different properties for each icon. Each icon you create for the same print device is a *logical printer*.

- Each logical printer you configure can have a different priority. The default priority is 1, which is the lowest priority. The highest priority is 99. A 99 priority interrupts a print job with a priority of 1.

- When print drivers are loaded on the server, they can be automatically downloaded to a client computer needing access to a print device. This feature is supported by only Windows 95, Windows NT Workstation, and Windows NT Server. You also must remember updates of print drivers can be downloaded to clients in the same way. If, for example, you update a print driver on the server, the clients who have previously downloaded the older version automatically receive the updated version the next time they access that print driver on the server.

- Ownership—You can take ownership of the printer. Remember taking ownership requires that you have the appropriate user rights. The Administrator group has the Take Ownership right by default. The ownership of a printer is assigned to whomever installs the printer. In most cases, this is the Administrators group, but not always. Remember the owner of something can't give ownership to someone else. To do this, someone with the rights of Full Control has to reassign ownership.

- One of the best features of printing with Windows NT is that you can stop or pause a document while printing.

- You can pause a printer and resume printing by clicking on Resume or Restart:

  Use Resume to start printing a document from the point it was paused. If paused after printing page 18 of a document, Resume would start printing at page 19.

  Regardless of where the document was paused, you can use Restart to start printing a document from page 1.

- To send print jobs to other servers, use the following method:

  1. Go to Start | Settings | Printers
  2. Select the printer that is not working.

3. Select Printers | Printer Properties.

4. Select Ports | Add Port.

5. Select Local Port.

6. Select New Port

7. Enter the UNC path to the printer you want to use temporarily (i.e., `\\printserver\hp`.)

- To connect a Unix operating system to a Windows print environment, you first must share the computer and install the TCP/IP Printing Services. The service is the *Line Printer Daemon* (LPD) and enables Unix clients to connect using the LPR command.

- The software driver may become corrupt. You will need to reinstall it. Doing this probably will not affect the system, so go ahead and do it if you're not sure of the nature of your problem. Remember to reboot after installation.

- If you are troubleshooting a printer problem, do not forget to check the Start | Programs | Administrative Tools | Windows NT Diagnostics | Resources properties, to see whether there is an IRQ or I/O conflict with the printer.

- The resource, or printer, trusts the user. There can be one-way or two-way trusts.

- Trusts are independent. A trust exists mutually between two domains. For three domains to have interdependent trusts, there must be a minimum of two trusts.

From Here

You may want to review Chapter 2, "Microsoft NT 4.0 Directory Services," and Chapter 4, "Windows NT 4.0 Installation," for more information. For a review of Windows NT group permissions, also see Chapter 8, "Managing Files and Directories," and Chapter 9, "Policies and Profiles." Chapter 16, "NetWare Connectivity," also has some discussion of printing.

CHAPTER 11

Remote Administration

The exam for Windows NT 4.0 Server in the Enterprise tests you on Administrative Tools. Do not be overly concerned about this topic. Most of the test questions do not dig any deeper than basic concepts. The following is a summary of the topics covered in this chapter:

- Remote administration
- Network Client Administrator
- Windows NT client server tools
- Windows 95 client server tools

Included on the Windows NT Server installation CD-ROM are utilities that enable you to administer your network remotely. You can install these utilities on Windows NT Workstation and Windows 95.

Once installed, Network Client Administrator and its respective tools enable you to administer your network from any client that supports this utility. Understanding the terminology is also important.

- *Local Administration*—Logged onto and administering the computer on which you are currently working.

- *Remote Administration*—Administering a computer on a network *other* than the computer on which you are currently working.

Network Client Administrator

When you use a server to administer a network, you use the *Network Client Administrator*. Nonserver clients give you several features to enable remote administration; however, the Network Client Administrator feature is available only on servers.

 Before setting up Network Client Administrator, you should prepare the information you'll need for the installation:

- User name
- Computer name
- Domain name
- Network adapter specifications
- Protocols being used on the network

During setup, you can specify whether the administrator starts automatically. If you choose not to start automatically, you can start the Administrator at the MS-DOS prompt on the client computer by typing `net logon`.

To start the Administrator shown in Figure 11.1, go to Start | Programs | Administrative Tools | Network Client Administrator.

For the MCSE test, you should know where to locate the administrator. Also, you should know about four options:

- Make Network Installation Startup Disk
- Make Installation Disk Set

Figure 11.1 The Network Client Administrator has four options.

- Copy Client-based Network Administration Tools
- View Remoteboot Client Information

Each of these options are discussed separately.

Make Network Installation Startup Disk

 When you boot the client with this disk, it installs the network adapter driver and lets you connect to the network share containing the operating system installation files. This option is used primarily for installing a small number of clients. Figure 11.2 shows the Share Network Client Installation Files dialog box.

Select the type of installation startup disk you are configuring as well as the drive letter for the boot floppy on the target computer. You also must select the model of network adapter card that is installed in the target computer. Figure 11.3 shows this dialog box.

The settings for the startup disk are displayed in Figure 11.4. Remember that if you are configuring TCP/IP on a routed network, you should have the IP address of the default gateway available when customizing these disks. The other option is to use DHCP to provide the IP address, subnet mask, and default gateway.

Remember that when creating this disk, you must format it with MS-DOS. You also must share the files you will be accessing. You can make a startup disk for only MS-DOS, Windows, and Windows 95 clients.

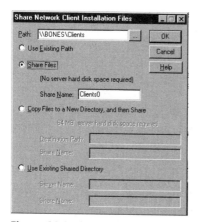

Figure 11.2 You designate either an existing share or create a share containing the network installation files.

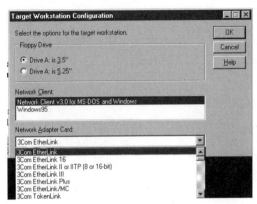

Figure 11.3 The floppy drive, the Network Client and the Network Adapter Card options are configured in the Target Workstation Configuration dialog box.

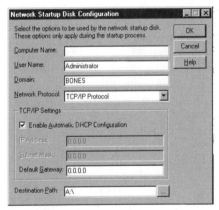

Figure 11.4 Enter the computer name and protocol configuration information on the Network Startup Disk Configuration dialog box.

Make Installation Disk Set

If you're doing a lot of client installations, this option creates a disk set. You enter the client information when each computer is booted, which creates a more personalized installation. Remember, that the path to create the disk set is Start | Programs | Administrative Tools | Network Client Administrator | Make Installation Disk Set.

You can make an installation disk set for the following clients:

■ Client for MS Networks 3.0 for MS-DOS and Windows

Figure 11.5   Use the Make Installation Disk Set dialog box to select which client or service and the destination drive.

- Remote Access for MS-DOS
- TCP/IP 32 for Windows for Workgroups 3.11
- LAN Manager 2.2c for MS-DOS and OS/2

The Make Installation Disk Set dialog box is shown in Figure 11.5. Select both the Network Client or Service and the Destination Drive. You also have the option to format the disks. The dialog box indicates how many disks will be required.

Copy Client-Based Network Administration Tools

This option creates a share containing the Windows NT Server administration tools for Windows 95 computers and Windows NT Workstations. You then connect to this network share from the target computer and install the tools. The installation process is discussed later in this chapter.

View Remoteboot Client Information

Remoteboot is a Windows NT service that provides the ability to remotely boot clients on the network from the server. This service can be used with MS-DOS, Windows 3.x, and Windows 95 clients. Remoteboot service is installed using the Services tab of the Network applet. This function enables you to see the information associated with each client regarding this ability.

Installation on Non-Server Clients

 As you'll recall, you get fewer network administrative tools when installing Windows NT Workstation clients and none of these with Windows 95. Keep in mind that installing the utilities on these computers does not give you immediate access. You must still have administrative rights on the domain when you want to administer the domain.

The minimum system requirements for this installation are shown in Table 11.1.

Table 11.1 Minimum System Requirements

	Windows 95	Windows NT Workstation
Microprocessor	486DX/33	486DX/33
RAM	8M	12M
Free Disk Space	3M	2.5M on system partition
Other	- - - -	Workstation service
	- - - -	Server service

As you might notice from Table 11.1, the minimum requirements are very similar. However, the services that are installed on the clients are quite different.

WINDOWS NT WORKSTATION

For Windows NT Workstation, the Network Client Administrator installs the following utilities:

- *DHCP Manager*—Used to manage the automatic assignments of IP addresses.

- *DNS Manager*—Helps to resolve domain names.

- *Remote Access Manager*—Configures the RAS service on the Windows NT server.

- *Remoteboot Manager*—Manages remoteboot on the server.

- *Server Manager*—The service used to administer the Windows NT server.

- *System Policy Editor*—Discussed in Chapter 9, "Policies and Profiles;" manages system and individual policies.

- *User Manager for Domains*—A Windows NT server service for managing the user and group accounts in a domain.

- *WINS Manager*—Manages the NetBIOS name resolution on a network.

To install the Network Client Administrator utilities on the Windows NT Workstation, do the following:

1. Place the Windows NT 4.0 Server disk in the CD-ROM of the workstation. Alternatively, you can install these tools from a network share.

2. Browse the following path on the CD:

   Clients folder | SRVTools folder | WINNT folder | SETUP.BAT

3. Select SETUP.BAT, and the installation proceeds automatically.

WINDOWS 95

Windows 95 receives considerably different tools to perform remote administration. You can use these tools to access the domain:

- *Event Viewer*—With this utility, you can view the logs (i.e., Event, Security, and Applications logs) discussed in Chapter 20, "Troubleshooting."

- *File Security*—This tool adds a FILE SECURITY extension to Explorer and My Computer. With it, you can manage the permissions assigned to resources on the network.

- *Print Security*—This tool enables you to add print security by creating permissions.

- *Server Manager*—This tool was added to Windows 95. This is *the* service used to managed the server.

- *User Manager for Domains*—This tool is used to manage user and group accounts remotely.

- *User Manager Extensions for Services for NetWare and File and Print Services for NetWare.*—These services enable you to interface with Novell NetWare from a Windows 95 client.

To install Network Client Administrator utilities on Windows 95, do the following:

1. Place the Windows NT 4.0 Server disk in the CD-ROM of the workstation. Alternatively, you can install these tools from a network share.

2. On the Windows 95 computer, go to Control Panel | Add/Remove Programs. Select the Windows Setup tab and click the Have Disk button. Browse the following path on the CD:

CLIENTS folder | SRVTools folder | WIN95

3. You are presented with a dialog box. Check the Windows NT Server Tools and click Install, and the installation proceeds automatically.

4. Edit `autoexec.bat` (or create an `autoexec.bat` as a text file if you have none). At the end of the path statement, type `;c:\srvtools`.

The computer must be rebooted to finish the installation.

Macintosh Services

For the MCSE exam, you should know that a Services for Macintosh option is also available. This option enables the two operating systems to share resources much like the way in which NetWare and Windows NT networks interface. With the Services for Macintosh option, you can do the following:

- Share printers
- Share files
- Manage NT and Macintosh networks from a Windows NT Server
- Support AppleTalk

The minimum requirements to run this service are as follow:

- Must be installed on Windows NT Server only
- NTFS partitions *only* on the Windows NT Server (no larger than 2G)
- 2M free disk space on the Windows NT Server
- Version 6.0.7 operating system on the MAC
- Macintosh must be running Appleshare

In studying for your tests, focus on understanding that this service exists and the basic things it facilitates.

For Review

- Network Client Administrator and its respective tools enable you to administer your network from any client that supports this utility.
- *Local Administration* means that you are logged onto and administering the computer from where you are currently working.

- *Remote Administration* means that you are administering a computer on the network *other* than the computer on which you are currently working.

- For the MCSE test, you should know where to locate the administrator: Start | Programs | Administrative Tools | Network Client Administrator

- The four components of the Network Client Administrator are as follow:

Make Network Installation Startup Disk

Make Installation Disk Set

Copy Client-based Network Administration Tools

View Remoteboot Client Information

- You must have *administrative rights* to administer the domain remotely.

- The Services for Macintosh option requires an NTFS partition on Windows NT Server for installation.

From Here

For more information on configuring and using policies and profiles, see Chapter 9. The Event Viewer is covered in Chapter 20, "Troubleshooting."

CHAPTER 12

Dynamic Host Configuration Protocol

To run a TCP/IP network, each computer, networked printer, router, and so on, must be assigned a unique IP address and a subnet mask. When TCP/IP was first implemented, the only way of accomplishing this task was to manually configure and track all IP addresses. This method continues today. To ensure that no duplicate addresses are issued, the administrator must do the following:

- Track all assigned addresses
- Manually configure each device that requires an IP address
- Maintain a list of unassigned addresses

This method can lead to problems with duplicate IP addresses being assigned. Troubleshooting duplicate IP address assignments can be an administrative nightmare. Although the client computer provides a message that an IP address conflict exists, the message identifies the conflicting computer by MAC address only. Because MAC addresses are seldom tracked, considerable time may be spent looking for the offending computer.

The *Dynamic Host Configuration Protocol* (DHCP) allows for the dynamic assignment of IP addresses and subnet masks as well as other options, such as the IP address of the default gateway. Using

DHCP also makes administration easier. Some of these advantages include the following:

- Each DHCP client is assigned a valid IP address.
- Typographical errors are prevented.
- Tracking of assigned and available IP addresses is simplified.
- Fewer configuration errors mean less time spent in troubleshooting network problems.

To implement DHCP on a network requires two components: the DHCP client software and the DHCP server. The DHCP server and the DHCP client must converse before an IP address is assigned by the DHCP server and accepted by the DHCP client. This process is referred to as *address acquisition*.

Address Acquisition

How does all this take place? How does a DHCP server lease an IP address to a DHCP client? The DHCP client first must request an IP address. Then a DHCP server must lease one to that client. This takes place in a four-packet broadcast-based conversation. These packets, which are shown in Figure 12.1 are the following:

- DHCPDISCOVER
- DHCPOFFER
- DHCPREQUEST
- DHCPACK

These packets are a special type of broadcast packet. These four packets take about a quarter of a second with a total size of 1.368

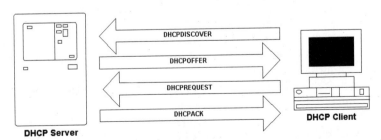

Figure 12.1 Address acquisition consists of a four-packet conversation between the DHCP client and the DHCP server.

bytes. These packets are forwarded by a router that supports the BOOTP protocol as defined in RFC 1542. Even so, DHCP traffic does not pose a significant bandwidth problem. The overall effect of this traffic on your network is determined by the length of the lease and routers forwarding DHCP packets to other subnets.

If your routers do not support BOOTP, there must be a DHCP server on each subnet of your network, or you need to install a DHCP relay agent on each subnet of your network that does not have its own DHCP server. The DHCP relay agent is discussed later in this chapter.

When a DHCP client boots, the client broadcasts a DHCPDISCOVER packet, asking for an IP address. Each and every DHCP server that receives this packet responds with a DHCPOFFER packet that contains an IP address and subnet mask that it is offering to the client.

The client responds to the first offer packet with a DHCPREQUEST packet accepting the offered IP address. The server then returns the DHCPACK packet to the client acknowledging assignment of the offered IP address. In addition, this packet contains any assigned options. These options are discussed later in this chapter.

After the client has received the acknowledgment packet from the server, TCP/IP is initialized, and the boot process continues. If the computer has multiple network adapter cards, this process is repeated for each. A unique IP address must be assigned to each network adapter card.

Address acquisition occurs when a DHCP client does not have an IP address, such as the following:

- When the client initializes for the first time
- If the client is moved to another subnet
- If the network adapter card in the client is replaced
- If the IP address has been manually released using ipconfig /release and then either the client is rebooted or the ipconfig /renew command is used.

Address Renewal

When a DHCP client receives an IP address, the DHCP server puts a time limit on how long the DHCP client may use that address. The time limit can be configured by the administrator depending on the needs of the network. This time limit is referred to as a lease. Something like leasing an apartment. When your apartment lease expires, you renegotiate the lease with the landlord or find some-place else to live.

When the lease on an IP address expires, the DHCP client also must renegotiate the lease. This lease or address renewal occurs via a two-packet conversation with the DHCP server. These two packets, DHCPREQUEST and DHCPACK, are shown in Figure 12.2.

These two packets are the same as the last two in the Address Acquisition conversation. If the address renewal takes place during the boot process, the packets are broadcast. However, directed packets are used when the DHCP client requests a renewal based on the amount of time that has elapsed. At this time, the DHCP client has TCP/IP up and running and knows the address of the DHCP server that assigned the IP address.

Address renewal occurs whenever the DHCP client boots and as a function of time based on the length of the lease. After half of the lease is expired, the DHCP client sends a DHCPREQUEST packet to the DHCP server that leased the address requesting to renew the lease.

If the DHCP server does not respond to this request; the DHCP client continues to use the same address; after all the lease has not yet expired. After 7/8 of the lease has expired, the DHCP client again tries to contact the DHCP server to request a lease renewal.

If the DHCP server still does not respond, the DHCP client waits until the lease expires and tries one more time to renew its lease. If the DHCP server still does not respond, then the DHCP client broadcasts a DHCPDISCOVER packet in an attempt to acquire a new IP address.

When the lease expires, the DHCP client no longer has an IP address, and TCP/IP will no longer function. Another IP address must be leased before TCP/IP can be used again.

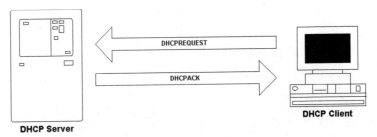

Figure 12.2 Address renewal consists of a two-packet conversation between the DHCP client and the DHCP server.

DHCP Client

 For a computer to be a DHCP client, it must be running one of the following operating systems:

- Windows NT Server 3.5 or later
- Windows NT Workstation
- Windows 95
- Windows for Workgroups 3.11
- Microsoft Network Client 3.0 for MS-DOS
- Microsoft LAN Manager 2.2c

A DHCP client is configured on the TCP/IP Properties dialog box as shown in Figure 12.3. The client may be configured as either a DHCP client, or an IP address is manually assigned. If the Specify an IP Address option is selected, this computer does not converse with the DHCP server.

If the Obtain an IP address from a DHCP Server option is selected, you can still specify additional parameters on the other tabs of the TCP/IP Properties dialog box. These parameters include assigning the address of a WINS server or DNS server. If these

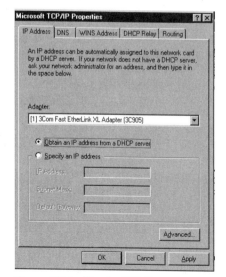

Figure 12.3   Use the TCP/IP Properties dialog box to configure your computer as a DHCP client.

entries are configured manually, they override any options sent to the client by the DHCP server.

TIP

Even when a computer is configured to be a DHCP client, you can still assign a default gateway address by clicking on the Advanced button on the IP Address tab of the TCP/IP Properties dialog box. This entry overrides any default gateway address sent by the DHCP server.

DHCP Server

The DHCP server must be installed on a computer running Windows NT Server. This computer must be configured with a static IP address and subnet mask. The DHCP Server may be installed on a domain controller or any member server.

TIP

A DHCP server cannot be installed on a computer that is a DHCP client. In fact, after installing DHCP server, the option to configure the computer as a DHCP client is disabled.

DHCP server is installed using the Network applet, Services tab. Click on the Add button and select Microsoft DHCP Server. When you click on the OK button, you receive a message that all adapters must be assigned a static IP address. When the necessary files have been copied from the installation share or CD-ROM, you must reboot your computer to finish the installation process.

After rebooting the computer, a new administrative tool is available—the DHCP Manager. When you first open the DHCP Manager, the DHCP server is listed as Local Machine on the left side. To enable dynamic IP addressing, a range of IP addresses, called a scope, and a subnet mask must be configured. Figure 12.4 shows the DHCP Manager.

Scope

The scope is a range of IP addresses that the DHCP server can assign to DHCP clients. Each DHCP server must have at least one scope that consists of the range of valid IP addresses and the associated subnet mask. Each DHCP server may be configured to manage multiple scopes.

On the menu in the DHCP Manager, select Scope | Create to display the Create Scope dialog box. Refer to Figure 12.5 to see the available fields that may be filled out.

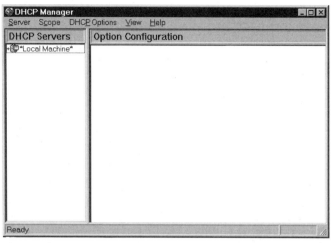

Figure 12.4 The DHCP Manager is used to configure and track the functions of the DHCP server.

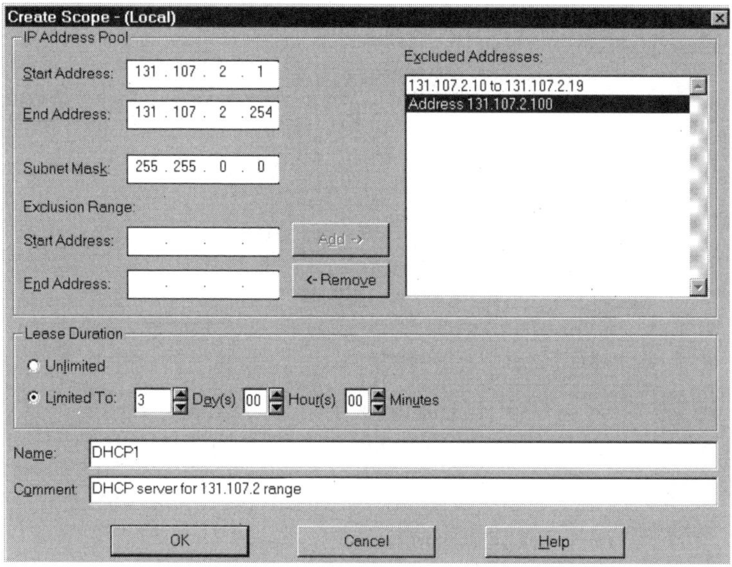

Figure 12.5 The Create Scope dialog box is used to create a new scope.

First, enter the Start Address and the End Address of the range of available IP addresses. You also must enter the appropriate subnet mask. All three of these fields are required fields.

The DHCP server needs to know whether any of the IP addresses in this scope have been assigned manually to a network device. These addresses must be excluded from the scope to prevent assigning a duplicate address. The DHCP server tracks when it assigns addresses from this pool but does not verify whether an IP address is being used before assigning it.

Exclusions

To not have conflicting IP address assignments, any manually assigned addresses must be excluded. Excluded IP addresses may be entered as either a single address or a range of addresses. Enter either a single IP address or the range of addresses in the Start Address and End Address boxes under Exclusion Range; then click the Add button. All excluded addresses are listed in the Excluded Addresses box on the right. Multiple ranges of IP addresses may be excluded.

Lease Duration

The next section of the Create Scope dialog box defines the lease duration. The lease may be unlimited or set to a maximum of 999 days, 23 hours, 59 minutes. The default lease duration is three days.

The problem with unlimited leases is that if a computer is moved to a new subnet, the administrator has to manually release the assigned IP address and have the computer acquire a new one. Although lengthening the lease period decreases traffic between the DHCP server and the DHCP client, the length of the lease is best determined based on the ratio of available IP addresses to DHCP clients.

TIP
If many more available IP addresses are available than DHCP clients, the lease can be lengthened. However, if the number of IP addresses is nearly equal to the number of DHCP clients, a shorter lease duration guarantees availability of leases when needed.

The bottom section of the Create Scope dialog box has a place to enter a name for the scope and a comment. If a name is entered, that name is displayed after the IP address in the DHCP Manager. Both of these fields are optional. Use the Comment box to enter text that defines the location of this scope.

When you are finished configuring the new scope and any excluded addresses, click the OK button. You then are presented with a message box asking whether you want to activate the scope. You may activate it at this time or wait until later. The scope must be activated before IP addresses from this scope may be assigned to clients.

Reservations

Computers, such as domain controllers, print servers, file servers, and application servers, need to have a static address assigned. These computers should not be DHCP clients. The most common way of handling this assignment is to manually configure the IP address on each of these computers.

An alternative method is to make these computers DHCP clients that always receive the same IP address. The DHCP server can be configured to reserve an address for a specific computer. This is called a *Reservation*. Reservations are configured by selecting Scope | Add Reservations from the DHCP Manager menu. This selection opens the Add Reserved Clients dialog box as shown in Figure 12.6.

In the IP Address box, type the IP address you want to assign to this computer. Enter the physical (MAC) address of the network adapter of this computer in the Unique Identifier box without the hyphens. Lastly, enter the computer's NetBIOS name in the Client Name box.

The advantage to using reservations is that all IP address configuration is administered centrally making it easier to track what IP addresses have been assigned to what computer. However, this approach is not without its downside. The advantages of central administration must be weighed against the disadvantages. The most important consideration is the effect on your network if the

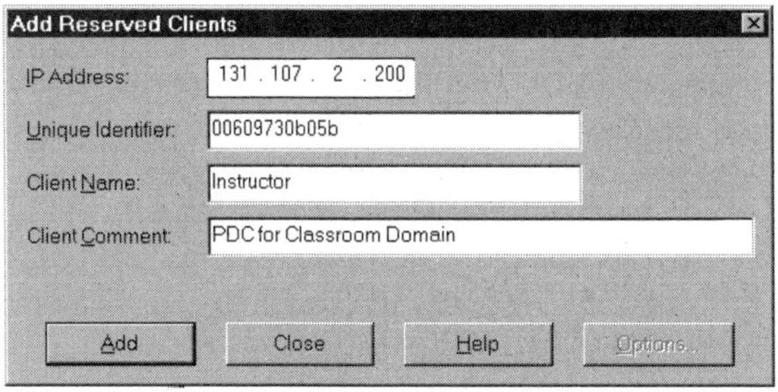

Figure 12.6   Use the Add Reserved Clients dialog box to assign an individual IP address to a specific computer.

DHCP server is down and the client computer cannot renew its address.

If the lease expires and if it cannot be renewed, then one of two things will happen. First, the client will attempt to acquire another IP address. If another DHCP server is not available, then TCP/IP is not initialized, and the computer is unable to communicate on the network. In either of these cases, clients may be unable to access the resources associated with this particular computer.

DHCP Options

 DHCP options are additional parameters that you want to have assigned to all computers. These options may apply to a specific scope or client reservation or be globally assigned. Options are actually TCP/IP parameters, most of which also can be assigned via the TCP/IP Properties dialog box.

The most common parameters that are assigned are as follow:

- Default gateway or router address
- DNS server addresses
- WINS server addresses
- NetBIOS node type

The default gateway or router address is the address the computer uses to deliver packets to remote IP addresses—that is, addresses located on a different subnet than the computer. See Chapter 14, "Domain Name System," for more information on the use of DNS servers and Chapter 13, "Windows Internet Name Server (WINS)" for further information on WINS servers and NetBIOS node type.

Options are configured from the DHCP Manager and may be designated as global or scope Options. Select DHCP Options from the DHCP Manager menu as shown in Figure 12.7.

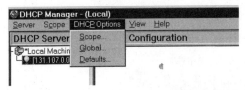

Figure 12.7   Select the type of options to configure from the DHCP Options selection on the DHCP Manager menu.

Global Options

Global scopes apply to the entire DHCP server; these options are sent to any client receiving an IP address from any of the scopes defined on that server. These options always are used unless either Scope or Client options have been configured.

Scope Options

These options are configured to apply to a specific scope. Any client assigned an IP address from the scope receives the options associated with it. If you have multiple scopes configured for separate subnets, then you need to be sure to assign a default gateway for each of these scopes.

Scope options override any global options set for the same parameter. That is, if a WINS server is configured as a global option and a different WINS server is configured as a scope option, the WINS server designated by the scope option is assigned to clients receiving an IP address from that scope.

Figure 12.8 shows the DHCP Options: Scope dialog box. In this instance, the 003 Router (Default Gateway) option has been selected. Its value has been entered by clicking on the Edit Array button.

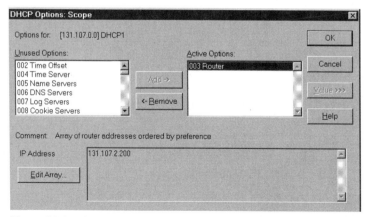

Figure 12.8 The DHCP Options: Scope dialog box is used to select options to be applied to the scope. This dialog box also is where you set the value for the selected options.

Client Options

Client options apply to a single client computer. These may be configured at the client computer or as a client reservation. To configure client options, first define the client reservation as described. Then under the DHCP Scope menu, select Active Leases.

Select the client for which you want to configure options and click on the Properties button. This selection displays the Client Properties dialog box as shown in Figure 12.9. Click on the Options button and select the options you want to configure.

> **TIP**
>
> Any options that have been manually configured either at a client or as a client reservation always override the options sent by the DHCP server. If an IP address for the WINS server has been entered at the client, when the DHCP server sends an address for the WINS server, it is ignored. Remember this when troubleshooting why a specific option is not working.

How do you determine that an IP address and the appropriate options have been set for a client? Use the utility `ipconfig.exe`. From a command prompt, type `ipconfig` to see the IP address and subnet mask assigned to that computer. If a default gateway has been assigned, it also is displayed.

Three switches can be used with `ipconfig`: *all*, *release*, and *renew*. Each of these have different effects on the computer.

- `ipconfig /all` displays all information on all the parameters or options that have been configured as well as the IP address and subnet mask. The information displayed here also includes the IP address of the DHCP server that assigned the IP address, when the lease was acquired, and when it will expire. `ipconfig /all` also

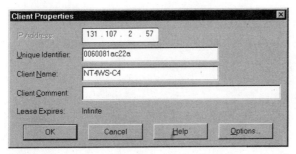

Figure 12.9   Use the Client Properties dialog box to configure individual client options.

can be used on a nonDHCP client. It displays the IP address, subnet mask, and any other options that have been configured for that client, such as a default gateway address.

- `ipconfig /release` notifies the DHCP server that the IP address will no longer be used by that client. At this point, TCP/IP is no longer usable until a new IP address has been obtained.

- `ipconfig /renew` causes the client to send a renewal request to the DHCP server that leased the IP address. If the IP address was previously released, the client will send a DHCPDISCOVER packet to acquire a new IP address.

TIP
When troubleshooting TCP/IP configurations, the `ipconfig` utility provides a quick look at how it is configured.

DHCP Relay Agent

 The DHCP Relay Agent provides a way to forward DHCP packets from one subnet to another across a router that does not forward BOOTP packets. Computers running Windows NT Workstation or Server can act as a DHCP Relay Agent.

The first step to install a DHCP Relay Agent is to install the DHCP Relay Agent Service. This is done through the Network Properties dialog box on the Services tab. After rebooting the computer, the DHCP Relay Agent is configured on the TCP/IP Properties dialog box using the DHCP Relay tab as shown in Figure 12.10.

Each DHCP Relay Agent must be configured with the IP address of one or more DHCP Server. The DHCP Relay Agent then acts as a proxy to forward address requests from DHCP Clients to the designated DHCP Server.

Multiple DHCP Servers

In the larger network, multiple DHCP Servers may be used to provide for load balancing. By installing two or more DHCP Servers, clients will not have to wait as long to receive an IP address. Multiple DHCP Servers also may provide a measure of fault tolerance. If one DHCP Server should be offline, the other DHCP server would be able to respond to requests for IP addresses.

The most common method of configuring multiple DHCP servers is to pair up two servers that are on different subnets.

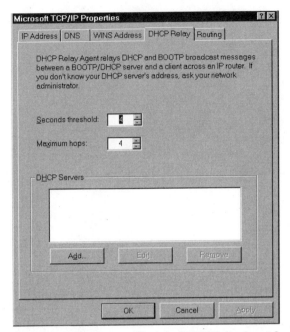

Figure 12.10   After installing the DHCP Relay Agent Service, configure the DHCP Relay Agent using the TCP/IP Properties dialog box.

Consider an example with two subnets, A and B, with a DHCP server on each one. To configure these servers to provide fault tolerance for each other, the available IP addresses should be split between the two. It is Microsoft's recommendation to configure a scope consisting of 75 percent of the IP addresses for the subnet that the server is on and another scope of 25 percent of the IP addresses for the other subnet.

TIP

When splitting a scope between two DHCP servers, be very careful that no duplicate IP addresses exist. Remember, a DHCP server does not talk to other DHCP servers. Also, a DHCP server does not verify that another computer is not using an IP address before it assigns that address to a client.

In the preceding example, DHCP Server 1 on Subnet A would be configured with a scope that includes 75 percent of the available IP addresses on Subnet A. It then would be configured with another scope that consists of 25 percent of the available IP addresses for Subnet B.

DHCP Server 2 on Subnet B then would be configured with the other 75 percent of the available IP addresses from Subnet B and 25 percent of the available IP addresses from Subnet A.

With this arrangement, if DHCP Server 1 should be offline at the time that a DHCP client from Subnet A requests an IP address, then DHCP Server 2 would be able to supply an appropriate IP address. For this to work, the router between Subnet A and Subnet B must be able to forward BOOTP packets.

The use of dynamic IP addressing can make one aspect of network administration less demanding. The DHCP server provides an easy method to configure TCP/IP on client machines. The DHCP server enables the administrator to better track assigned and available IP addresses.

For Review

- Address acquisition occurs through a four-packet conversation.

- Address renewal occurs through a two-packet conversation.

- The minimum configuration requirements for a DHCP server is a range of IP addresses and a subnet mask.

- The range of IP addresses and its associated subnet mask is called a *scope*.

- Options can be configured on the DHCP server to provide additional parameters.

- Any options configured at the client override options assigned by the DHCP server.

- Reservations can be configured to have the DHCP server assign a specific IP address to a specific DHCP client.

- Use the `ipconfig` utility to verify TCP/IP configuration.

- Use the DHCP Relay Agent to facilitate sending DHCP requests across a router that does not forward BOOTP packets.

- When configuring DHCP servers to provide fault tolerance, configure the scopes to contain 75 percent of the IP addresses from the home subnet and 25 percent of the IP addresses from the other scope.

From Here

For more information on WINS and NetBIOS node type, see Chapter 13, "Windows Internet Name Service (WINS)." DNS is covered in Chapter 14.

CHAPTER 13

Windows Internet Name Service (WINS)

Computers identify each other by a numerical address. On the TCP/IP network, this address is the IP address. People, however, prefer to use easy-to-remember names for their computers. These names are NetBIOS names.

To communicate with other computers using these easy-to-remember names, you need a way to resolve the name to the associated IP address. The *Windows Internet Name Service* (WINS) provides this function.

When a Windows NT computer boots, the computer registers its name and IP address in order to ensure that both are unique on the network. In this chapter, we cover NetBIOS names and how WINS handles name registration and name resolution.

NetBIOS Names

A NetBIOS name is a unique 16-character name used to identify a network resource. The first 15 characters are the name entered during installation. This portion of the NetBIOS name can be changed later. The 16th character is reserved to identify the specific service or application being registered, such as the server or workstation service, a username, or a domain controller.

TIP
The name you select for your computer must be a unique NetBIOS name. This name may be up to 15 characters in length and cannot contain / \ * , . " @ or a space.

NetBIOS Name Resolution

Using easy-to-remember, meaningful names simplifies attaching to network resources either by using the net use command or Windows NT Explorer. However, a TCP/IP network uses the IP address to communicate with these resources. The conversion of a NetBIOS name to an IP address is referred to as *name resolution*.

Windows NT operating on a TCP/IP network can use several methods to resolve computer names to IP addresses. These methods are as follow:

- *NetBIOS name cache*—This local cache contains the local computer names as well as computer names that have been recently resolved to IP addresses.

- *WINS*—This application provides resolution of NetBIOS names to IP addresses.

- *Broadcast*—A name resolution query may be sent to discover the associated IP address.

- *LMHOSTS file*—This text file is located on the local machine that maps the NetBIOS name to the IP address. (LMHOSTS files are discussed later in this chapter.)

- *HOSTS file*—This text file is located on the local machine that maps hosts names to IP addresses. HOSTS files are discussed in Chapter 14, "Domain Name System."

- *Domain Name Server* (DNS)—This server consists of a database that maps host names to IP addresses. See Chapter 14, "Domain Name System," for further information on the use and configuration of a DNS.

NetBIOS Name Resolution Modes

The order that each of these resources is used to provide NetBIOS name resolution over TCP/IP is determined by the computer's name resolution node type. These types as listed in Table 13.1 are defined in the *Request for Comments* (RFCs) 1001 and 1002.

Table 13.1 NetBIOS over TCP/IP Name Resolution Modes

Mode	Description
b-node (broadcast)	Uses broadcasts for name registration and resolution
p-node (peer to peer)	Uses a NetBIOS Name Server (i.e., WINS) for name registration and resolution. If the WINS server is offline, then name registration and name resolution fail.
m-node (mixed)	This mode is a combination of b-node and p-node. First broadcast is used for name registration and name resolution. If name resolution fails, then the WINS server is queried.
h-node (hybrid)	This mode is also a combination of b-node and p-node. However, the WINS server is used for name registration and name resolution. If a name cannot be resolved by the WINS server, then broadcasts are used.
Microsoft enhanced b-node	This enhanced b-node uses the LMHOSTS file for name resolution if efforts to resolve a name by broadcasts fail. (This capability is further discussed in the "LMHOSTS File" section.)

LMHOSTS File

The LMHOSTS file is a static file that maps NetBIOS names to IP addresses. A NetBIOS name to IP address mapping in the LHHOSTS file enables that NetBIOS name to be resolved for a remote computer that cannot respond to name query broadcasts. Computers can use the LMHOSTS file to obtain the name to IP address.

Enhancements to the LMHOSTS File

When the LMHOSTS file was introduced, the file could not be used to provide logon validation across subnets or when designing a domain that included multiple subnets. These limitations were removed by introducing a few keywords in the LMHOSTS file. The keywords and their functionality are described in Table 13.2.

Table 13.2 LMHOSTS Keywords

Keyword	Description
#PRE	When **#PRE** is added after an entry, that entry is preloaded into the NetBIOS name cache. The entry stays in the NetBIOS name cache and does not time out.
#DOM:<*domain*>	When added after an entry, #DOM associates that entry with the domain specified by <*domain*>. This keyword affects how the browser and logon services behave in routed TCP/IP environments. To preload a #DOM entry, you also must add the #PRE keyword to the line.
#INCLUDE <*filename*>	This keyword forces the system to seek the specified <*filename*> and parse it as if it were local. The #INCLUDE keyword enables you to use a centralized LMHOSTS file located on a server. In this way, a centrally maintained LMHOSTS file can be treated as though it were located on the local computer.

Before a b-node broadcast is used for name resolution, the NetBIOS name cache is checked. If a name query fails using broadcast and WINS, the LMHOSTS file is parsed to see whether the requested NetBIOS name is contained. An example of an LMHOSTS file is as follows:

```
131.107.2.5    server2    #print server
131.107.2.7    server3    #SQL server
131.107.2.2    server1    #PRE #DOM:domain1    #Domain controller
```

NOTE
Use the # sign to mark text as comments. When the LMHOSTS file is used for name resolution, it is parsed one line at a time starting with the first line. To optimize the use of LMHOSTS, put the most frequently used resource as the first entry, keep comments to a minimum, and list any entries with the #PRE keyword at the end.

The greatest limitation associated with using an LMHOSTS file is that it is a static file. Because this file is static, entries have to be updated if the name or the IP address of the computer changes. This means updating the LMHOSTS file on each and every computer. An LMHOSTS file may be created or edited with any DOS editor and must be saved to `%SYSTEMROOT%\system32\drivers\etc`.

NOTE

A sample LMHOSTS file (`LMHOSTS.SAM`) is saved to your hard disk when Windows NT is installed. This file is located in `%SYSTEMROOT%\system32\ drivers\etc`.

WINS Clients

When Windows NT is first installed, the node type is set as Microsoft enhanced b-node. This setting can result in a large amount of broadcast traffic that may have significant effects on the functioning of your network. In addition, in the segmented network, resources located across a router cannot be located without an LMHOSTS file or a HOSTS file located on the local computer.

The addition of a WINS server to provide for name resolution can greatly reduce the amount of broadcast traffic associated with name registration and name resolution. When a client is configured to use a WINS server, its node type is changed to h-node.

 A WINS Client may be any computer running one of the following operating systems:

- Windows NT Server or Workstation 3.5 or later
- Windows 95
- Windows for Workgroups 3.11 running Microsoft TCP/IP-32
- Microsoft Network Client 3.0 for MS-DOS with the real-mode TCP/IP driver
- LAN Manager 2.2c for MS-DOS

 The WINS Client must be configured with the IP address of the WINS Server. The client can be configured either dynamically via a DHCP server or manually. Figure 13.1 shows the WINS Address tab of the TCP/IP properties box. Use this tab to manually configure the use of WINS for name registration and name resolution.

The IP address of both a primary WINS server and a secondary WINS server may be entered. In this way, if the primary WINS server is offline or if name resolution fails, an alternative WINS server may be queried.

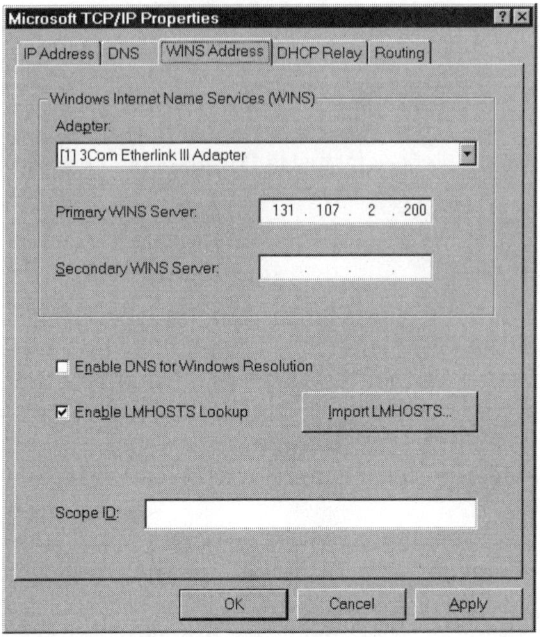

Figure 13.1 The WINS Address tab of the TCP/IP Properties dialog box is used to designate the WINS server or servers that the client is to use for name registration and name resolution.

You also can configure your computer to use an LMHOSTS file for name resolution by checking the Enable LMHOSTS Lookup box. Use the Import LMHOSTS button to designate the location of an alternative file.

When a WINS client starts, it registers its NetBIOS name and associated IP address with the designated WINS server. This registration is repeated for each of the NetBIOS names that the computer wants to register.

Later, when the WINS client needs to communicate with another computer using its NetBIOS name, the name query is sent to the WINS server. The WINS server, in turn, looks up the name in its database and returns the IP address to the client making the request.

Name Registration

When the WINS Client boots, it sends a Name Registration Request to the WINS server. The WINS server accepts or rejects the name registration by issuing a positive or negative name registration response to the requesting node.

If the name does not exist in the database, it is accepted as a new registration. The name is entered in the WINS database, and a positive name registration response is sent.

When the name exists in the WINS database but has a different IP address than that being requested and has been released, the WINS server treats the request as a new registration and a positive name registration response is sent.

If, however, the entry is in the *active* state, the WINS server sends a name query request to the device registered in the database. If the device still exists, the device sends a positive name query response back to the WINS server. The WINS server sends a negative name registration response to the computer attempting to register the name rejecting the name registration. If no response is received, a positive name registration response is returned, and the name is registered in the database as a new registration.

Name Release

When the WINS client shuts down, it sends a Name Release notification to the WINS server with which it registered. The WINS server marks the database entry as *released*.

WINS Server

The Windows Internet Name Service was designed to overcome the limitations of using an LMHOSTS file thereby simplifying administration. A WINS server is a dynamic database for registering and resolving names. The WINS server in installed on a Windows NT server running TCP/IP. This computer must have a static IP address. The address may be a domain controller or a member server.

The WINS Server is installed using the Services tab of the Network Properties dialog box. Click on the Add button and select Windows Internet Name Service. When you click on the OK button, the appropriate files are copied from the Windows NT Server CD or the network share containing the installation files. After this, your computer has to be rebooted for the service to start.

After the computer has been rebooted, the WINS Manager can be located from the Start menu as part of the Administrative Tools group under Programs. The WINS Manager is used to configure and manage the WINS Server and to view the database containing the names and IP addresses of the WINS Clients that have registered with it. Figure 13.2 shows the WINS Manager.

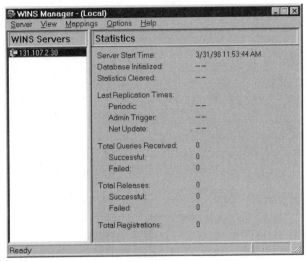

Figure 13.2 The WINS Manager is used for configuration and management of the WINS Server.

Because WINS is a dynamic service, as soon as you start it entries are added to the database. These entries may be viewed by selecting Mappings | View Database from the WINS Manager menu. As clients register with the WINS Server, their NetBIOS names and associated IP Addresses are added to the database. Figure 13.3 shows what this database looks like.

To provide name resolution for computers that are not capable of dynamic name registration, the WINS system also allows the registration of *static* names. WINS distinguishes between dynamic and static entries by using the WINS Manager and selecting Mappings | Static Mappings from the menu. The Add Static Mappings dialog box is shown in Figure 13.4.

TIP

Use static entries for any non-WINS computers, such as those running Unix, to provide name resolution for requests from WINS clients attempting to connect to these resources.

Replication

With larger networks or segmented networks, you may want to add WINS Servers to provide for more efficient name resolution and to keep name resolution traffic on the local segment. The disadvan-

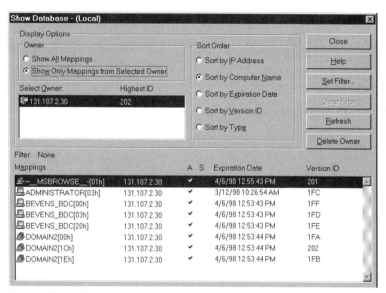

Figure 13.3 The WINS database contains the NetBIOS names and IP addresses for each of the registered computers.

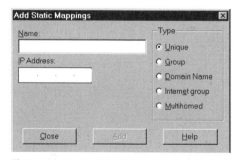

Figure 13.4 The Add Static Mappings dialog box is used to enter a static entry.

tage of multiple WINS Servers is that WINS Clients may be using a WINS Server, which does not contain the address of the desired resource, for name resolution.

To overcome the disadvantages of multiple WINS Servers, configure the servers to share their databases with each other. This process is called *replication*. Replication is configured using the WINS Manager as shown in Figure 13.5.

Two types of replication partners exist, Push Partners and Pull Partners. WINS replication can be configured using any combination of these, such as Push/Pull, Pull/Pull, or Push/Push partnerships. Select

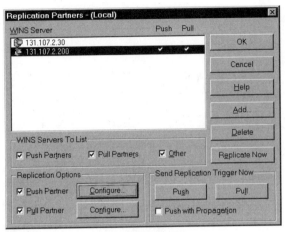

Figure 13.5   Select Server | Replication Partners on the menu of the WINS Manager to open the dialog box to configure replication.

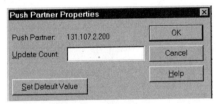

Figure 13.6   Enter the number of changes to occur before replication with a Push Partner is triggered.

the type of replication you want to use based on the speed of the connection between the two WINS Servers.

TIP
If the link between the two WINS Servers is a slow one, such as a WAN link, use Pull replication rather than Push.

Push replication is based on the number of changes that have been made to the WINS database before replication occurs. The default is 25 changes. Figure 13.6 shows the dialog box used to configure push replication.

Pull replication is based on the amount of time to elapse before replication occurs and when replication is to begin. The interval is entered as hours, minutes, and seconds. Figure 13.7 shows the dialog box used to configure pull replication.

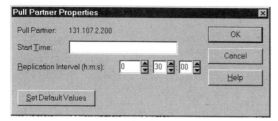

Figure 13.7 Enter the amount of time to elapse before replication with a Pull Partner is triggered.

By using replication, each of the WINS Servers has the same information in its database as all others. This information includes both dynamic and static entries. In this way, a computer that uses WINS Server1 is still able to successfully resolve names of computers that registered with WINS Server2. The entries from WINS Server2's database are copied to WINS Server1.

WINS Proxy Agent

When dealing with the multiplatform network, provisions for name resolution must include the capability of non-WINS clients to resolve NetBIOS names. Non-WINS clients, such as Unix and NetWare, cannot query the WINS server for the IP address of a WINS client. The WINS Proxy Agent was designed to address this lack.

The WINS Proxy listens for name resolution requests from the non-WINS clients. The WINS Proxy then forwards these requests to a WINS Server. The WINS Server resolves the name to an IP address and sends this information to the WINS Proxy. The WINS Proxy then forwards this information to the client making the request.

 For a computer to be configured as a WINS Proxy, it must be a WINS client. This configuration is accomplished by editing the registry entry as follows:

```
HKEY_LOCAL_MACHINE\SYSTEM\CurrentControlSet\Services\Netbt \
Parameters\EnableProxy
```

The value type for this key is a REG_DWORD and can be set as 0 (false) or 1 (true).

TIP

A computer configured as a WINS server cannot also be configured as a WINS Proxy agent.

The use of WINS Servers on your network has many advantages:

- Reduction of broadcast traffic associated with name registration and name renewal
- Name resolution in the segmented network does not need to use LMHOSTS files.
- Browsing and logon validation can occur across the segmented network.

For Review

- A NetBIOS name is 16 characters long, but only 15 of the characters are user configurable.
- The NetBIOS modes are b-node, p-node, h-node, and m-node.
- The LMHOSTS file is a text file that associates NetBIOS names to IP addresses.
- A WINS server resolves a NetBIOS name to an IP address.
- WINS servers may be configured as a push or pull partner.

From Here

The other name resolution service to study is DNS. See Chapter 14 for information on installation and configuration of a DNS server and how to use a HOSTS file.

CHAPTER 14

Domain Name System (DNS)

Connecting computers to share resources is only half of the job. To use the resources, a method must be created that provides for locating the necessary files, printers, and so on. One such resource is the Domain Name System. This tool provides for locating local resources as well as those located on the Internet.

This chapter addresses the purpose of the Domain Name System and how DNS helps locate network resources. This chapter also covers the installation and configuration of the DNS Server service. The DNS Server can also be configured to work with WINS Server to improve name resolution in your network.

What Is DNS?

Before 1980, the ARPANET maintained a file called `Hosts.txt` on a computer located at the *Stanford Research Institute's Network Information Center* (SRI-NIC) in Menlo Park, Calif. Each computer then could download the file as needed.

Because only a few hundred computers were networked, this arrangement worked well. The `Hosts.txt` file needed to be updated only every day or two. In addition, the `Hosts.txt` file was small enough that downloading it did not take long.

As more and more locations connected to the Internet, however, this system became unwieldy. Problems that appeared included the following:

- The Hosts.txt file became too large.
- Administration became extremely time consuming as the file needed to be updated more than once a day.
- The increased network traffic resulted in the SRI-NIC becoming a bottleneck for the entire network.
- Because the Hosts.txt was a flat file, every computer on the network had to have a unique name.

As a result of these problems, the governing body of the ARPANET created the DNS, which is a hierarchically organized, distributed database that provides a method of naming and locating hosts on the Internet.

The hierarchical nature of the DNS means that each host or computer no longer needed to have a unique name. By having a distributed database, no one computer is responsible for maintaining the needed information.

The purpose of the DNS is to resolve computer names to IP addresses. The Domain Name System has three components. The DNS clients are called *resolvers*, and the servers are called *name servers*. The third component is the domain name space.

The Internet domain is different than Microsoft's domain. A domain as defined by Microsoft refers to how computers, users, and resources are organized. The Internet domain is how host names are organized.

The Internet domain consists of the type of domain or top-level domain, such as com, edu, org, and so on, and the second-level domain. A computer's name is a combination of the host name and the domain name referred to as a *Fully Qualified Domain Name* (FQDN). For example, the FQDN server1.myplace.com is composed of the host name (server1) and the domain name (myplace.com).

NOTE
The term *domain* when used in DNS refers to an Internet domain, which is different than a domain as used in relation to Windows NT Directory Services. Internet domains are controlled by the *Internet Network Information Center* (InterNIC) and must be unique. More information on this subject can be found at http://www.internic.net.

HOSTS File

The HOSTS file is a text file that maps a host name to an IP address. This file maintains compatibility with the Unix HOSTS file. The HOSTS file can be used to map both local and remote hosts. Its biggest disadvantage is that it is a static file, which means the file must be updated manually. Any typographical errors result in failure in name resolution.

 The HOSTS file must be located on each host computer that needs to do name resolution. The HOSTS file is located in the %SYSTEMROOT%\system32\drivers\etc folder. An example of a HOSTS file is as follows:

```
127.0.0.1      localhost      loopback
131.107.2.2    server1.mycorp.com   #PDC
131.108.3.3    server2
100.1.10.10    unix
```

Entries in the HOSTS file are not case sensitive and are limited to 255 characters. Use any text editor to create or edit the HOSTS file.

DNS Server Service

The DNS Server service resolves a FQDN to its IP address. This information then is used by the computer making the request to locate the desired resource. When you use Internet Explorer to access a Web page, a DNS server resolves the friendly name to its IP address so that the Web page can be displayed.

Although both DNS and WINS resolve names to IP addresses, some basic differences exist. DNS resolves a FQDN or Internet to its IP address. WINS on the other hand resolves the NetBIOS name to its IP address.

The biggest difference between DNS and WINS has to do with configuration and maintenance issues. WINS is dynamic. Every WINS client registers its name and IP address when the client boots up. In this way, if the IP address changes, it is automatically updated.

DNS server, however, is static. Each computer name and its IP address must be manually entered into the DNS database. If the IP address or name changes, then these changes must be manually maintained.

Some advantages to using a DNS server include the following:

- Unix-based systems and other non-WINS enabled clients are more easily integrated into your network. They can be accessed using friendly names, and the non-WINS enabled machines can query the DNS Server to locate Windows-based systems.

- Name resolution on the Internet requires a DNS Server rather than a WINS Server. This functionality can be extended to include access to an organization's intranet.

- In the larger organization, a DNS Server provides for a hierarchical naming system across the entire network.

How It Works

Each DNS Server contains a portion of the DNS database. This database is referred to as a zone and is the administrative unit for the DNS. The DNS server is a name server that does the actual name resolution. Each DNS server may manage more than one zone. The clients requesting information are referred to as *resolvers*. A resolver may be the DNS client or another DNS Server. The steps that a DNS Server performs in resolving a name to IP address are as follow:

1. A client or resolver sends a request to the DNS Server.

2. The DNS Server first checks its database. If it has the requested information, the server sends that information to the resolver.

3. If the DNS Server does not have the requested information, it then queries other name servers. This process may take several forwarded requests before the desired information is located.

4. When the desired information is located, it is sent back through the same path that the request traveled until it reaches the resolver, who originally issued the request.

Domain Name Space

The DNS database is organized in an hierarchical manner with various levels, each with specific relationships with other levels. This structure is illustrated in Figure 14.1. The uppermost level is referred to as the *root*. Under the root are the various top level domains (nodes) such as org, edu, com, net, uk, and so on. Each of the top lev-

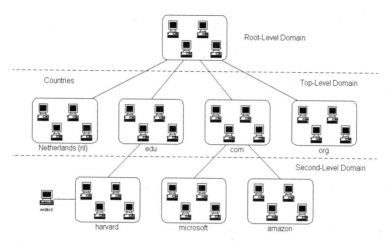

Root-Level Domain

Countries   Top-Level Domain

Netherlands (nl)   edu   com   org

Second-Level Domain

wizkid

harvard   microsoft   amazon

Figure 14.1 The domain name space can be thought of an upside down tree. The domains are referred to as nodes.

els may have several second level domains. These second level domains, in turn, may contain hosts and/or multiple subdomains. Domains are separated by a period.

In Figure 14.1, *harvard* is a subdomain of the top level domain *edu*. This subdomain contains a computer named *wizkid*. Therefore, the FQDN for this computer is `wizkid.harvard.edu`.

TOP-LEVEL DOMAINS

Both the root and the top-level domains are managed by InterNIC. In the United States, these top-level domains are organizational in nature and are represented by a three-letter name such as *org* for organizations, *com* for commercial, and *edu* for educational institutions.

NOTE

The organization of the top-level domains is presently being examined. Due to the rapidly increasing popularity of the Internet, the demand for domain names is rapidly exceeding the present system. Additional top-level domains probably will be available shortly.

In the rest of the world, the top-level domains are two-letter names for geographical locations such as *uk* for the United Kingdom.

ZONES

InterNIC delegates administrative responsibility for domains below the top level to other organizations. These organizations then may delegate administrative tasks to other organizations. The administrative unit for DNS is the zone that can consist of a single domain or a domain with multiple subdomains. Figure 14.2 shows two zones. Zone 1 contains three second-level domains: horse.com, cow.com, and chicken.com. Zone 2 contains only one second-level domain, pigs.com.

FULLY QUALIFIED DOMAIN NAMES

Each node in the DNS name space must have a unique name referred to as its FQDN. This name results from combining the various node names with a period separating each one. The names are assigned from the bottom up to the root.

When a DNS Server resolves a name, it resolves the from right to left. For example, when a DNS Server resolves the FQDN rover.mydomain.com, it first contacts the root server, which forwards the request to the name server in control of the top-level domain com.

The request then is passed by this server to the name server that administers the second-level domain mydomain. This server then returns the IP address for the host rover back through the same route from which the request originally traveled.

DNS Server Installation and Configuration

 Microsoft's DNS Server service can be installed on a computer with Windows NT Server. This computer must be using the TCP/IP protocol and be configured with a static IP address. The DNS Server service is installed using the

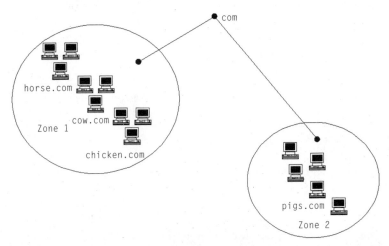

Figure 14.2   A zone may contain one or more domains. In addition, a zone may contain only part of a domain.

Network applet from the Control Panel. On the Services tab, click on the Add button and then select the Microsoft DNS Server.

After rebooting your computer, the DNS Manager is available via Start | Programs | Administrative Tools. All configuration of the DNS Server is done using the DNS Manager. Figure 14.3 shows the DNS Manager.

The first step in configuring your DNS Server is to add your server to the DNS Manager by selecting DNS | New Server from the menu and adding the server as shown in Figure 14.4.

The next step is to create the zone for this server by selecting DNS | NewZone from the menu. You then define the zone as a *primary zone* and enter its name. When this has been done, two resource records are created as shown in Figure 14.5.

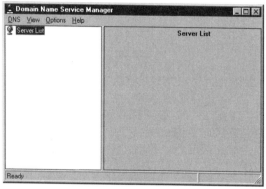

Figure 14.3   The DNS Manager tool is used for managing your DNS Server.

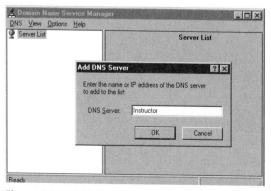

Figure 14.4   Add your server to the DNS Manager by entering either the computer's name or IP address.

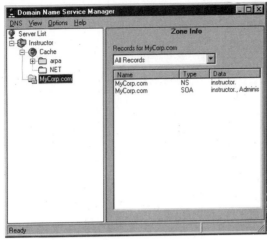

Figure 14.5   As a result of creating the new zone, two resource records are created as shown here.

The principal object of the DNS that you will configure is the *Resource Record* (RR). The RR contains the information managed by the DNS. Every RR has three properties in common:

- *Owner*—The name of the DNS domain to which the RR applies.

- *Class*—The defined family of RR types.

- *TTL*—How long the information in the RR remains valid.

Other objects of the DNS include the following:

- *DNS Domain*—This node is on the DNS tree and contains the Resource Records for that domain.

- *DNS Zone*—This part or subtree of the DNS database is administered by one DNS Server. This zone may be a complete domain or only a portion of a domain. A zone, however, may not span multiple DNS Servers.

- *DNS Server*—The software interface that manages one or more zones.

- *Server List*—This list of DNS servers can be administered from one DNS Manager. Additional servers may be added as needed.

NOTE
The order that servers are added to the DNS Manager is important. When Windows NT searches the DNS database for a computer name, it searches each DNS Server in the order they appear in the DNS Manager.

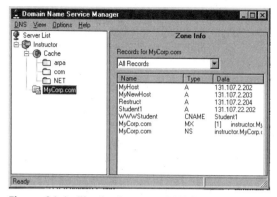

Figure 14.6 The database on a DNS Server may contain several different types of records.

The building block of the DNS database is the Resource Record. These records may be of varying types. The most common ones are as follow:

- *Start of Authority Record* (SOA)—The SOA is the first record in any DNS database and defines the characteristics for the DNS zone.

- *Name Server Record* (NS)—This record lists any additional name servers.

- *Host Record* (A)—This record associates the host name to IP address. A host record should be created for all hosts in the zone.

- *MX*—This record designates the mail server for the domain.

- *Canonical Name Record* (CNAME)—This record often is referred to as an alias. This record associates more than one host name with a single IP address.

A sample DNS database with various types of records is shown in Figure 14.6.

NOTE
All database record types are defined in RFCs 1034, 1035, and 1183. Copies of these RFCs can be found at the InterNIC site.

Configuring a DNS Client

Operating systems that can be configured as DNS clients include the following:

- Windows NT Server
- Windows NT Workstation
- Windows 95
- Windows for Workgroups 3.11 with TCP/IP-32

These clients may be configured to use DNS to resolve host names either manually or automatically using DHCP. To have the client configured using DHCP, configure the *006 DNS Servers* option for the appropriate scope. For more information on using DHCP, see Chapter 12, "Dynamic Host Configuration Protocol."

Use the Network applet to manually configure the client to use a DNS Server to resolve host names. Select the Protocol tab and either select TCP/IP and click on the Properties button or double-click on TCP/IP to open the Microsoft TCP/IP Properties dialog box. Figure 14.7 shows this dialog box.

This dialog box may be used to indicate a host name that is different from the NetBIOS name of the computer; however it is recommended to use the default host name. The name of the domain that the computer belongs to is also entered in this dialog box.

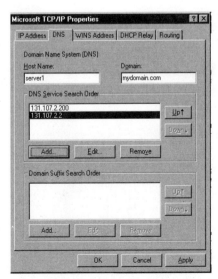

Figure 14.7 Enter the IP address of one or more DNS Servers to be used for name resolution.

The IP address of one or more DNS Servers is entered by clicking on the Add button. The order that the IP addresses are entered is the order that the DNS Servers are searched.

Integrating WINS and DNS

The DNS database is a static structure that must be manually updated whenever changes are made. For example, if a host machine moves from one domain to another, then this change must be entered by an administrator. Failure to maintain an up-to-date database may result in either a failure to resolve a name or resolving the name with incorrect information.

This administrative overhead becomes even more of a problem when IP addresses are dynamically assigned using DHCP. Using a WINS Server partially overcomes this problem. Every time a WINS client starts up, it registers its IP address with the WINS Server. Then when a WINS client wants to resolve the name of another WINS client, the information it obtains is current.

The problem occurs when a non-WINS client needs to obtain the address of a WINS client. The non-WINS client queries the DNS Server for the IP address, but if an entry has not been created, the query fails. If an entry has been created, the information returned may be incorrect, especially if the WINS client is using DHCP.

One method of addressing this problem is to configure the Windows NT DNS Server service to use WINS for host name resolution. This integration results in a type of dynamic DNS Server service. Use the DNS Manager to configure DNS to use WINS to resolve the host name of a FQDN.

The Zone Properties dialog box is opened by right-clicking on the zone that should query the WINS server. On the WINS Lookup Tab, check the *Use WINS Resolution* checkbox. Then enter the IP address of the WINS Server to use.

When a DNS server running on Windows NT receives the query, it then passes the host name (far left portion of the FQDN) to the WINS Server. The WINS Server, in turn, responds with the associated IP address. This answer then is passed back to the resolver (DNS client). This process, which is invisible to the resolver, is illustrated in Figure 14.8.

The advantage of using WINS for host name resolution is that the DNS Server appears to have a dynamic database. In addition, non-WINS clients can resolve NetBIOS names while using the DNS Server. For more information on using WINS, see Chapter 13, "Windows Internet Name Service."

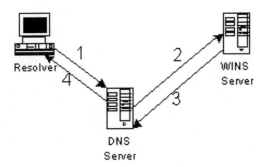

Figure 14.8 The DNS Server receives a query for an IP address (1). The server then forwards the host name as a NetBIOS name to the WINS Server (2). The IP address is returned by the WINS Server (3) to the DNS Server, which then forwards it to the client (4) who issued the request.

For Review

- The Domain Name System is a hierarchical, distributed database used to resolve a host name or FQDN to an IP address.

- A HOSTS file is a static text file used to resolve host names to IP addresses.

- DNS resolves names from the right to the left.

- A zone is the administrative unit for DNS.

- A DNS Server may manage more than one zone.

- The DNS Server service may be installed on a computer running Windows NT Server 4.0 with a static IP address.

- The DNS Manager is used for configuring the DNS Server service.

- The Resource Record is how information is entered in the DNS database.

- The most common Resource Record types are SOA, A (Host Record), NS (Name Server Record), MX (Mail Server Record), and Canonical Name Record (CNAME).

- DNS is static unlike WINS, which is dynamic.

- DNS can be configured to use WINS for host name resolution.

From Here

For more information on using WINS for name resolution, see Chapter 13, "Windows Internet Name Service."

CHAPTER 15

Remote Access Server

The *Remote Access Server* (RAS) enables users to dial into a remote network using the telephone lines. The RAS acts as a gateway giving the remote user access to network resources as though directly wired to the network.

In the enterprise network, the RAS enables an organization to expand its network to include remote offices. This expansion is more economical than installing dedicated lines, and it works where high-speed access is not available.

The client side of RAS is called *Dial-Up Networking* (DUN). This chapter covers the installation and configuration of both RAS and DUN.

Overview of RAS and DUN

RAS and DUN interact to connect a network over different locations. RAS enables organizations to use the Public Telephone System and digital services such as ISDN, X.25, and the Internet to extend their networks.

Remote clients can use the network as though they were directly connected to it. RAS supports Windows NT security features, protocols, and WAN connections. WAN connectivity may be achieved in several different ways.

Modems

Windows NT can detect installed modems. If detecting a modem is a problem, a modem may be installed manually using the Modem applet in the Control Panel. RAS uses standard modem connections over the telephone lines to establish communication between RAS and the client. In addition, DUN can be used to connect to an Internet Service Provider (ISP).

A special kind of access line is an *Integrated Services Digital Network* (ISDN), which is faster than using the public telephone system. To use an ISDN connection, a digital "modem," rather than an analog one, must be installed.

X.25

X.25 uses a packet-switching protocol for transmitting data. DUN clients can access the X.25 network using an X.25 *packet assembler/disassembler* (PAD) and the telephone number of the PAD service. RAS provides access in one of two ways:

- If the operating system is Windows NT or Windows 95, a PAD is installed.
- If the network is Windows NT only, an X.25 smart card may be used instead.

Point-to-Point Tunneling Protocol

The *Point-to-Point Tunneling Protocol* (PPTP) enables the use of the Internet to securely access your remote network. PPTP enables the use of IP, IPX, or NetBEUI over a TCP/IP network by encapsulating the data. PPTP also provides for data encryption.

The biggest advantages of using PPTP are lower costs and less administrative time involved in providing for remote access. Because the Internet is used, a large number of modems is not required. In addition, no dedicated leased lines are needed for a secure connection. Less hardware means less time spent managing access.

Protocols

RAS supports two types of protocols, LAN and WAN protocols. LAN-based protocols are TCP/IP, IPX/SPX, and NetBEUI. WAN, or remote access, protocols are PPP, SLIP, and Microsoft RAS protocol.

See Chapter 5, "Network Configuration," for more information on the LAN protocols.

Serial Line Internet Protocol (SLIP)

SLIP was first developed in 1984 to provide TCP/IP access over slow, serial connections. Limitations of SLIP include the following:

- The inability to use DHCP or WINS
- Supports only TCP/IP, preventing the use of other protocols
- Authentication information, such as username and password, are transmitted as clear text.

TIP
Windows NT RAS server cannot act as a SLIP server, only as a SLIP client.

Point-to-Point Protocol (PPP)

PPP was developed as an enhancement to SLIP. PPP allows for the use of DHCP and WINS and supports most protocols. In Windows NT, PPP supports TCP/IP, IPX, and NetBEUI.

When RAS is installed, it binds to the protocols already installed on the server. If needed, additional protocols can be added. Each protocol is individually configured.

Microsoft RAS Protocol

Older versions of RAS supported only connections from clients using NetBEUI as the protocol. Currently, the Microsoft RAS protocol provides a gateway to access network resources running any of the three supported protocols.

Gateways

RAS acts as a gateway in different situations and provides access to resources using NetBIOS. RAS also has the capability to act as an IP or IPX router to link networks, both LANs and WANs.

Installation of RAS

RAS can be installed on Windows NT 4.0 Server or Windows NT 4.0 Workstation. A version also runs on Windows 95. The minimum hardware requirements to install RAS are as follow:

- A network adapter card
- One or more modems
- If using an ISDN line, an ISDN "modem"
- If using an X.25 network, an X.25 smart card

RAS also can be configured to directly connect two computers using a null modem cable attached to a serial port.

RAS may be installed at the same time that Windows NT Server is installed. RAS also can be installed after installation of the operating system from the Network Applet | Services tab. Before installing the service, collect the following information:

- The type of communications port
- The modem model and any required modem settings
- Whether the RAS server supports Dial-In Only, Dial-Out Only, or both Dial-In and Dial-Out
- The protocols to be installed

Figure 15.1 shows the Remote Access Setup dialog box. This box is presented during installation if you select to install RAS at that time. If changes need to be made later, access this box by highlighting the RAS Service on the Services tab of the Network Properties dialog box and click on the Properties button.

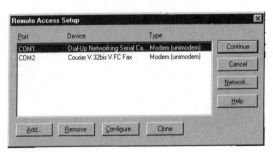

Figure 15.1 The Remote Access Setup dialog box is used to configure the server.

The first step in configuring a RAS server is to set up the hardware that the RAS server will use, including the port and type of modem. The configure button at the bottom of the dialog box is used to specify whether the port will be used for dial-in and/or dial-out purposes. The Configure Port Usage dialog box is shown in Figure 15.2.

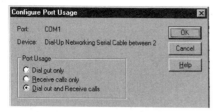

Figure 15.2 Choose dial out only, receive only, or both.

If multiple modems are installed on the RAS server, each one must be configured separately using the Configure Port Usage dialog box.

PROTOCOL CONFIGURATION

Clicking on the Network button displays the Network Configuration dialog box that allows for configuring each installed protocol. Configuring the dial-in protocols determines the amount of network access a user will have when calling in using that protocol.

TCP/IP

When configuring TCP/IP, two parameters are configured, Network access and IP address, as shown in Figure 15.3. Access may be limited to the RAS server only or granted to the entire network.

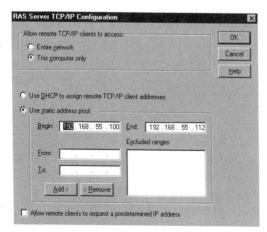

Figure 15.3 Configuring network access and IP address.

You can assign an IP address to a RAS client in two ways. If a DHCP server is running on your network, RAS can be configured to obtain the IP addresses from the DHCP server and assign them to the client. See Chapter 12, "Dynamic Host Configuration Protocol," for more information on using DHCP.

The second way to assign client IP addresses is by creating a pool of addresses on the RAS server. The RAS server then assigns an IP address to each client upon connection. Remote clients may request a reassigned IP address if the *Allow remote clients to request a predetermined IP address* check box is checked.

IPX/SPX

Remote IPX/SPX clients may be allowed to access only the RAS server or the network, as when configuring TCP/IP.

Parameters for IPX/SPX are configured from the same dialog box. A network number may be automatically assigned, or a static number may be entered. By default, *Allocate network numbers automatically* and *Assign same network number to all IPX clients* are selected. Unless you have a specific need, leave these settings as they are. See Chapter 5, "Network Configuration," and Chapter 17, "Internet Information Server," for more information on configuring IPX/SPX.

NetBEUI

The only configuration necessary for NetBEUI is the amount of user access, like with the previous protocols, TCP/IP and IPX/SPX. If the client is running NetBEUI, the RAS Server acts as a gateway to allow access to network resources running either TCP/IP or IPX/SPX.

AUTHENTICATION CONFIGURATION

In addition to configuring the protocols, this dialog box also is used to set the authentication level and to enable multilink. Three levels of authentication are as follow.

■ *Allow any authentication including clear text.* This option is used to enable access to the RAS server by clients unable to use a higher level of security. This authentication level is the least secure of all. Select this option to support the largest variety of clients.

TIP

Additional security can be added by installing an intermediary security host. This host is located between the RAS clients and the RAS server. The client must enter a password or code before gaining access to the RAS server. This type of host is a good choice when you need to provide access to a variety of clients but still want to have a higher level of security.

- *Require encrypted authentication.* This option permits a connection using any type of authentication. The type is requested by the client. Passwords are encrypted when using this option.
- *Require Microsoft encrypted authentication.* The only type of authentication that will be accepted is MS-CHAP. When selecting this level of user authentication, you also may have all data sent across the connection encrypted by checking the *Require data encryption* check box.

> **TIP**
> Most questions on authentication levels are scenarios. Select the most secure type of authentication that will provide access to all RAS clients. Be sure and pay attention to the operating system being run by the clients before making your decision.

MULTILINK

Multilink provides the ability to combine multiple connections to provide increased bandwidth. Multilink will work with modems, ISDN, or X.25 and must be configured on both the RAS Server and the RAS Client. In fact, multilink also works with a combination of connection types. The RAS server can be configured to use multilink by checking the *Enable Multilink* checkbox in the Network Configuration dialog box.

> **TIP**
> If RAS is configured for call-back security, multilink will not work. Only one phone number may be installed in a user's account, and only that number is called; thereby bypassing the multilink capability.

Dial-In Access Rights

After RAS is installed and configured, users must be granted the right to connect to the RAS Server. This can be done either using the RAS Admin utility, User Manager (Workstation), or User Manager for Domains (Server).

Figure 15.4 shows the Remote Access Permissions dialog box. This box may be opened via Users | Permissions from the RAS Admin utility menu. The top part of the box lists all users. Select the desired user account and check the *Grant dial-in permission to user* check box.

On the bottom of the Remote Access Permissions dialog box are the options to configure *Call Back*. Providing for call back increases the security of the RAS server. After a call is received and the user authenticated, the RAS server disconnects and then dials the user back. The three options are as follows:

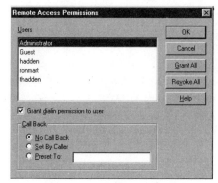

Figure 15.4 The Remote Access Permissions dialog box.

- *No Call Back.* The user continues with the session after the connection has been established and authentication is completed. The user then disconnects when finished with the call.

- *Set By Caller.* After authentication, the user is prompted to enter a call back number. This is helpful for supporting traveling users. The cost of the call then is covered by the organization.

- *Preset To.* This option is the most secure of the call back options. When a user connects to the RAS server, the RAS server calls back to a preconfigured number.

When using User Manager or User Manager for Domains, select the user to configure access rights and open the Properties dialog box. Clicking on the Dialin button opens the dialog box used to grant rights. This box provides the same functionality as when using the RAS Admin utility. The only difference is that only that user's access status is displayed when using User Manger. The RAS Admin utility lists all users. This way to individualize multiple users' access rights is quicker.

Installation of Dial-Up Networking

Connection to a RAS server is made from the client through the use of Dial-Up Networking. After the connection is made, the DUN Client functions as though directly connected to the remote network.

Dial-Up Networking is automatically installed during installation if Remote Access Services are installed. Dial-Up Networking can be installed after the installation of the operating system the same way as RAS. On the Services tab of the Network Properties dialog box, select *Remote Access Services*. If only DUN is to be installed, configure the modem for Dial Out connections only.

DUN has the same hardware requirements as those for installing a RAS server. After all, DUN is merely one portion of the RAS Server's capabilities. After DUN is installed, several options may be configured:

- Telephony API
- Phonebook entries
- Remote logon
- Auto-dial

Telephony API (TAPI)

TAPI acts as a device driver for the telephone system, thereby enabling the use of the telephone system as an extension to your computer. TAPI configures the dialing properties for your system. DUN is a TAPI-aware application. TAPI configuration is done during installation of DUN. This configuration can be altered later by using the Telephony applet in the Control Panel.

LOCATIONS

A location is set up to configure how TAPI dials numbers to establish a connection. A location may be related to a geographic location but also may be related to a particular site in a geographic location such as a hotel room. The information needed to configure a location includes the following:

- Area or city code
- Country code
- How to access an outside line
- Calling card information

Figure 15.5 shows the My Locations tab of the Dialing Properties dialog box. Use this dialog box to create, modify, or remove Locations. A location may be used by any TAPI-aware application, not just DUN.

When creating a location, use a meaningful name. This name is selected when configuring Phonebook entries (see "Phonebook Entries" later in this chapter). If dialing from a location outside of the United States, enter the City Code in the Area Code text box.

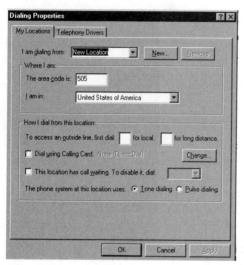

Figure 15.5   The Dialing Properties dialog box is used to configure Location parameters.

The Country Code is configured by selecting the country name from the *I am in* drop-down box.

If dialing an additional number is necessary to access an outside line, such as through a PBX, enter that number. Different entries for accessing a local line and a long-distance line may be entered.

Two optional parameters may be configured:

- *Dial using Calling Card.*   This number is stored in a scrambled format and is not displayed again after entering. Multiple calling cards may be configured.

- *This location has call waiting. To disable it, dial:*   If Call Waiting is not disabled, the connection may be severed when a second call comes in.

You also must specify whether the phone system you are attached to uses either tone or pulse dialing.

PHONEBOOK ENTRIES

Phonebook entries contain all the information to establish a connection. These entries then are stored in a phonebook. Phonebooks may be individual or shared by multiple users.

Phonebook entries may be configured using the New Phonebook Entry wizard or manually by selecting I know all about phonebook entries and would rather edit the properties directly. A new phonebook entry is created by opening Dial-Up Networking and then clicking on the New button. Figure 15.6 shows the New Phonebook Entry dialog box.

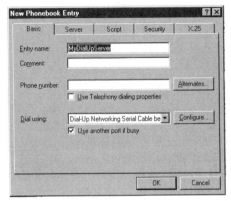

Figure 15.6   The New Phonebook Entry dialog box has five tabs and is used to record the settings necessary to establish a connection.

Enter a name for this entry that is meaningful in the Entry name text box. An optional comment also may be entered. If the *Use Telephony dialing properties* option is not checked, the fields for Country Code and Area Code are not displayed.

TIP
Multilink may be enabled by selecting multiple lines in the *Dial using* box. The number of telephone numbers to dial determines how many phonebook entries need to be created. For example, if calling an ISDN with two channels that have the same phone number, only one entry is required.

Enter the phone number to be called and the modem to be used. Multiple phone numbers may be configured by clicking on the Alternates button. If multiple modems are available, check the *Use another port if unavailable* checkbox.

Use the Server tab to select the type of dial-in server. Protocols also are included on this page and may be configured if necessary depending of the type of server being called.

The Script tab is used to indicate whether a script should be run before or after dialing to establish a session. Using a script bypasses the need for manual intervention to establish the connection. Alternatively, a terminal window can be configured to pop up after a connection is established.

The Security tab is used to configure the type of Authentication and Encryption Policy. These choices correspond to the authentication methods discussed earlier in this chapter:

■ Accept any authentication including clear text

■ Accept only encrypted authentication

■ Accept only Microsoft encrypted authentication

If the last option is selected, the *Require data encryption* and *Use current username and password* options become available. Encrypting the data transferred across the connection provides for a more secure connection. If the username and password on the DUN client correspond to the username and password on the remote network, using this option automates the logon process.

The last tab, X.25, is used to specify the network provider and its address. Optionally, user and facility information may be entered.

Remote Logon

Windows NT enables the use of Dial Up Networking for logging into a domain by placing this option on the logon dialog box. If this option is checked, the user can select which phonebook entry to use to establish a connection.

To configure the logon parameters, click on the More button in Dial-up Networking. Then select Logon Preferences to display the Logon Preferences dialog box shown in Figure 15.7.

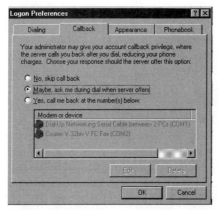

Figure 15.7 The Logon Preference dialog box is used to configure how a logon occurs.

The Dialing tab is used to configure the number of redial attempts, how long to wait between attempts, and the idle time before hanging up. The Callback Tab, shown in Figure 15.7, is where the DUN client is configured for call back.

The Appearance tab configures the user's interaction during logon. An individual phonebook or the system phonebook is selected using the Phonebook tab.

When logging onto a Windows NT domain using a roaming profile, the profile is downloaded to the client computer. This downloading can result in a very slow logon process using DUN. One way to prevent this slowdown is to specify that the locally cached profile is used rather than the server-based one. To specify use of the locally cached profile, use the System applet from the Control Panel on the User Profiles tab. See Chapter 9, "Policies and Profiles," for more information on using profiles.

AutoDial

RAS AutoDial maps network addresses to phonebook entries in the AutoDial mapping database. The database can include IP addresses, NetBIOS names, or Internet host names.

AutoDial is enabled by default. To disable AutoDial, use the User Preferences dialog box accessed by clicking on the More button in Dial-up Networking. Then select User Preferences to display the User Preferences dialog box shown in Figure 15.8.

Figure 15.8   The User Preferences dialog box is used to enable or disable AutoDial.

Troubleshooting

Several common types of errors may occur when using RAS. Various approaches are used to diagnose and correct the problems. One tool frequently used to diagnose problems is the Event Viewer. RAS events are logged in the System Log.

- *Problems with PPP Connections.* A ppp.log file can be created to help diagnose problems related to authentication over PPP. To enable logging, edit the registry parameter \HKEY_LOCAL_MACHINE\ System\CurrentControlSet\Services\Rasman\PPP\Logging and change its value to 1.

- *Authentication Problems.* Try the lowest authentication on both the server and the client. If a successful connection is achieved, try the next higher type of authentication.

- *Dial-Up Networking Monitor.* The Dial-Up Networking Monitor displays the status of the connection and is helpful in diagnosing problems.

By using a RAS Server, you can expand the size of your network by connecting remote offices. The RAS Server also provides network access for users who travel.

For Review

- RAS enables the use of the public telephone system to connect remote users to your network.
- PPTP provides a secure connection using the Internet.
- RAS supports TCP/IP, IPX/SPX, and NetBEUI protocols.
- WAN connections can be made using SLIP, PPP, or Microsoft RAS protocols.
- RAS supports three levels of authentication: Clear text, Encryption, and MS CHAP.
- The use of multilink increases bandwidth by combining two or more lines.
- Users must be granted access to connect to the RAS server.
- TAPI is configured by creating or modifying locations.
- Create a phonebook entry for each server to be called.
- RAS may be used to log on remotely to a Microsoft domain.

- The Event Viewer and the Dial-Up Networking Monitor may be used to troubleshoot problems with RAS.

From Here

Chapter 5, "Network Configuration," and Chapter 17, "Internet Information Server," contain additional information on installing and configuring protocols. See Chapter 9, "Policies and Profiles," for information on working with profiles. Chapter 12 covers using DHCP.

CHAPTER 16

NetWare Connectivity

Windows NT Server and Novell NetWare are the leading PC-based networking operating systems. As a result, many large networks use both. Replacing pre-existing NetWare networks with Windows NT may be desirable. Microsoft has provided various tools designed to ensure compatibility with existing installations of NetWare and offers simple methods to migrate from NetWare to Windows NT.

Windows NT Server comes with the NWLink IPX/SPX Compatible Transport protocol and *Gateway Services for NetWare* (GSNW). In addition, *File and Print Services for NetWare* (FPNW) and *Directory Services for NetWare* (DSNW) are available as free add-ons to make coexistence easier and to simplify administration.

This chapter covers these features and products. A basic overview of NetWare features with which the Windows NT administrator needs to be familiar also is presented.

NDS versus Bindery

Prior to release of NetWare 4.0, NetWare used a bindery to store security and resource information. The bindery was located on each NetWare server. A user needing access to resources on a NetWare server would specify the NetWare server housing the resource and a valid user account and password for that NetWare server. Novell changed this specification with the release of NetWare 4.0. NetWare 4.0 uses *NetWare Directory Services* (NDS) for housing the security and resource information for all machines in a group similar to a Windows NT domain. This arrangement is referred to as a *tree* in NetWare terms, and the information is stored in one location.

This arrangement creates a single user logon to access resources from multiple servers. A user needing to access resources with NDS must specify the tree and the context (a location within the tree) using a valid user account and password, which is an improvement in contrast to having a username and password for every server containing the needed resources.

NetWare 4.x servers can run in bindery emulation mode, the security model for NetWare versions older than 4.x. This mode was required for NetWare servers to be accessible to previous versions of Windows NT. Many older programs designed around older versions of NetWare require this mode. Bindery emulation mode is the default for NetWare 4.x servers

Bindery emulation may be disabled by changing the Bindery Context setting on the NetWare server. Leaving bindery emulation mode enabled allows applications designed for the older bindery mode to properly function. However, this setting also disallows browsing of the NDS tree.

Windows NT 4.0 connects to NetWare via bindery emulation or using the newer tree and context method. If no programs that require bindery emulation are being used, disabling emulation mode allows Windows NT machines to navigate the NDS tree structure.

NWLink Protocol

NWLink is Microsoft's answer to Novell's IPX/SPX protocol suite, and, in fact, Microsoft went to great lengths to ensure complete compatibility. (Independent tests have shown that NWLink actually is faster than the original IPX/SPX.) When installing GSNW, NWLink protocol is automatically installed (if not currently installed) on the workstation.

TIP

The installation of NWLink IPX/SPX Compatible Transport alone on a Windows NT Server allows NetWare clients to run an application located on the Windows NT Server. The installation of a redirector such as GSNW is not necessary to access these applications.

The use of NWLink is not limited to Microsoft networks that want to connect to NetWare machines. In fact, NWLink can be used on networks without any Novell resources on them. NWLink has several advantages over the use of either NetBEUI or TCP/IP. NWLink is routable, unlike NetBEUI, allowing for its use in larger networks. The current release of NWLink is faster than TCP/IP for Windows machines, and the administration of NWLink is significantly less.

The major drawback to the use of NWLink on a network is the Internet's growing popularity and its use of TCP/IP. Many administrators still use NWLink as a primary transport protocol, binding TCP/IP as a second protocol only on machines that need Internet access. Using NWLink helps limit the exposure a firm's machines have to intrusion risks from the outside world.

When NWLink is installed, Windows NT Server adds two entries to the network protocols list, NWLink IPX/SPX Compatible Transport and NWLink NetBIOS, which is for the Session layer NetBIOS that runs on top of the NWLink transport. NWLink automatically runs NetBIOS on top of IPX/SPX at the OSI session and presentation layers.

TIP
The installation of NWLink IPX/SPX Compatible Transport alone on a Windows NT Server does not allow the use of file and print services on a Novell NetWare server. The installation of a redirector such as GSNW is necessary to access these services.

Only the IPX/SPX Compatible Transport has any configurable properties. These properties are the frame type and the network number. Incorrectly configuring either of these two properties results in an inability to communicate with other computers on the network.

Frame Type

The IPX protocol enables the use of several types of frame. The frame type describes the type of headers added to data prior to transmission. Windows NT supports four frame types for IPX with Ethernet:

- 802.2
- 802.3

- Ethernet II
- Ethernet *SubNetwork Access Protocol* (SNAP)

Novell NetWare versions prior to 3.12 used Ethernet 802.3 as default. NetWare 3.12 and later versions use Ethernet 802.2 as default.

TIP
The network interface card in use with a computer may be able to handle only a limited number of frame types. This restriction is particularly true with older network cards and may cause problems when configuring the Windows NT Server computer to communicate with a NetWare server.

The frame type should be set to Auto Detect initially. Auto Detect automatically sets the frame type and the network number based on the traffic detected on the network when the workstation is started. If no traffic or a mix of traffic is detected, the frame type and network number should be set manually. The frame type also must match among all computers that will communicate.

TIP
A major cause of problems on an IPX network is incorrect frame types, due to different NetWare versions having different defaults. Ensure that all NetWare servers are set to the same frame type. Alternatively, multiple frame types may be bound to the Windows NT Server's network adapter to minimize this problem.

The administrator also can use multiple frame types on the Windows NT Server, if a mix of frame types is being used on existing servers on the network. Additional information on NWLink and frame types can be found in Chapter 5, "Network Configuration."

Network Number

The network number is an eight-digit hexadecimal number set by the network administrator. This number is associated with the network cable or segment and all the computers attached to that segment.

The number is bound to the specific network adapter attached to the cable, not the NetWare server itself. Therefore, to communicate, every NetWare server and workstation attached to the same cable must have the same number associated with the network adapter attached to the cable.

If the frame type is set manually, the network number can be left to its default of 0. This setting enables automatic detection of the network number. If the default of 0 is not used, then the administrator must ensure that the network number matches with the number for the adapter on the NetWare server for which the Windows NT Server needs access.

Gateway Services for NetWare (GSNW)

Gateway Services for NetWare is the redirector used on Windows NT Servers to access the file and print resources of NetWare networks. In addition to these client services, GSNW also allows the Windows NT Server to provide access to Windows NT client machines without having to reconfigure the clients or install any additional software.

Client Services

NetWare file and print services are accessed in the same manner as resources on Microsoft Windows based systems. The GSNW acts as a *Transport Driver Interface* (TDI) compliant NetWare compatible redirector that interfaces with NWLink at the Transport layer. NWLink interfaces with NDIS-compliant network adapter drivers completing the journey down the OSI model to the physical layer.

GSNW requires NWLink as a transport protocol and installs NWLink if it is not already installed. Additionally, the Server and Workstation services also are required for GSNW. The Workstation service is required for any network service request to be sent from a client machine to a server. The Server service is necessary to provide gateway access.

When using the client services part of GSNW, access to resources is controlled by the NetWare server by user-level security. This security level is provided by the Windows NT Server user, who provides a user account and password that is valid on the NetWare server at each logon to Windows NT. When using the Gateway portion of GSNW, access to NetWare resources by Windows NT clients is controlled by the Windows NT Server housing the gateway.

 GSNW can be installed during installation of Windows NT Server from the Services screen (see Figure 16.1).

1. Open the Network Applet from the Control Panel.
2. Choose the Services tab.

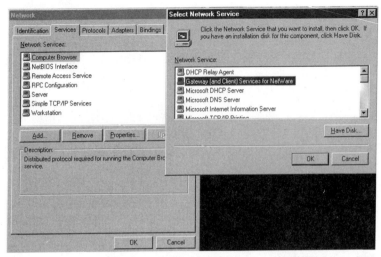

Figure 16.1 Use the Services tab of the Network Properties dialog box, click on the Add button, and select Gateway (and Client) Services for NetWare.

3. Select Add

4. Choose Gateway (and Client) Services for NetWare from the list.

5. Shut down and restarting Windows NT.

On restarting, a user may be able to immediately use NetWare services. The default settings of no preferred server and Auto Frame Detection attach the user to the first available NetWare server using bindery emulation mode.

TIP

If a user account, which matches the user's Windows NT user account in name and password, exists on the NetWare server, the user has access to the server without providing further information. Otherwise, the user is presented with an additional dialog box to log on to the NetWare server.

The user must specify either the server or tree and context to which they are attempting to log on. If the user is logging into a NetWare 3.x server (or a NetWare 4.x server running in bindery emulation mode), s/he should choose the Preferred server radio button and specify the server that contains the user account. If the user is attempting to log on to NetWare 4.x, s/he should specify a tree and context.

GSNW installs a Control Panel applet (see Figure 16.2) that enables the user to specify the following:

- Preferred server or default tree and context

- Print options

- Optional running of the NetWare login script

- Gateway configuration options

Specifying a preferred server or default tree causes Windows NT to attempt to connect the user to the specified server or tree first. If a user does not specify one, Windows NT attempts to connect the user to the nearest server or tree.

Three print options are used to specify settings for how NetWare will treat a print job.

- *Add Form Feed*—This option adds a form feed after each print job printed. This option is needed with some older applications to ensure that the printer ejects the last page.

- *Notify when printed*—This option notifies the user after the job has been printed.

- *Print Banner*—This option prints an announcement page prior to the actual job. This separator sheet frequently contains the user-name of the individual who submitted the print job.

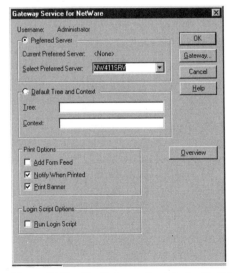

Figure 16.2 The Gateway Services for NetWare Applet enables you to con-figure which server you want to log on to.

The user can run the NetWare login script associated with the user account specified for logging into the NetWare server.

Gateway Services

GSNW is an easy method of enabling Windows NT clients access to NetWare resources. After GSNW is installed and configured on a Windows NT Server, NetWare resources appear to Microsoft clients as ordinary shares on the Windows NT Server machine.

To configure a gateway, select the Gateway button on the Gateway Services for NetWare dialog box. Figure 16.3 shows the Configure Gateway dialog box.

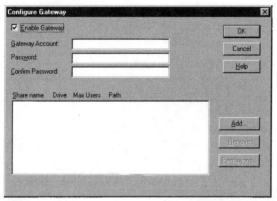

Figure 16.3 The Configure Gateway dialog box is used to set up the gateway between the Windows NT server and the NetWare server.

By default *Enable Gateway* is checked. The Gateway Account must exist on the NetWare server. In addition, this account must be a member of the NTGATEWAY group. Enter the password for this account in both the Password and Confirm Password text boxes.

The next step is to create the share to enable access to the files on the NetWare server. Click on the Add button to display the New Share dialog box. This dialog box is shown in Figure 16.4. Assign a Share Name that is meaningful to those users who will access files from the NetWare server.

Type the path to the directory that you want to share. Both the name of the NetWare server and the directory path must be entered. A drive letter also can be selected. After clicking on OK, you are returned to the Gateway Services for NetWare dialog box.

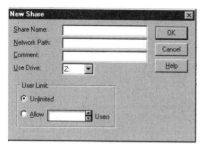

Figure 16.4 The New Share dialog box is used to create the share that will provide access to NetWare resources.

Use the Permissions button to assign access permissions to the newly created share.

A user on the Windows NT network needs to browse the Network Neighborhood of the Windows NT Server with the shared NetWare resource. Otherwise, the user treats it as any other shared resource. Printing to a NetWare printer appears the same as printing to a Windows network printer.

One limitation that can occur with GSNW is that each resource a user wants to access must be set up in a share. An administrator must configure each share using the GSNW Gateway dialog box. On a large network, this process may become burdensome. Additionally, downtime of the server with GSNW affects all Windows users attempting to access NetWare resources, unless they also have Client Services for NetWare (CSNW) installed and configured on their local workstation (CSNW is another free add-on available on the Windows NT Server installation CD-ROM).

The primary advantage of GSNW over the use of CSNW in a network is the centralization of control. GSNW requires installation only on a single server. Each client machine that wants access to NetWare resources needs to have network access only to the Windows NT Server configured with GSNW. This configuration requires neither NWLink nor the client redirector to be installed on the client computers.

The Windows NT Server with GSNW installed does have an additional load. If a large number of clients need access to NetWare resources, the installation and use of CSNW on specific client machines rather than GSNW may be warranted.

Additionally, GSNW uses Windows NT share security to determine access to NetWare resources. CSNW relies on NetWare security to limit access to NetWare resources.

TIP
When choosing between using GSNW on a server or CSNW client services on the clients, consider the amount of access required by the clients. In addition, when presented with a scenario note whether any limitation is imposed on installing additional software on the client computers.

Migration Tool for NetWare

The Migration Tool for NetWare is included with Windows NT Server. This tool enables the administrator to migrate users, groups, and files from one or more NetWare servers to Windows NT. To use the Migration Tool for NetWare, the migration must be made to a Windows NT server.

When migrating users from a NetWare server, the migration must be performed to the PDC. Remember, this copy of the SAM is the only one that can be edited. To preserve file permissions and ownership, files must be migrated to an NTFS partition. This partition may be on any Windows NT Server.

The Migration Tool may be used to migrate more than one NetWare server at one time. Configurable options are as follow

- How to handle duplicate usernames and groups
- Set up passwords on user accounts that are migrated
- Maintain logon scripts
- Select which files and directories are to be migrated and their destinations

TIP
When migrating users from multiple NetWare servers, use a mapping file to control how each user and each group is migrated on a case-by-case basis.

The Migration Tool for NetWare makes the conversion from a NetWare-based network to a Windows NT-based network a much easier task.

File and Print Services for NetWare

Microsoft's *File and Print Services for NetWare* (FPNW) enable you to integrate NetWare clients into a Windows NT network without installing any additional software on the client computers. FPNW does not come with Windows NT but is an add-on.

After installing FPNW on a Windows NT Server, the Windows NT Server appears as a NetWare 3.12 compatible server. The NetWare clients then can access files and printers located on the Windows NT Server. In addition, by installing FPNW on an application server, such as one running Exchange, NetWare clients can then access the application.

Directory Services for NetWare

Directory Services for NetWare provides central administration of a network consisting of both Windows NT and NetWare servers. DSNW is compatible with NetWare 2.x, 3.x, and 4.x (running in bindery emulation mode).

DSNW copies NetWare user accounts to the PDC with DSNW installed. In addition, user accounts that exist in the domain are then copied to the NetWare server. In this way, all user accounts may be administered from one location. Any changes made are copied back to the NetWare server.

By using DSNW, you, as an administrator, can do the following:

- Specify which users and groups should be copied from the NetWare server to the PDC. Each of these accounts must comply with the domain account policy.

- Specify which Windows NT accounts are copied to the NetWare server.

- Combine multiple NetWare user accounts into a single account providing for a single user logon to access all resources.

DSNW does not come with Windows NT but is an add-on. In the heterogeneous network environment, DSNW provides for a single user logon for both Windows NT and NetWare clients to access all network resources, whether hosted on a NetWare server or a Windows NT Server.

For Review

- NWLink is compatible with Novell NetWare's IPX/SPX protocol suite.
- The frame type used must match on all machines.
- Not all frame types are available on all network adapter cards.
- NetWare 3.11 and earlier use Ethernet 802.3 as a default.

- NetWare 3.12 and later use Ethernet 802.2 as a default.
- The network numbers assigned to adapters of communicating machines must match.
- NWLink and the Server and Workstation services must be installed for GSNW to function.
- A valid NetWare user account and password must be provided before use of NetWare resources.
- Printing to a NetWare printer is identical as printing to a Windows printer.
- NWLink must be installed on any machine with CSNW or GSNW installed.
- If GSNW is used, it is installed only on the Windows NT Server that acts as the gateway to the NetWare server with the resources needed.
- Accessing file and print resources through GSNW is the same as accessing resources through a network share.
- GSNW does not require any software to be installed on Windows NT client workstations to access NetWare resources.
- When migrating users from NetWare to Windows NT, the migration must be to the PDC.
- When migrating files from NetWare, the destination must be an NTFS partition.
- A Windows NT Server with FPNW installed appears as a NetWare 3.12 server to NetWare clients.
- DSNW provides synchronization of Windows NT and NetWare users and accounts.

For Review

For more information on configuring a network, see Chapter 5, "Network Configuration."

CHAPTER 17

Internet Information
Server

R ecent years have seen the growth of the Internet from a network primarily accessed by universities to a household word.
As an offshoot of this phenomenon, intranets have become
common in many organizations. This chapter covers the differences between the Internet and intranets as well as the Internet services that come with Windows NT 4.0.

Internet versus Intranets

The Internet is a global network of computers all running a common protocol. The World Wide Web provides the capability of
delivering graphic documents using the *hypertext transfer protocol*
(HTTP). These documents or Web pages are delivered by a Web
server. Each document has a unique address called a *Uniform
Resource Locator* (URL).

An intranet is a network contained within an organization that
takes advantage of HTTP to deliver a wide variety of documents to
the users of the organization's network. However, this network is
not connected to the Internet, which is the first major difference
between the two. Organizations may elect to connect to the Internet but to keep the intranet separate.

Windows NT comes with two versions of the Internet services. When installed on Windows NT Server, the product is called *Internet Information Server* (IIS). When installed on Windows NT workstation, it is called *Peer Web Services* (PWS).

PWS is actually a scaled-down version of IIS. The features available in IIS but not with PWS include the following:

- Logging to an ODBC database
- Hosting virtual servers
- Controlling access by using IP addresses
- Managing available bandwidth
- 128-bit encryption

The biggest consideration when selecting between IIS and PWS is with licensing. Windows NT Workstation enables only up to 10 simultaneous connections. If PWS is run as a Web server and if the number of connections exceeds 10, then you would be in violation of your license.

Installation

As stated before, Internet publishing services may be installed on Windows NT Server or Workstation running TCP/IP. Besides the hardware required by the operating system, no other hardware is required. The amount of available hard disk space required is dependent upon which services are installed.

Before installing IIS, decide which publishing service(s) and components you want to use. Figure 17.1 shows the Microsoft Internet Information Server Setup dialog box. IIS provides three publishing services, WWW, FTP, and Gopher. Additional components that may be installed include the following:

- Internet Service Manager
- WWW Service Samples
- Internet Service Manager (HTML)
- ODBC Drivers & Administration

Each of these components are discussed further in this chapter. IIS and Web documents must be installed on NTFS partition(s) in order to take advantage of file-level security.

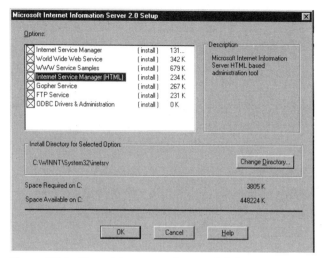

Figure 17.1 The total amount of required disk space is dependent on which services and components are installed.

The installation process is begun by opening the Network applet and clicking on the Add button of the Services tab. Select Microsoft Internet Information Server.

When IIS is installed, any configuration changes are made using the *Internet Service Manager* (ISM) as shown in Figure 17.2

Double-click on either the service or the server name to open the property box for a particular service. Figure 17.3 shows the WWW Service Properties dialog box. This dialog box contains four tabs used for configuring the WWW service.

SERVICE

The Service tab has several configurable parameters as shown in the following list. The top part contains parameters that manage connections.

- TCP Port
- Connection Timeout
- Maximum Connections

The next section contains the username and password used to authenticate anonymous users. By default, an account is created, and a randomly generated password is created. The default user account is IUSR_<computername>.

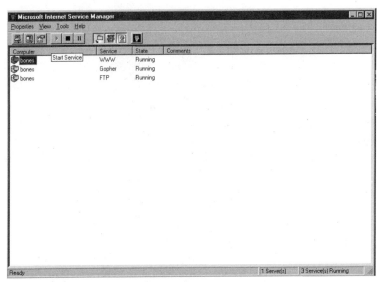

Figure 17.2   The Internet Service Manager is used to configure all installed Internet services.

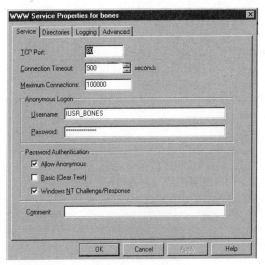

Figure 17.3   Configure each service via its Properties dialog box. This dialog is for the WWW Service.

TIP

What user account is used for anonymous connections does not matter as long as the rights are appropriately set. In fact, separate user accounts could be used for each service. However, it is *very* important that the password entered here matches the password set in User Manager. If they do not match, then anonymous access fails.

DIRECTORIES

When users access your Web site, you may want to be able to give access to some information and restrict access to other information. One of the ways to control this access is to designate a default document to be displayed when a user connects. You may want the user to see a listing of files or browse a directory. Both of these options are configurable on the Directories tab as shown in Figure 17.4.

Figure 17.4   The Directories tab is used to configure directories and how they respond when an anonymous user tries to connect.

The other use of the Directories tab is to create a 'virtual' directory structure of your Web site. A virtual directory is an alias pointed to an actual path and may exist on the Web server or on another server entirely.

Create a virtual directory by clicking on the Add button to display the Directory Properties dialog box as shown in Figure 17.5. The steps to create a virtual directory are as follows:

1. Enter the path to the directory. The path may be local or use UNC to connect to a remote directory.

2. Enter the alias, the name the user enters to access the directory.

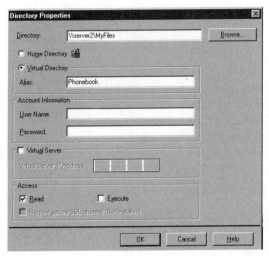

Figure 17.5 Use the Directory Properties dialog box to create either a virtual directory or a virtual server.

3. Set the permissions to read and/or execute. More on permissions later.

IIS can host multiple domain names. The additional domain names are hosted on a virtual server. Creating a virtual server is a little more involved:

1. An IP address must be obtained for the domain either from InterNIC or your ISP.

2. The domain name must be associated with this IP address by adding an entry to database on the appropriate DNS Server.

3. Bind the IP address to the NIC on the Web server.

4. Associate the IP address with the home directory for the domain.

See Chapter 14 for more information on DNS Servers and Chapter 5, "Network Configuration," for details of working with protocols.

LOGGING

IIS can log to either a text file or an ODBC-compliant database, such as SQL Server. When saving to a text file, the log can be restarted either daily, weekly, monthly or based on size as shown in Figure 17.6.

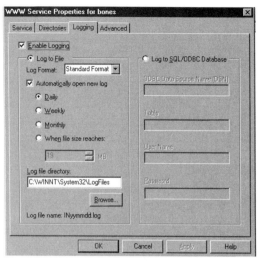

Figure 17.6   Use the Logging tab to configure the type of logging desired.

TIP

Logging to an ODBC-compliant database has the advantage of placing the log in a format that can be easily manipulated. The disadvantage is that this places an additional load on the Web server and may slow it down. A better approach is to log to a file and later import that file into a database or even a spreadsheet for analysis.

ADVANCED

The last tab is the Advanced tab. Two parameters are configured on this tab. The first is the ability to control access to the Web server based on the IP address of the client accessing your Web site. This control can be accomplished either by individual IP address or a range of addresses. Using the Advanced tab, either grant or deny all access and then define the exceptions. Figure 17.7 shows the Advanced tab.

The second parameter is the amount of bandwidth that the server may use. This parameter gives the administrator the option to prevent the Web server from saturating the network. This may be advantageous when administering an intranet to make sure that users have the necessary bandwidth for purposes other than viewing Web pages.

NOTE

Any changes made to the bandwidth affect *all* Internet services for that particular Web server.

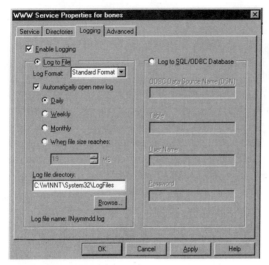

Figure 17.7   Using the Advanced tab is one way to increase the security of your Web site.

IIS Security

IIS has several features that address security concerns. The majority of the security features of IIS are those of the underlying operating system, Windows NT Server. See Chapter 7, "User Manager for Domains," for information on managing account policies. Recommendations for securing your site include the following:

- Use NTFS partitions.
- Require passwords with a minimum length of six characters.
- Keep a password history.
- Change passwords frequently.
- Lockout accounts after a specified number of unsuccessful attempts to logon.
- Do not reset lockouts automatically, rather than require the administrator to unlock accounts.
- Disconnect users with limited hours.
- Allow Anonymous access.
- Use Anonymous access only to your FTP site.

ANONYMOUS ACCESS

Allowing anonymous access as a security measure may seem contradictory. When a user attempts to connect to your Web site using anonymous access, the Internet user account is used to grant access. The IUSR_<computername> account is created during installation of IIS. This account is made a member of the Guests group. When a remote user attempts to anonymously access resources that user is authenticated as IUSR_<computername>. Set the appropriate access rights for this user using NTFS permissions, thereby controlling what anonymous users can access. See Chapter 8, "Managing Files and Directories," for further information on using NTFS permissions.

TIP
FTP is an older technology and does not support encrypted authentication. This means that usernames and passwords are sent over the Internet in clear text. To maintain security, enable *only* anonymous access to your FTP site.

IIS also can be configured to require a username and password for access to certain directories. The WWW service may be configured to use one of two types of authentication:

- Basic authentication sends usernames and passwords as clear text only. Although this authentication is supported by any type of client, it may lead to a breach in security.

- Windows NT Challenge/Response authentication provides for a secure logon. The client must be running a browser capable of participating in this type of authentication such as Microsoft Internet Explorer 2.x or newer.

Use of either IIS or PWS provides for the capability to use the Hypertext Transfer Protocol to provide access to various network resources. This service can be used either via the Internet or to set up an intranet for an organization. The advantages are that the user needs to learn only one application, a Web browser, to access multiple types of information.

For Review

- IIS installs on Windows NT Server; PWS installs on Windows NT Workstation.

- IIS can be installed with three different publishing services, WWW, FTP, and Gopher.

- Use the *Internet Service Manager* (ISM) to configure each of the publishing services.

- A user account is created for anonymous access during installation.

- If the password for the anonymous account is changed using the ISM, the password also must be changed using User Manager or User Manager for Domains.

- Virtual directories are aliases referencing a directory located on the Web server or on a remote server.

- Virtual servers allows for multiple domains to be hosted from one Web server.

- IIS can log to either a text file or an ODBC-compliant database.

- Access to the Web site can be controlled by the user's IP address.

- Implement security features to secure your Web site.

From Here

See Chapter 7, "User Manager for Domains," for information on managing account policies and Chapter 8, "Managing Files and Directories," for information on NTFS permissions.

CHAPTER 18

Server Optimization

This chapter leads you through several procedures to optimize Windows NT Server in the Enterprise. The topics include the following:

- Bottlenecks
- Virtual memory
- Caching
- Multiprocessors
- Thread priority
- Performance Monitor
- Windows NT Diagnostics
- Task Manager
- Memory dumps
- Optimizing the environment
- Background and foreground applications

When Microsoft designed Windows NT, their goals included creating a more dependable operating system. In most cases, Windows NT has fulfilled that goal. Some aspects of the operating system have been completely redesigned. In fact, the system can even troubleshoot some of its own problems. The following sections discuss a few of the self-tuning options you have with Windows NT 4.0 Server in the Enterprise.

NOTE
You must complement your study of this chapter with a complete review of Chapter 19, "Tuning the Network." The optimization benefits you receive depend on your understanding of the concepts presented here, as well as how to capture data with Network Monitor, as described in Chapter 19.

Bottlenecks

As a three-lane highway reduces to two lanes, the traffic slows and sometimes stops. In networking, this scenario is referred to as a *bottleneck*. A bottleneck is any device or program that slows network performance.

Network bottlenecks occur for a variety of reasons. Inadequate CPU, inadequate RAM, or an overwhelmed network adapter card are examples of possible bottlenecks. Yet finding the source of the trouble is not an easy thing to do. Applying solutions haphazardly, without a clue to the cause, can be expensive. In many cases, haphazard network troubleshooting does not work.

The more complex a network, the more difficult finding the bottleneck becomes. Having the right tools may not solve the problem, but at least these tools give you the ability to develop a working strategy. Your skill in understanding how to capture and analyze data will make the difference in discovering the cause of network bottlenecks.

To be a system administrator, you should have or develop detective skills. Here is how you will need to equip yourself:

- A basic understanding of the problem so that you can determine which diagnostic or monitoring tool to implement.
- Who? What? Where? When? How? How much? and so on.
- You must analyze the data you generate from the tools in Windows NT.
- Develop a proposed solution.
- Create a plan to implement the solution.

Make changes to your system one at a time and document those changes. If you think a problem has two causes, change only one facet and test it. Assure yourself that the change you made is reversible before going forward. Unnecessary changes can adversely affect system performance and cause you even more problems.

 Before you begin any monitoring, establish a baseline. A baseline establishes a standard for judging network performance. The exams ask you about the best times to do this. Remember these rules:

- High traffic times, like the morning logons, are bad times to establish *isolated* baselines.
- Sample network traffic at various times throughout the day.
- Take baseline samples for several days.

Remember the purpose of monitoring is to sample the network as a whole. Bottlenecks can occur, even in the best systems. In tuning your network servers, the goal is most often a consistently dependable system that reduces the likelihood of bottlenecks or other traffic problems.

 If you get a question about hard page faults, remember that page faults are only a problem if they are ongoing. Hard page faults, indicating a lot of disk writing, are common. It's only if hard page faults continue and become overwhelming that they should concern you.

Virtual Memory

Virtual Memory enables the computer to simulate RAM more slowly on the hard disk. The official Microsoft name for this process is *demand paging*, which uses the Pagefile.sys file as a repository for the temporary storage and exchange of data that is in use currently or was recently used. Pagefile.sys is also known as a *SWAP file*.

Physical RAM cannot always contain all of the *pages* of memory that are open at any given time. Therefore, the swap file holds the *inactive* pages of memory, awaiting their summons for execution by the CPU.

Swapping, however, can significantly compromise system performance. Every time a hard disk performs swapping, the hard disk must execute a write operation. This operation is significantly slower than RAM, which performs more quickly and with much less overhead.

Consequently, the larger the physical RAM, the less time the system spends on *swapping* pages, and the healthier the system performance. In real life (as opposed to the exam environment) Windows NT likes RAM, and more RAM almost always makes Windows NT perform more quickly.

For the MCSE exams, you should remember that more RAM or physical memory is often necessary to reduce paging.

If you are getting *OUT OF MEMORY* error messages, try reconfiguring your Virtual Memory settings.

To configure Virtual Memory, go to Start | Settings | Control Panel | System | Performance | Change.

You can configure both the virtual memory and the server speed optimization from the screen shown in Figure 18.1.

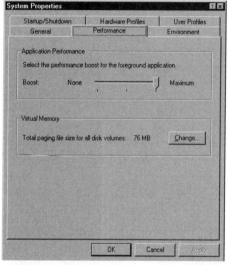

Figure 18.1 Foreground application priority and page file size and location both influence performance.

For Windows NT 4.0 Server, you cannot configure the Pagefile.sys to be less than 2M. By default, the size is set to the amount of RAM on the computer. The maximum size for a page file is the amount of free space on the hard disk. Additionally, each hard disk on a computer can have all or part of the page file.

If you add an application to a disk where the maximum free space is used for paging, do not forget to change the paging file size.

If you accept the default minimum, which is the size of the RAM, and the free disk space falls below that minimum, problems will occur. For example, if you have 48M of RAM on the computer, 48M will be your default minimum page file size. If your free space on the disk falls to 40M, then you must reenter the minimum and maximum sizes. Or, move the pagefile to a faster disk with more free space.

 If the server's paging file expands beyond its specified maximum size, the paging file fragments the disk and increases the start time and response time for applications. Disk fragmentation slows down performance; page file fragmentation can seriously affect performance.

Caching

An explanation of the self-tuning aspects of virtual memory would not be complete without a discussion of *caching* (pronounced cashing.) In the preceding section on "Virtual Memory," you read about paging and the delaying effects of disk writes on system performance. Windows NT sets aside a portion of the physical RAM for caching, which helps reduce the effects of paging.

Two types of caching are possible, but only write-back caching is used in Windows NT. The data is always available for reading. Data is sent to cache before being paged. As cache fills, it moves older data to the page file.

Think of this as data being *pushed* through memory as shown in Figure 18.2.

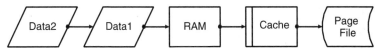

Figure 18.2 Windows NT keeps data available for reading, either from the cache or the page file.

Write-through caching is *not used* in Windows NT. In this method, shown in Figure 18.3, the data is written to the page file and cache simultaneously.

 Adding RAM gives a boost to your system performance by increasing caching and reducing paging.

Multiprocessors

 A Windows NT 4.0 Server can sustain up to four microprocessors as it is sold.

By distributing the system requirements across multiple processors, the server can balance requests and perform

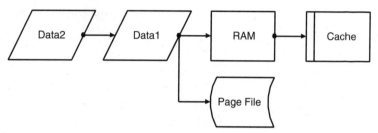

Figure 18.3 Windows NT does not use write-through caching.

with more stability. This distribution provides multithreaded applications the opportunity to maximize their output. Keep in mind, multithreaded applications running across multiprocessors do not necessarily mean more speed. Thread performance is inter-dependent; that is, applications execute threads based on the out-put of another thread. Therefore, threads still wait for each other. The potential for increased speed exists. Remember that single thread applications still execute only on a single processor.

Self-tuning systems were designed to take advantage of this type of load balancing. Running in the background, the system opti-mizes itself, freeing you, as the system administrator, for other important tasks.

Thread Priority

In addition to multiprocessing, Windows NT prioritizes threads. You can accept the default values of 8 (the range is 0–31), or you can change the way the system prioritizes. The self-tuning part of the task manager utility enables the system to vary the default value of 8, +/– 2 degrees, depending upon system requirements.

For the procedures to change the priorities, see "Task Manager" and "Background and Foreground Applications" later in this chapter.

 In configuring these priorities, remember these two things:

- Any user can configure values up to 23 for any process. The com-mands to begin these are

Start /low (priorities 4–7)

Start /normal (priorities 8–12)

Start /high (priorities 13–23)

- Only administrators can configure values of 24 or higher. The command is

Start /realtime (priorities 24 - 31)

The values of 24–31 are reserved for real-time processes. For the exam, you need to know that a real-time event requires the CPU's complete attention. These high priorities can *hog* the system resources, however, which is why only administrators have the right to use the high-end values.

Review the "Task Manager," section later in this chapter. As you make efforts to optimize your own particular network, use Task Manager to change the thread priorities of processes currently executing. The thread priorities translate to the applications' priorities described in the preceding paragraph. Using Task Manager gives you the opportunity to see how thread priority can improve or adversely affect your system performance.

Be careful, however, because executing a thread in a real-time mode can slow system performance.

RECAP OF SELF-TUNING

 The following are the essential self-tuning devices built into Windows NT:

- *Virtual Memory & Caching*   Remember additional RAM decreases paging in virtual memory and caching.

- *Multiprocessors*   Windows NT supports up to 4 microprocessors.

- *Thread Priority*   Users can configure priorities up to 23. Only administrators can configure priorities greater than 23, which are reserved for real-time processes.

Performance Monitor

Launch the Windows NT 4.0 Performance Monitor, shown in Figure 18.4, as follows:

Start | Programs | Administrative Tools | Performance Monitor

The Performance Monitor is a powerful tool that depends *entirely* on your ability to configure it. When you start the monitor, you get

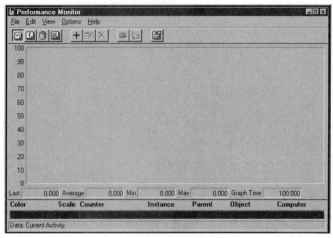

Figure 18.4 The Windows NT 4.0 Performance Monitor.

a blank screen just as you see in Figure 18.4. One of your future goals should be to learn each counter and what it can do. For the time being, however, your review should focus on the counters that you may encounter on the MCSE exam.

The first obstacle you need to overcome in Performance Monitor is the cryptic description given to each counter. Although some of the names are straightforward (e.g., % Processor Time); others, like System: Processor Queue Length can intimidate the beginner. Microsoft assists you by putting the counters in groups, also known as *objects*. These groupings are determined by what is monitored.

For example, one group is *processor,* which contains all counters related to the CPU. For the exams, know these major counter groups:

- Processor—CPU-related counters
- LogicalDisk—Relates to logical disk partitions
- Memory—Collects data about all memory configurations
- PagingFile—Anything related to the swapping process
- PhysicalDisk—Collects information relating to any hard disk
- Server—Services and processes of the server

Other groups exist, but these groups are the most important.

Learning Performance Monitor is crucial for troubleshooting network problems and identifying bottlenecks. Take some time to experiment with Performance Monitor.

Performance Monitor can slow network performance. Because Performance Monitor is a monitor, it does not interact with or interfere with any system process.

However, Performance Monitor uses system resources like any other application. Therefore, the more counters you initiate, the more resources are required. Depending upon your system resources, this impact can be minimal or adverse.

In the Enterprise, you can monitor 25 servers simultaneously. You can determine the effect on the system. In log view, take a reading using manual update. Select the `Update Counter Button` and take another reading. The difference is the load that monitoring places on your server.

Logical Disk versus Physical Disk

Although it may be obvious, differences exist between logical and physical disks. A clear understanding of these concepts is vital before undertaking the MCSE exams:

- *Physical disks*—The hard disk is seen as one unit. For purposes of monitoring, the physical disk counters record read/writes to and from a whole disk drive.

- *Logical disks*—Mapped network drives, volume sets, and so on. Logical disks can combine physical disks or be a part of them. For example, a volume set combines physical disks into a single unit, which is a logical disk.

Add a Counter to the Screen

As you develop more sophisticated skills with Performance Monitor, you learn which counters give you the information you need. You also will develop a deeper understanding of how to use the counters together for comparisons of different system processes.

In the beginning, you may find yourself adding more counters to the screen than you need. Beware of this tendency. Overloading the screen with counters creates clutter, demands system resources, and can negate many of the good things monitoring can achieve. One alternative option is to launch several instances of Performance Monitors at once, each with fewer counters. You can save the monitors you find most useful and retrieve them as you would with any file.

Before adding a disk-related counter, you may need to *initialize* the system with diskperf. Disk counters can use significant system resources, so you must take deliberate steps to enable them. To do this, complete the following steps:

1. Start | Programs | Command Prompt
2. Type diskperf -y or diskperf -ye if monitoring RAID disks
3. Reboot

You can add a counter to the Performance Monitor in two ways:

- Select Add from the Edit drop-down menu, shown in Figure 18.5. Select a counter to add to the screen.

- Click the + sign on the toolbar, shown in Figure 18.6. Select a counter to add to the screen.

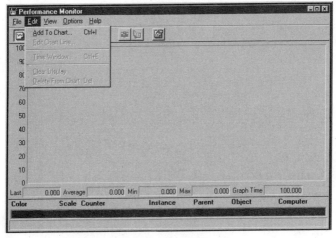

Figure 18.5   Add counters from the Edit menu.

Immediately after adding a counter, a recap of its name and default properties is placed at the bottom of the screen. You will want to check the values associated with the counter. If the minimums and maximums values are too low, for example, no reading may be displayed on the screen.

The counter begins sampling the system at once. A line appears on the screen to indicate the readings it is taking. Keep in mind that these readings are real-time.

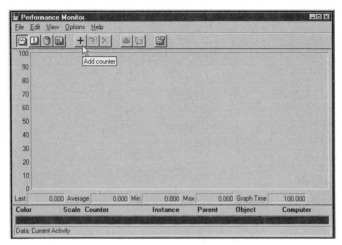

Figure 18.6 Add counters by clicking on the plus.

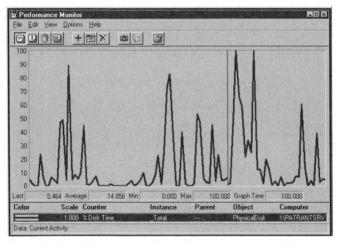

Figure 18.7 Disk time varies from almost nothing to 100 percent.

Notice the readings in the counter for % Disk Time, shown in Figure 18.7, which is determining the amount of time the hard disk is interacting with the processor.

Counters

You need to know several counters for the MCSE exams. Most likely, questions about what system components the counters measure will be asked. Solutions will be requested if the counter determines there is a system problem. The following is a comprehensive list of the counters you need to know for the MCSE exam:

- Processor: % Processor Time

    DEFINED: Measures the processor activity in percentage form. If the processor is *constantly* running above 80 percent capacity, you have a problem. The key word here is *constantly*. For the processor to go to 80 percent or higher is normal; it just should not stay there for an extended period.

    SOLUTIONS:

    - Add a faster microprocessor (Pentium at a minimum)

    - Add another microprocessor (NT Server will support up to 4)

 To monitor the page-swapping process, enable the following counters:

- PROCESS: PageFileBytes
- PROCESS: PageFileBytes_Total
- System: Processor Queue Length

DEFINED: Always remember when you see QUEUE in a counter that something is waiting, just like the real world. In this instance, threads are awaiting processing by the processor.

 If the counter sustains a reading of two or greater, there is a problem.

SOLUTIONS:

- Add a faster microprocessor (Pentium at a minimum)

- Add another microprocessor (NT Server supports up to 4)

- Memory: Pages/sec

    DEFINED: This counter measures the pages written to the hard disk.

    SOLUTION: Add RAM if the Pages/sec counter ever sustains a rate in the 70–100 range. If you have multiple hard disks, you might consider creating multiple paging files.

    If you combine this counter with the Average Disk Sec/transfer, and the reading is greater than 10 percent, you have excessive paging. Adding RAM or reconfiguring the paging files are possible solutions.

■ % Disk Time

DEFINED: This counter measures the effects disk requests have on the processor.

SOLUTION: Reduce disk requests by adding RAM.

  If you must guess about a solution, adding RAM is the best answer.

■ Current Disk Queue Length

DEFINED: This counter measures the queue for data waiting to be moved to the hard disk.

SOLUTIONS:

■ Increase the disk speed by adding RAM, which increases your disk cache and reduces swapping. Adding RAM clears the path for application disk requests to write to the disk.

■ Consider upgrading your hard disk. Older disks can be slower and less efficient in writing data. Primarily a function of the disk controller, technology has increased the speed at which they perform.

■ Add multiple hard disks. Although an expensive solution, writing data across multiple disks can dramatically improve system performance. Consider implementing a Stripe Set to facilitate this method.

 If you suspect RAM problems, use the Pages/sec and Available Bytes counters.

Saving Files, Alerts, and Reports in Performance Monitor

The graphical interface of Performance Monitor is not the only way you can view the data. You can save the files for viewing later. All you need to do is select the File drop-down menu and select Save As, entering the path for the files.

You must know how to set up an alert in Performance Monitor. See Figure 18.8:

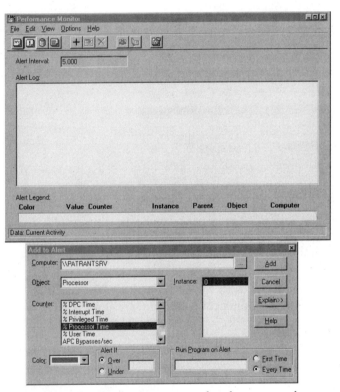

Figure 18.8 The Alert log is empty; no alerts have occurred.

1. Select the ! icon from the Performance Monitor taskbar.
2. Select the + icon to add the counters to be monitored.
3. Configure the information in the screens.

You can configure the alert to signal a user or computer by going to Server Manager.

Log View

This view records your data into a file, which you can export to other applications.

Report View

Using a predetermined format, this view puts the data selected into a nongraphic report.

Windows NT Diagnostics

To start the Windows NT Diagnostics, shown in Figure 18.9, go to Start | Programs | Administrative Tools | Windows NT Diagnostics.

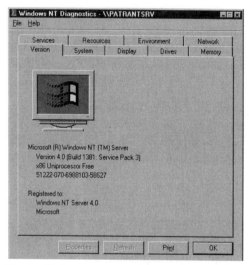

Figure 18.9   Windows NT Diagnostics provides an abundance of useful information.

The Diagnostics utility is an enhanced version of the System screen in the Control Panel. As a tool for troubleshooting, this applet is an excellent starting point for viewing configuration details about your system.

The following is a recap of the tabs in Windows NT Diagnostics:

- *Services*   This screen reviews the services the current system supports.

- *Resources*   You will use this screen when you need to troubleshoot hardware conflicts. This screen reviews all system hardware, including IRQ, I/O ports, DMA, memory, and devices.

- *Environment*   Information the system uses as a landmark for applications to configure themselves based on current settings.

- *Network*   This screen displays the current domain model, including the domain name, current logon, and servers.

- *Version*   Miscellaneous recap of the system version and its components.

- *System*   You will find information about the manufacturer of your CPU and computer here.

- *Display*   This screen displays the configurations of your video.

- *Drives*   Here, you will find information about your *local* machine's hard and logical drives, including the file system used.

- *Memory*   This valuable tool is used when you need a recap of how your *local* system is using memory. In addition to RAM, you can view the page file and its allocation. You also can view threads and running processes.

NOTE
Remember that you can view and print the diagnostics information only from the Windows NT Diagnostics applet.

Task Manager

The most used method to go to the Task Manager is by pressing Ctrl-Alt-Del simultaneously.

You might find it beneficial to start and then minimize the Task Manager so that you can monitor the system at any time. However, minimizing Task Manager while it is in the Performance mode does not display it on the taskbar as normal. Instead, the Task Manager appears as a green icon next to the time displayed on the taskbar.

Three options are available in Task Manager:

- *Applications*   This tool is useful for displaying all of the applications running on the system. The bottom of the screen displays the number of processes running, as well as the CPU and memory usage.

Note the three buttons displayed at the bottom of Figure 18.10.

- End Task   This button enables you to end any application you select.

- Switch To   After highlighting an application, this button enables you to go directly to it.

- New Task   This button enables you to start running a new application from this screen.

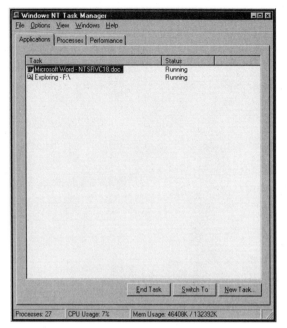

Figure 18.10   This dialog box enables you to end tasks, switch to other open applications, or even start a new task.

- *Processes*   The screen shown in Figure 18.11 displays the background tasks the operating system is using. Remember the distinction between applications (the previous screen) and processes. Also, note your only option here is to end a proccess by highlighting it and clicking on the End Process button.

  Do not end a Process unless you know why you are doing it and what effect ending it will have on the system.

- *Performance*   The performance tab, shown in Figure 18.12, is graphical and similar to the Performance Monitor (see previous section in this chapter.)

  Two counters in Task Manager are available from the Performance tab. Each counter is presented in both graphical and written, or log formats:

  - *CPU Usage*—As a real-time view of system resources, Task Manager eliminates the task of starting Performance Monitor counters. This section gives a great recap of threads and processes.

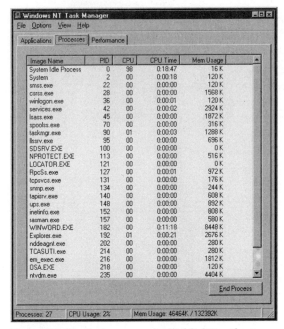

Figure 18.11 End a process by highlighting the process and clicking on the End Process button.

- *MEM Usage* This review displays itself in two modes. Note in Figure 18.12, however, that the graphical portion displays the *total* memory usage, as opposed to these two written logs:

  Physical Memory displays the Total, Available, and cache memories. This log is especially useful for troubleshooting page file problems.

  Kernel Memory gives an excellent recap of the queue for system paging.

Memory Dumps

The recovery feature of Windows NT Server is available for major system failures called *stop errors*. To configure this option, as shown in Figure 18.13, go to:

Start | Settings | Control Panel | System | Startup/Shutdown

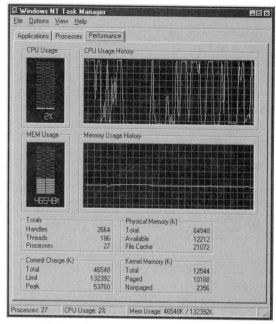

Figure 18.12   Memory use, CPU use, and their histories are displayed.

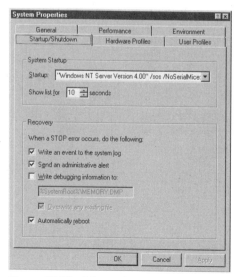

Figure 18.13   Microsoft technical support may request that you obtain a memory dump to help troubleshoot stop errors.

In the bottom portion of this screen, you can see the Recovery feature. Following the statement, When a STOP error occurs, do the following:, are four check boxes:

■ Write an event to the system log When you check this option, stop errors are recorded in the *system log*, which is viewed in Event Viewer. By selecting the View drop-down menu and then Detail, a full explanation is available.

NOTE
The authors intended to present a figure from Event Viewer showing the event detail of a stop error. However, in the past several months of operation, none of the computers running Windows NT Server or Workstation on this network have experienced a Blue Screen of Death (BSOD), and therefore, no recorded log entry was available for display.

While researching system problems, don't forget that Event Viewer also has the capability to filter, arrange, search, and save log files.

 ■ Send an administrative alert using the dialog box shown in Figure 18.14. You can configure a user to receive an alert when a stop error occurs. To set this up, go to

Control Panel | Server | Alerts or
Start | Administrative Tools | Server Manager.

Knowing about alerts is not only important to the test, but also is a way to optimize your system. If you suspect there is a problem with any component of the server or the network, configuring an alert can tip you off before a major problem occurs.

Alerts are also good for power losses, printer problems, and security.

■ Write debugging information to: The default location for this file, as shown in the figure, is %SystemRoot%\Memory.Dmp. The debugging file can be sent to Microsoft for analysis.

 To use this recovery feature, do not move the page file from the boot partition. (The boot partition contains the WINNT directory.)

However, if the recovery feature is not required, you can boost system performance by moving the page file off the physical disk containing the boot partition.

■ Automatically reboot This final check box allows the system to reboot whenever a stop error occurs.

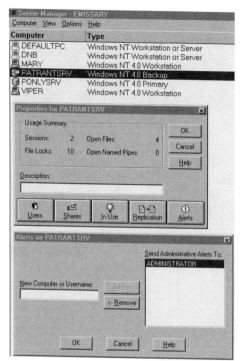

Figure 18.14   Administrative alerts on this BDC are sent to the Administrator only.

In the recovery section, note the option to `Overwrite any existing file`, which is grayed out in the figure. If you check this option, any existing dump files are destroyed. Do not check this box if you want to keep the older dump files.

Look again at Figure 18.13; here are two more features available on the System Properties | Startup/Shutdown menu tab.

The STARTUP option shown in Figure 18.13 enables you to configure which operating system starts by default. In a dual boot configuration, this is where you would configure Windows NT, Windows 95, or whatever should boot automatically.

The Show List For option enables you to configure the time that the *dual boot list* displays before the default operating system loads.

Optimizing the Environment

You can optimize the Windows NT Server environment, shown in Figure 18.15, from the same system properties page reviewed in the previous sections. To go there, select the following:

Start | Settings | Control Panel | System | Startup/Shutdown

Just as user profiles and system policies have a hierarchy, so do the settings of the environment. In this case, the order is as follows:

- *User*—Highest priority. Any settings here take precedence over the system and autoexec settings.
- *System*—Overrides autoexec. Only user settings override system settings.
- *Autoexec*—Lowest priority. A setting here is superseded by settings in system and user.

As you can see from the screen, there are two variables:

- *System*—Only the administrator can make changes here, which affect the entire system.
- *User*—A change here affects a local user.

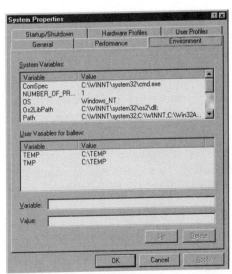

Figure 18.15   Administrators may enter System variables and values.

Background and Foreground Applications

Windows determines that some applications have priority, while others lie dormant in the background. You can change these priorities to fit the needs of your system by going to

Start | Settings | Control Panel | System | Performance

Earlier in this chapter, you reviewed the bottom section of this screen, Virtual Memory. Now, look at the upper portion, Application Performance.

The most unusual feature of this configuration is that it uses a *sliding* dial. Although it may appear that you could set the slider at any point along the range, you cannot. No numbers are showing, and only the three positions marked with notches are valid. The three notches correspond to settings in the registry as follows:

- MAXIMUM (right notch); (Registry) 2

  This notch gives the foreground application the highest priority available. The foreground application comes first. The CPU maintains the background applications but relinquishes their resources if the foreground application requests additional CPU attention.

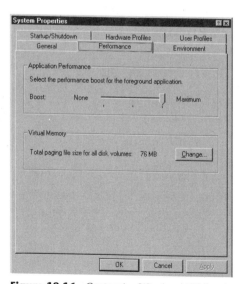

Figure 18.16 Customize Windows NT for the applications and needs of your sytem.

- IN THE MIDDLE NOTCH; (Registry) 1

  This setting increases the CPU's responsiveness to foreground applications slightly. In this instance, the background applications are not deserted quite so quickly.

- NONE (left notch); (Registry) 0

  All applications are treated equally by the CPU

If you change the priority of foreground applications, the change affects only *dynamic* applications. Real-time applications, which include the essential operating system files, are not affected.

For Review

- Microsoft NT 4.0 Virtual Memory is a method that enables the computer to simulate RAM on the hard disk. The official Microsoft name for this process is *demand paging.*

- Swapping, however, can significantly compromise system performance. Every time a hard disk performs swapping, the hard disk must execute a write operation, which is significantly slower than RAM, because RAM performs with much less overhead. For the MCSE exams, remember more RAM or physical memory is necessary to reduce paging.

- If you are getting OUT OF MEMORY error messages, reconfigure your Virtual Memory settings. To configure Virtual Memory, go to Start | Settings | Control Panel | System | Performance | Change.

- For Windows NT Server, you cannot configure the Pagefile.sys to be less than 2M. By default, this file is set to the amount of RAM on the computer. The maximum size for a page file is the amount of free space on the hard disk. Additionally, each hard disk on a computer can have its own paging files.

- If the server's paging file expands beyond its specified maximum size, the paging file fragments the disk and increases the start time for applications.

- Before you begin any monitoring, establish a baseline. A baseline is a standard against which everything else is judged. The exams ask you about the best times to do this. Remember these rules:

  High traffic times, like the morning logons, are bad times to establish baselines.

  Sample network traffic at various times throughout day.

Take baseline samples for several days.

- Remember the purpose of monitoring is to sample the network system as a whole. Bottlenecks always occur, even in the best systems. In tuning your network server, the goal is a consistently dependable system.

- If you get a question about hard page faults, remember page faults are only a problem if ongoing. Hard page faults, indicating a lot of disk writing, are common. However, consistent hard page faults in excess of five per second require attention.

- A Windows NT Server can sustain up to four microprocessors. Keep in mind, multithreaded applications running across multiprocessors do not necessarily mean more speed. Thread performance is interdependent; that is, applications execute threads based on the output of another thread.

- For the exams, know the major counter groups:

  Processor—CPU-related counters

  LogicalDisk—Relates to logical disk partitions

  Memory—Collects data about all memory configurations

  Paging File—anything related to the swapping process

  PhysicalDisk—Collects information relating the any hard disk

  Server—Services and processes of the server

- *Performance Monitor can slow network performance.* Because Performance Monitor is a monitor, it does not interact with, or interfere with any system processes. However, Performance Monitor uses system resources like any other application. Therefore, the more counters you initiate, the more resources are required. Depending upon your system resources, this effect can be minimal or adverse.

- Before adding certain disk-related counters, you must *initialize* the system:

  1. Start | Programs | Command Prompt

  2. Type `diskperf -y` and reboot.

- To monitor the page swapping process, enable the following counters:

  PROCESS: PageFileBytes

  PROCESS: PageFileBytes_Total

- If the `System: Processor Queue Length` counter sustains a reading of *two or greater, you have a problem.*

- If you have to guess about a solution, RAM is the best answer.

- If you suspect RAM problems, use the Pages/sec and Available Bytes counters.

- The three parts of the Task Manager are Applications, Processes, and Performance.

- The values of 24–31 are reserved for real-time processes. For the exam, you need to know that a real-time event requires the CPU's complete attention. These high priorities can hog the system resources, however, which is why administrators are the only users with the right to use these high-end values.

- *Send an administrative alert*—You can configure a user to receive an alert when a stop error occurs. To set this up, go to Control Panel | Server | Alerts.

- To use the recovery feature, do not move the page file from the boot partition. (The boot partition contains the WINNT directory.) However, if the recovery feature is not required, you can boost system performance by moving the page file off the boot partition.

- MAXIMUM FOREGROUND PRIORITY gives the foreground application the highest priority available. The foreground application comes first. The CPU maintains the background applications but relinquishes their resources if the foreground application requests additional CPU attention.

From Here

All components of Windows NT Server in the Enterprise can have an effect upon system performance. However, the following chapters contain the most important items for optimization of the server:

- Chapter 2, "Microsoft NT 4.0 Directory Services"
- Chapter 3, "Planning for Fault Tolerance"
- Chapter 4, "Microsoft NT 4.0 Installation"
- Chapter 5, "Network Configuration"
- Chapter 11, "Remote Administration"
- Chapter 19, "Tuning the Network"

CHAPTER 19

Tuning the Network

When planning for installing a Windows NT based network, spend time planning the network's configuration and the number and types of servers to be installed. As time goes by, servers are upgraded or added to the network. Additional networked services and applications are also added.

Monitoring and optimizing your servers has been covered earlier in this book. This chapter addresses how to assess your network load. The tools you use and what you can do to improve performance also are covered.

Network Traffic

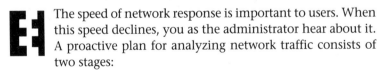

The speed of network response is important to users. When this speed declines, you as the administrator hear about it. A proactive plan for analyzing network traffic consists of two stages:

- *Optimization*   You should consider two factors when optimizing your network: available bandwidth and available network services. Increasing bandwidth results in faster response time. Increasing available network services results in increased traffic and possibly slower response time. A compromise between the two is necessary.

- *Capacity Planning*   Various factors must be considered when trying to predict future network needs. An administrator needs to predict the effect of adding new services and plan how to minimize any adverse effects of the new service.

When examining the health of an existing network or planning for increasing network services, the type and frequency of network traffic and its impact on the network are important to determine. This can be done by doing the following:

1. Use an isolated network segment to prevent other traffic from creating inaccurate results.
2. Use a network tool that can capture and examine the traffic such as Network Monitor.
3. Capture the traffic created by the service you are analyzing.
4. Examine and identify each frame that is captured.

Network Frames

The traffic that is captured is composed of frames. Each frame contains addresses, protocols, and data. The three types of frames are as follow:

- Broadcast frames are sent to all computers and have a destination address of FFFFFFFFFFFF. Each computer on that segment captures and processes these frames.
- Multicast frames are sent to a designated group of computers.
- Directed frames are sent to a specific address. These frames are processed only by the computer to which they are addressed.

Each frame, no matter the type, has several fields:

- *Preamble*   Notifies you when data is coming and is eight bytes in length
- *Destination address*   *Media Access Control* (MAC) address of target computer and is six bytes in length
- *Source address*   MAC address of the source that last sent the frame and is six bytes in length

- *Type or length* Specifies protocol or data size in the frame and is two bytes in length
- *Data* Up to 1,500 bytes in length
- *Cyclic Redundancy Check* (CRC) A checksum used to determine accuracy of data delivered

The last factor to consider is the type of transport protocol being used. Certain protocols send the majority of their data using broadcast frames while others use primarily directed frames. NetBEUI uses only broadcast frames while TCP/IP primarily uses directed frames to deliver data over a routed network. (See Chapter 5, "Network Configuration," for more information on protocols.) For this reason, the protocol is an important factor when analyzing network traffic.

Microsoft Network Monitor

Many different kinds of tools are used to analyze network traffic. These tools can be a combination of hardware and software or entirely software-based. No matter which kind you use, it should have three basic abiliities:

- Ability to capture data
- Ability to save captured data
- Ability to examine captured data

Microsoft's Network Monitor is a software-based tool used to capture, send, and analyze network traffic. Two versions of Network Monitor are available. The basic version is included with Windows NT Server. The full version is included with Systems Management Server.

The difference between the two is the extent that data can be captured. The basic version enables capture of data sent to and from the computer running Network Monitor. The full version enables the capture of all traffic on the entire network segment.

Installation

 The basic version of Network Monitor requires Windows NT Server for installation. The full version, however, also can be installed on Windows for Workgroups 3.x, Windows 95, and Windows NT Workstation. The only hardware requirement for Network Monitor is a supported network card.

Network Monitor consists of two components:

- Network Monitor Application is the component that saves and/ or displays captured frames.

- Network Monitor Agent is the component that enables the capturing of network data. The Agent can be run on a remote computer on a separate segment to allow for remote monitoring.

On the Services tab of the Network applet, click the Add button and select Network Monitor Tools and Agent to install the basic version.

To install the full version of Network Monitor, run the `setup.exe` command from the Systems Management Server CD. This command installs the Network Monitor Application. Also install the Network Monitor Agent.

Figure 19.1 displays the Network Monitor Interface seen while capturing data. Four panes display various realtime statistics about the captured data.

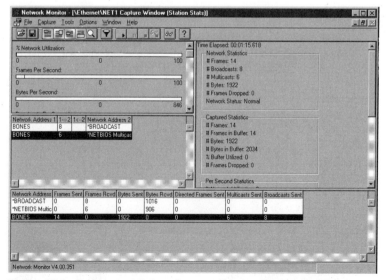

Figure 19.1 Real-time statistics of captured data is displayed by Network Monitor.

Graph Pane	Five bar charts are displayed, which show the percentage of Network Utilization, Frames Per Second, Bytes Per Second, Broadcasts Per Second, and Multicasts Per Second. The maximums for each of these is marked with a line.
Session Statistics Pane	Designates which host is sending broadcasts and multicasts and displays a summary of communications between two hosts.
Total Statistics Pane	Total statistics for all traffic captured on the segment.
Station Statistics Pane	Summary of the type and total number of frames sent by a host.

Each pane is updated dynamically during a capture. A capture may be started by one of three methods:

- Select Capture | Start from the Menu.
- Click the Start Capture button on the toolbar.
- Using the F10 function key.

You can stop a capture in one of three methods:

- Select Capture | Stop from the menu.
- Click the Stop Capture button on the toolbar.
- Using the F11 function key.

The amount of data being captured can be controlled by using a capture filter. These filters can be configured to only capture data using a specific protocol or based on source or destination address.

Working with Captured Data

Captured information may be displayed immediately or saved for later analysis. The captured frames are displayed in three frames as shown in Figure 19.2.

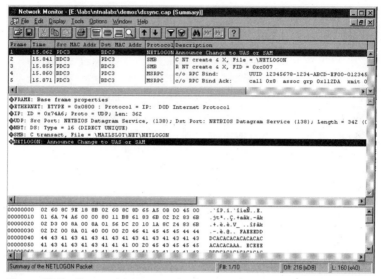

Figure 19.2 Captured frames are displayed in three different formats.

Summary Pane	Lists all frames contained in the capture. Highlighting a frame here causes the corresponding information to be displayed in the Detail and Hexadecimal Panes. The order of the frames displayed here can be sorted by columns.
Detail Pane	Protocol information is displayed here from the outermost layer to the innermost one. If a + sign is shown, clicking on it reveals additional data.
Hexadecimal Pane	Information is displayed in hexadecimal format. When part of a frame is highlighted in the Detail Pane, the corresponding data is highlighted here.

The Summary Pane is shown in columnar format. These columns can be sorted.

- *Frame*—Sequence number indicating in what order the frame was captured.

- *Time*—Time relative to the start of the capture. It also can display the time of day the frame was captured or the elapsed time from the last captured frame.

- *Src MAC Addr*—Source's MAC address.

- *Dst MAC Addr*—Destination's MAC address.

- *Protocol*—What protocol was used to send the frame.

- *Description*—Summary of the contents of the frame.

- *Src Other Addr*— The network address of the sending host, such as an IP or IPX address.

- *Dst Other Addr*—The network address of the destination host such as an IP or IPX address.

- *Type Other Addr*—What type of address is shown in the prior two columns.

A filter may be applied when analyzing captured data. This filter allows for the display of a portion of the captured file. Filters may be applied based on the protocol used or the address of the source or destination host.

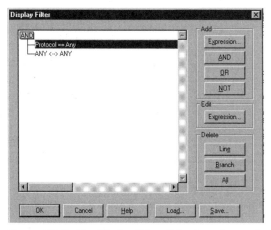

Figure 19.3   The Display Filter dialog box shows whether any filters are already configured.

Filters may be applied by selecting Display | Filter from the menu or using the Filter icon on the Toolbar. Figure 19.3 shows the Display Filter dialog box. Double-click on `Protocol==Any` to access the Expression dialog box as shown in Figure 19.4.

All filters are enabled by default. When configuring a filter, disabling all protocols and then enabling the protocol you want displayed is often easier. A filter may also be configured to display frames based on source or destination address.

324 MCSE NT Enterprise Server

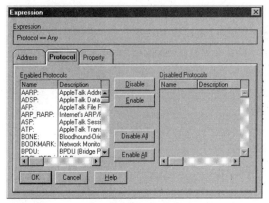

Figure 19.4   Use the Expression dialog box to configure a display filter.

Using Network Monitor

Although all network services have an impact on network function, three of significance to the administrator are DHCP, WINS, and domain synchronization. The amount of network traffic generated by these services can have a significant impact on available bandwidth for the user. Each of these are examined and methods of improving network performance are suggested.

DHCP Traffic

DHCP is covered in Chapter 12. This service provides for the dynamic assignment of IP addresses. When analyzing the effect of a network service, the type of traffic and its frequency are both important factors. Because the communication between a DHCP Server and DHCP Client is primarily broadcast based, you might expect that the use of this service would decrease available bandwidth.

As mentioned in Chapter 12, the process of address acquisition consists of a four-frame communication:

- DHCPDISCOVER

- DHCPOFFER

- DHCPREQUEST

- DHCPACK

Figure 19.5 shows Network Monitor with a DHCPDISCOVER packet open. The size of the frame is 342 bytes ; the total size of all

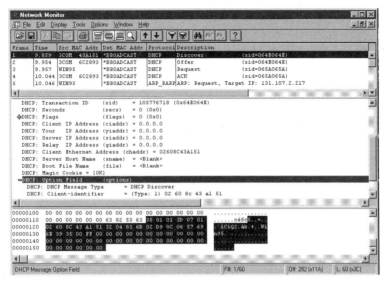

Figure 19.5   Address acquisition consists of four frames.

four frames is 1,368 bytes. It takes less than 1/4 of a second for this conversation to occur. Because IP address acquisition should only occur once, this traffic is not of significance.

Address renewal takes two frames

■ DHCPREQUEST

■ DHCPACK

Although this process is half the size of address requisition, it occurs more frequently. This process occurs on startup of the computer or as a function of the length of the lease. An IP address is renewed at 50 percent, 87.5 percent, or 100 percent of the lease duration.

In the majority of situations, this traffic occurs no more frequently than once a day. The amount of traffic generated this way is minimal and should have negligible effect on the network.

TIP
If the DHCP client is separated from the DHCP server by a slow link, the boot process of the DHCP client may appear slow. If this is the case, installing a DHCP server on the same side of the link as the DHCP client could solve the problem.

WINS Traffic

After a computer has received an IP address and initialized TCP/IP, the next step is to register its NetBIOS name. This process becomes directed rather than broadcasted by using WINS. Four different processes are involved in using WINS:

	Frequency	Number of Frames	Total Size
Name Registration	Each startup	2	220 bytes
Name Renewal	Every 3 days	2	214 bytes
Name Resolution	Variable	2	196 bytes
Name Release	Every shutdown	2	214 bytes

Name Registration occurs upon startup for every service or application that uses NetBIOS. A frame 110 bytes long is sent from the client, and a response of 110 bytes in size is sent from the WINS server. Because each client typically registers three or four names, the total traffic generated by name registration is between 660 bytes and 880 bytes per client.

Name Renewal occurs for each registered name every three days. This process consists of two frames, a request from the client, and a response from the server and generates 214 bytes of traffic. If the client has four registered names, the total traffic would be 856 bytes every three days. Not much to worry about.

Name Release occurs when a service or client shuts down. This conversation consists of two frames for a total size of 214 bytes. This traffic usually occurs no more frequently than once a day and has little effect on network traffic.

Name Resolution generated traffic occurs every time the WINS client needs to access a resource. Each name resolution results in 196 bytes of network traffic. Because this activity is apt to occur frequently during the day, it has the greatest impact on network traffic of the four processes.

WINS traffic can be optimized by the following:

- *Increase the NetBIOS Name Cache* Edit the registry entry `HKEY_LOCAL_MACHINE\System\CurrentControlSet\Services\NetBT\Parameters\Cache Timeout` and increase the value.

▪ *Use an LMHOSTS file*   Preloading the most frequently accessed NetBIOS names prevents WINS being consulted for name resolution.

This network traffic can be a significant issue when it occurs across a slow link such as a dial-up connection. One way to address the issue is to install a WINS server at the remote location. This installation brings up the issue of the amount of traffic generated by WINS replication.

TIP
When configuring WINS replication across a WAN link, configure the partners as Pull partners. In this way, you can control when replication occurs. By scheduling the timing of replication, the effect on network response time can be optimized.

Three factors determine the amount of network traffic generated by the WINS replication process:

▪ *Establishment of the relationship between partners*   This process takes about 20 frames for a total size of 2,000 bytes.

▪ *Verification of database version number.*   When a trigger is issued to replicate the database, the first step is to compare database versions. This generates 900 bytes of data in 12 frames.

▪ *Size of the records being replicated*   Most records require only a single frame, and the amount of network traffic is dependent on the number of records to be replicated.

See Chapter 13 for more information on WINS and replication.

Domain Controller Synchronization

When changes are made to the PDC, these changes are sent to a BDC by a process of synchronization. A log of changes made is maintained to prevent having to send the entire database during synchronization. See Chapter 2, "Microsoft NT 4.0 Directory Services," for more information on domain controllers.

Factors that affect the amount of data to be synchronized and that can be used to calculate the amount of traffic synchronization will generate include the following:

▪ Number of password changes per month
▪ Number of new user accounts per month

- Number of groups that are changed per month
- Number of new computer accounts per month

The steps of synchronization are as follow:

1. The PDC announces a change.
2. The BDC establishes a secure channel to the PDC.
3. The BDC verifies its copy of the database.
4. Updated data is transferred to the BDC.

Several parameters may be changed in the registry to control how synchronization occurs. These parameters may be found at HKEY_ LOCAL_MACHINE\SYSTEM\CurrentControlSet\Services\Netlogon\Parameters. See the following table for their description and possible values.

	Default Value	Value Range	Description
PulseConcurrency	20	1–500	Maximum number of BDCs that will be notified of changes at one time.
Pulse	300 sec.	60–3600	Amount of time that will elapse between update notices being sent by the PDC.
Randomize	1 sec	0–120	How long the BDC waits after receiving an update notice before contacting the PDC for changes.

TIP
When users complain of slow logons across a WAN link, consider placing a BDC on the far side of the link. Before doing this, consider the effect of synchronization on the link.

When synchronization occurs across a WAN link, the registry may be edited to decrease the effect on available bandwidth. Add the Replicaton Governor parameter to the registry entry HKEY_LOCAL_

`MACHINE\System\CurrentControlSet\Services\Netlogon\Parameters`. The acceptable values for this parameter are 1 to 100, which represents the percentage of bandwidth available for synchronization. Lowering this value results in synchronization taking longer. However, bandwidth is still available for users.

Analyses of network traffic should be an ongoing endeavor. By comparing the present function of the network with a baseline record, a decrease in performance can be identified and appropriate changes made before it becomes a disaster.

This analysis of network performance is especially important when considering the effect of network traffic on WAN links. The slower the link, the more important it is to optimize network services.

For Review

- Network management includes optimization and capacity planning.

- The three types of frames are broadcast, multicast, and directed.

- Network Monitor provides a way to capture and analyze network traffic.

- The two versions of Network Monitor are basic and full.

- When using DHCP, address acquisition consists of four frames. Address renewal takes up two frames.

- Every service or application that uses NetBIOS registers its name with WINS.

- Placing a WINS server on both sides of a WAN link results in faster name resolution.

- When replicating across a WAN link, configure for Pull replication.

- The amount of synchronization traffic is dependent on the number of changes made to the SAM.

- Placing a BDC on the far side of a WAN link improves logons but creates synchronization traffic across the link.

From Here

See Chapter 2, "Microsoft NT 4.0 Directory Services," for more information on domain controllers and Chapter 13 for managing WINS servers.

CHAPTER 20

Troubleshooting

T he most successful troubleshooter is one with experience and
knowledge: experience with the software and the hardware.
Knowledge includes knowing where to go for more information when faced with a new problem. This chapter covers the basics
of troubleshooting and available resources.

Possible sources of additional information include the following:

- Microsoft's TechNet
- Web sites, those hosted by Microsoft as well as others
- Classes and training materials
- Microsoft resource kits
- Consultants

In addition, newsgroups and newsletters are available that cover
almost every aspect of Windows NT.

The first step in troubleshooting is to have a systematic approach
to diagnosing and solving the problem. Steps that you might take
include the following:

- Did it ever work?
- If it did work, what has changed since the last time it worked?

- Gather specifics about the problem.
- Consider possible approaches to solving it.
- Try one possible solution at a time. If it works, great. If it does not work, then try another approach.

One of the most important aspects of troubleshooting is documentation. Be sure to document the details of the problems and attempted solutions. It is important to record any solution attempted whether it works or not.

Troubleshooting Tools

Many tools are supplied with Windows NT that are helpful in troubleshooting problems. Some of these tools have already been covered and are not reviewed here. They include the following:

- Event Viewer (Chapter 18)
- Performance Monitor (Chapter 18)
- Network Monitor (Chapter 19)
- Server Manager (Chapter 11)
- User Manager and User Manager for Domains (Chapter 7)

One of the most common troubleshooting problems is access to resources. Chapter 8, "Managing Files and Directories," and Chapter 10, "Printing," cover this problem. Additional tools and methodologies are covered in the remainder of this chapter.

Installation Problems

When troubleshooting installation problems, some major areas should be examined:

- Hardware compatibility
- Hardware configuration
- Reviewing logs
- Viruses

Hardware Compatibility

The most frequent problems with installation result from incompatible hardware. Check the Hardware Compatibility List, a copy of which is included on the Windows NT Server Installation CD-ROM_in the \support folder, the filename is hcl.hlp. It is best to consult the most recent version of the HCL, which is available for download from Microsoft's Web site.

In addition, Microsoft provides the Windows *NT Hardware Qualifier* (NTHQ) utility on the CD. The NTHQ detects what hardware is installed on the computer. Use this list to validate that the hardware is on the HCL.

TIP

An NTHQ disk is created by running makedisk.bat which is found on the Windows NT CD-ROM in the \support\hqtools directory. After creating the disk, reboot your comoputer with the disk in the A: drive.

CD-ROM

Often the CD-ROM may not be compatible with Windows NT but can be accessed under an alternative operating system, such as Windows 95 or MS-DOS. If this is the case, boot that operating system and copy the installation files to the hard drive. You then can install Windows NT from the copy on the hard drive.

As an alternative solution, if a network connection is available, the installation can be accomplished by using the network share.

Hardware Configuration

When installing Windows NT, make sure that no conflicts exist between hardware devices. This is especially true when installing on a computer that has been running Windows 95.

Remember, Windows NT 4.0 is not plug'n'play compatible. Many hardware devices are designed to be plug'n'play and work well under Windows 95. However, these same devices may not be recognized by Windows NT.

Other devices are either plug'n'play or manually configured. Configurable settings include I/O addresses and interrupts. Check to see whether manual configuration has been done properly.

Use Windows NT Diagnostics to determine what resources are being used by what hardware devices, as shown in Figure 20.1. Other versions of WINMSD can be used when installing Windows NT on a computer running an alternative operating system. A version of WINMSD can be run under Windows 95. A nongraphical version also comes with newer versions of MS-DOS.

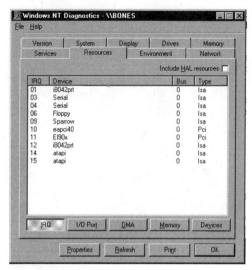

Figure 20.1   WINMSD provides a wealth of information about your system.

Logging

Create a log file of the installation process by using the /l switch during installation. This forces the creation of a log file called $winnt.log, which contains any errors encountered.

Viruses

Many types of viruses exist, some of which can affect the system partition. Make sure that no viruses are present. These can often corrupt an installation of Windows NT or prevent installation entirely.

Boot Problems

Next to installation, the most common problem with Windows NT has to do with being unable to boot. Three main types of problems can occur during boot:

- Corrupted or missing boot file
- Incorrect or corrupted device driver
- Memory incompatibilities resulting from applications

Understanding the boot process is helpful when troubleshooting boot problems. By knowing where in the boot process the error occurs, the cause of the problem may be more easily identified. A successful boot does not occur until a logon has been completed. Assuming that Windows NT is the selected operating system, the process consists of four steps:

1. *Power On Self Test* (POST). This portion is where the computer performs a self-test. The boot portion of the hard disk is located, and NTLDR is initialized.

2. *Boot Loader Phase.* During this phase NTLDR consults the BOOT.INI file for the operating system that is to be started and the location of the system files. Next, NTDETECT.COM is used to determine what hardware is installed, and a list of the appropriate device drivers is created.

3. *Kernel Phase.* NTLDR turns over control to NTOSKRNL.EXE. During this phase device drivers are loaded, services started, and the page file is initialized.

4. *Logon Phase.* The last phase of a successful boot is completion of the logon sequence. See Chapter 7, "User Manager for Domains," for more information on logging onto a Windows NT computer.

The approaches to boot problems are varied depending on the cause and when they occur during the boot process. The following section covers the most common approaches to solving boot problems.

Last Known Good Configuration

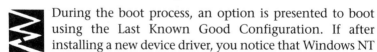 During the boot process, an option is presented to boot using the Last Known Good Configuration. If after installing a new device driver, you notice that Windows NT does not boot correctly, select Last Known Good Configuration. When a user successfully logs on to a Windows NT computer, the configuration in effect at that time is copied to be used whenever Last Known Good is selected. For this reason, if a new piece of hardware or an updated device driver is installed, do not log back on after rebooting if you suspect that the system is not functioning properly.

Repair Process and the Emergency Repair Disk

If you find that using the Last Known Good option does not allow you to successfully boot the machine, then the next option is to attempt a repair of your installation:

1. Boot your computer with the Windows NT Setup Disk, #1.
2. After inserting Disk #2, you will be given the opportunity to repair your installation.
3. Insert the Emergency Repair Disk when prompted.

CREATING AN EMERGENCY REPAIR DISK (ERD)

During installation, you are prompted to create an ERD. After installation you can use the rdisk.exe utility to create an ERD. Run this utility from either the RUN line or from a command prompt. You then are presented with the Repair Disk Utility as shown in Figure 20.2.

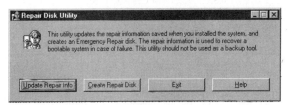

Figure 20.2   The Repair Disk Utility provides the ability to create a new ERD or update repair information.

The Repair Disk Utility has two options, to either update the repair information or to create a new repair disk. If you choose to update the information, you are prompted to create an ERD after the update is complete.

When creating an ERD, the information contained in %SYSTEM-ROOT%\Repair directory is used. This information is written during installation and is not updated automatically.

> **TIP**
> If you use the information saved to the Repair directory during installation to create an ERD, when you use that ERD, the system will be returned to its original configuration. Any users or groups that have been created or changed will be lost. Also, any system configuration changes will also be lost.

The repair process presents you with four options. Select the appropriate options and then continue with the repair process. The available options are as follow:

- *Inspect Registry Files.* You are prompted for verification of replacement of each registry file.

- *Inspect Startup Environment.* Inspects the `boot.ini` file and verifies that Windows NT is a valid option.

- *Verify Windows NT System Files.* Compares existing system files with the version on the CD. You are prompted to replace any differing files.

- *Inspect Boot Sector.* Checks to make sure that *Ntldr* is referenced by the primary boot sector. This is helpful if the `sys.com` utility has been used on the partition, such as if Windows 95 or MS-DOS were installed after Windows NT.

Reinstall

If repairing the installation does not work, then your only choice is to reinstall the operating system. After successfully reinstalling Windows NT, the system can be returned to its original configuration by using the ERD or restoring the registry from a recent backup.

"Blue Screen of Death"

The most infamous problem associated with troubleshooting Windows NT is the stop screen affectionately known as the *Blue Screen of Death* or *BSOD*. A stop screen is displayed whenever Windows NT encounters a fatal error.

These stop screens are blue screens that contains debugging information. This information is helpful in identifying what caused the problem and how to correct it. They are not as daunting as they appear. There are five sections to this information:

- `Debug Port Status Indicator`   This information appears in the upper right corner of the screen if a modem or serial cable is connected and the debug option has been turned on.

- `BugCheck Information`   This section begins with the word `STOP` and contains the most helpful information. The most common stop codes are hardware related. Record this and consult TechNet or Microsoft Technical Support for further information.

- `Driver Information`   The next section contains three columns containing the base address, time stamp, and the name of each loaded driver. This section often provides information as to the address of the instruction that caused the error.

- `Kernel Build Number and Stack Dump` This section contains the build number and lists the range of addresses in the stack. This might indicate the component that caused the crash.

- `Debug Port Information` This section confirms whether a dump file was created.

Windows NT may be configured to create a memory dump whenever a stop error occurs. This is configured using the System applet in the Control Panel on the Startup/Shutdown tab. Two utilities are available for analysis of a crash dump. They are as follow:

- `dumpchk` Verifies that all memory addresses in the memory dump file are valid

- `dumpexam` Creates a text file called `memory.txt` from the information contained in the memory dump file

Both of these utilities are on the Windows NT Server CD and are specific to the platform of the involved computer.

Dr. Watson

Dr. Watson is an application debugger that is part of Windows NT. This utility writes its information to the Application Log and can be examined using the Event Viewer.

Troubleshooting Windows NT can be less of an obstacle if you know the software and the hardware on which the operating system is running. By taking a systematic approach, any troubleshooting question becomes less of a roadblock. The more experience you have with troubleshooting problems, the easier it becomes.

For Review

- Use a systematic approach to all troubleshooting problems.

- Record what worked and what did not work for all problems. This will help you solve future occurences of this problem faster.

- Use the tools that come with Windows NT for troubleshooting. They include Event Viewer, Performance Monitor, and Network Monitor.

- An incompatible CD-ROM does not mean you cannot install Windows NT.

- Use the NTHQ to verify that installed hardware is on the Windows NT HCL.

- Verify hardware configuration, looking especially for resource conflicts.

- Determine where in the boot process a problem exists to help in solving it.

- After you log on, the Last Known Good Configuration is overwritten by the present configuration.

- Keep an up-to-date ERD available at all times.

- If you have to reinstall Windows NT, use the ERD or restore a backup to return your computer to its prior configuration.

- Examine the information displayed by the BSOD for valuable information.

- Dr. Watson records application errors in the Application Log.

From Here

Additional troubleshooting information is available in Chapters 18, "Server Optimization," Chapter 19, "Tuning the Network," and Chapter 11,"Remote Administration." Also see Chapters 7, 8 and 9 for managing and troubleshooting access to resources.

Index

access control
file/directory management,
142–145
installing Windows NT 4.0,
77
Internet information server
(IIS), 287
Microsoft NT 4.0 Directory
Services, 43
network configuration, 103
account policies, file/directory management,
142–145
accounts
Administrator accounts,
119
creating accounts, 123–124
creating names for
accounts, 120
creating user accounts, 117
default user accounts, 117,
119
deleting accounts, 121
Dialin option, 129–130
directory replication,
110–111
domain accounts, 117–118
Gateway Services for NetWare (GSNW), 274
groups, 126, 130–138
Guest accounts, 119

Hours/access time, 127,
128
Internet information server
(IIS), 283–285
local accounts, 117, 118
local logons, 128, **129**
local path, 127
lockout accounts, 288
Logon To restriction, 128
managing user accounts,
125–130
modifying accounts,
123–124
names, 120
network configuration, 94,
103
passwords, 120, 124, 125
planning accounts,
119–124
profiles, 126–127, **126**
remote logons, 128, **129**
renaming accounts,
120–121
restrictions, 120
templates for accounts,
121–123, **122**
temporary user accounts,
128–129
universal naming convention (UNC), 125
user accounts, 125–130

341

About the Authors

Dave Kinnaman, MCSE, a writer in Austin, Texas, has co-authored many books and articles about computers and the Internet. Dave is particularly involved in information access issues, including Internet filtering software, disability access, and retirement issues on the Internet.

Theresa Hadden, MCSE, MCT, has over 10 years of System Administration experience using Novell, Unix, and Windows NT. She is presently teaching in the MCSE program at a local college where she teaches core courses and Internet products, both in the classroom and via the Internet. In addition, she does consulting for organizations with Windows NT and Novell networks. She is actively involved in the design and implementation of online courses which include instructor access utilizing audio conferencing via the Internet. She is the mother of two sons and lives in New Mexico.

Patrick Terrance Neal, MCSE, MCT, owns The Windsor Group, a network consulting and training business in Tampa, Florida. After 12 years in the publishing industry, he is now focusing his career on writing about the MCSE certifications as well as emerging technologies.